Improving Classroom Learning with ICT

D1390596

Improving Classroom Learning with ICT examines the ways in which ICT can be used in the classroom to enhance teaching and learning in different settings and across different subjects.

Weaving together evidence of teachers' and learners' experiences of ICT, the authors:

- explain why the process of integrating ICT is not straightforward;
- discuss whether hardware and infrastructure alone are sufficient to ensure full integration and exploitation of ICT investment;
- emphasise the pivotal role that teachers play in supporting learning with ICT across the curriculum;
- argue that teachers need a greater understanding of how to put ICT to use in teaching and learning;
- highlight that out-of-school use of ICT has an impact on in-school learning;
- discuss what kinds of professional development are most effective in supporting teachers to use technologies creatively and productively.

Case studies are used to illustrate key issues and to elaborate a range of theoretical ideas that can be used in the classroom.

This book will be of interest to all those concerned with maximising the benefits of ICT in the classroom.

Rosamund Sutherland is Professor of Education at the University of Bristol, UK.

Susan Robertson is Professor of Sociology of Education at the University of Bristol, UK.

Peter John is Vice-Chancellor of Thames Valley University, UK.

Improving Learning TLRP

Series Editor: Andrew Pollard, Director of the ESRC Teaching
and Learning Programme

Improving Classroom Learning with ICT

Rosamund Sutherland,
Susan Robertson and
Peter John

with Nick Breeze, Roger Dale,
Keri Facer, Marina Gall, Elisabeth
Lazarus, Sasha Matthewman,
John Morgan, Federica Olivero,
Dan Sutch, Celia Tidmarsh
and Pat Triggs

 Routledge
Taylor & Francis Group

LONDON AND NEW YORK

First published 2009
by Routledge
2 Park Square, Milton Park, Abingdon, Oxon OX14 4RN

Simultaneously published in the USA and Canada
by Routledge
270 Madison Ave, New York, NY 10016

Routledge is an imprint of the Taylor & Francis Group, an informa business

Typeset in Charter ITC and Stone Sans by
Florence Production Ltd, Stoodleigh, Devon
Printed and bound in Great Britain by
CPI Antony Rowe, Chippenham, Wiltshire

British Library Cataloguing in Publication Data
A catalogue record for this book is available from
the British Library

Library of Congress Cataloging in Publication Data
Improving classroom learning with ICT /
   Rosamund Sutherland . . . [et al.].
   p. cm. – (Improving learning TLRP)
   Includes bibliographical references and index.
   1. Computer-assisted instruction.   2. Educational technology.
   3. Information technology.   4. Education–Effect of
   technological innovations on   I. Sutherland, Rosamund, 1947–
   LB1028.5.I434 2009
   371.33′4–dc22   2008025406

ISBN10: 0–415–46173–1 (hbk)
ISBN10: 0–415–46174–X (pbk)
ISBN10: 0–203–88534–1 (ebk)

ISBN13: 978–0–415–46173–3 (hbk)
ISBN13: 978–0–415–46174–0 (pbk)
ISBN13: 978–0–203–88534–5 (ebk)

Contents

Illustrations

Figures

Tables

Acknowledgements

The InterActive Education project (2000–4) was made possible by a grant from the Economic and Social Research Council (ESRC). It was one of the Teaching and Learning Research Programme projects and we are indebted to the ESRC and the TLRP for their support. Mary O'Connell was the administrator for the project and has continued to support the writing of this book. We are deeply grateful to Mary for her loyalty, creativity and absolute commitment to the project and know that the book would not have been finished without her contribution.

The InterActive project was a partnership between teachers and researchers, and we would like to thank the following people for the major contribution they made to the project: David Badlan, Dave Baker, Linda Baggott La Velle, Rebecca Ball, Dick Bateman, Bryan Berry, Rob Beswetherwick, Raj Bhakerd, Andrew Bigg, Chas Blacker, Adrian Blight, Kate Bouverie-Brine, Jan Bovill, Stephanie Bower, Helena Brazier, Linda Bridgeman, Chris Carter, Charmaine Clarke, Andrew Cleaver, Ruth Cole, Sarah Curran, Chris Davies, Ian Davies, Liz Dunbar, Rachel Edwards, Thamir Elzubaidi, Alan George, Stephen Godwin, Louise Hamilton, Phil Hamilton, Gary Handley, Andrew Harman, Catherine Harvey, Jo Heppinstall, Natalie Heysham, Ben Houghton, Judi Johnston Hubbold, Nick Jones, Rod Jones, Marie Joubert, Pam Kelly, John Lang, Liz Lang, Nicky McAllister, Sam Mills, Simon Mills, Heidi Moulder, Suzanne Nash, Ros O'Connor, Pat Peel, Sven Rees, Catherine Roberston, Andrew Rome, Muriel Saffon, Emma Scott-Cook, Joe Sharp, Ian Shedden, Tim Shortis, Richard Shotton, Baldev Singh, Paul Stephens-Wood, Daniel Such, Jude Swailes, Paul Taylor, Maria Thompson, Ian Thomson, Toby Tyas, Nigel Varley, Geof Warnock, Marnie Weeden, Aled Williams, Paul Wilson, Jocelyn Wishart, Rachel Yates, Rachel Zewde.

Finally our greatest debt is to the students and young people who participated in "learning with ICT" and were key to the success of the project.

Contributors

Nick Breeze, Graduate School of Education, University of Bristol.

Roger Dale, Graduate School of Education, University of Bristol.

Keri Facer, Education & Social Research Institute, Manchester Metropolitan University.

Marina Gall, Graduate School of Education, University of Bristol.

Peter John, Thames Valley University, London.

Elisabeth Lazarus, Graduate School of Education, University of Bristol.

Sasha Matthewman, Graduate School of Education, University of Bristol.

John Morgan, Graduate School of Education, University of Bristol.

Federica Olivero, Graduate School of Education, University of Bristol.

Susan Robertson, Graduate School of Education, University of Bristol.

Dan Sutch, Futurelab.

Rosamund Sutherland, Graduate School of Education, University of Bristol.

Celia Tidmarsh, Graduate School of Education, University of Bristol.

Pat Triggs, Graduate School of Education, University of Bristol.

Authors' preface

This publication is a whole book written by several authors who all worked together on the InterActive Education project. As a team we came to the project with different ideas about teaching and learning with information and communication technology (ICT), ideas that to a certain extent converged throughout the project. The process of writing the book has been a collaborative one, with members of the team taking responsibility for writing different chapters. We have also given voice to the teacher researchers within the project through a series of vignettes and case studies that are threaded throughout the book. We value its multi-voiced nature and have not attempted to suppress differences in order to reach a synthesis. In this sense we see the book as a polyphony, where conflicting views and characters are left to develop unevenly into a crescendo. We hope that you will engage with and enjoy the whole book, while resonating with the parts that are particularly relevant for your own work.

Part 1

What are the issues?

Within the first part we set the scene for the whole book, identifying the challenges, issues and questions which it addresses. We start by presenting statistics on the penetration of new technologies into schools and discuss why overcoming the technical obstacles is necessary but not sufficient. We introduce the InterActive Education project which took up the challenge of expanding teachers' practice and empowering them in their uses of ICT for teaching and learning. We explain why we believe that to change practice and achieve a long-term shift in conceptions of how ICT can enhance teaching and learning, the traditional relationship between teachers and researchers has to be changed. We present an overview of the theoretical ideas that underpin the book as a whole and begin the process of illustrating these ideas with case studies of teachers learning to use ICT.

Chapter 1*

A holistic approach to understanding teaching and learning with ICT

Computer-based technologies can be powerful pedagogical tools – not just rich sources of information, but extensions of human capabilities and contexts for social interactions.

(Bransford *et al.* 2000, p. 218)

What is the issue?

The keynote quotation for this chapter presents a vision for the use of ICTs in teaching and learning that we share. It is ten years since Bransford and his colleagues articulated this idea of digital technologies as 'powerful pedagogical tools'. How near are we today to releasing the potential of new technologies to enhance teaching and learning in different settings and across different subjects?

Statistics show that between 2000 and 2006 large and ongoing government investment in technology resulted in a steady improvement in computer: student ratios in primary and secondary schools in the UK. In 2006, on average, there was one computer for every six students; in secondary schools there was one computer for 3.6 students.[1] Laptops became more available along with an increase in wireless connectivity.[2] Interactive whiteboards became a feature of many classrooms, especially in secondary schools. The central commitment to technology has been and remains a feature of educational policy documents. However, throughout this period the consistent message is that new digital technologies were and are being incorporated only inconsistently by practitioners in UK schools.[3]

Surveys do show a sharp increase in the use of ICT resources in lessons since 2005, but this is mainly accounted for by the rapid spread and adoption of interactive whiteboards. Teachers quickly saw the possibilities of whiteboards for whole-class teaching; their use of

* This chapter has been authored by Pat Triggs and Rosamund Sutherland.

presentation software and word processing, of downloaded and online resources in lesson planning and delivery increased. Aside from whole-class activity, uses of ICT remain in general limited to word processing and Internet search.[4] These tools appear deceptively transparent, while other technologies are perceived as more complex and challenging to use. However, assumptions that these more familiar uses of technology are unproblematic in relation to learning require examination.

Measures of the 'e-maturity'[5] of schools show wide variations in the extent to which use of technology is embedded in teaching and learning. School inspectors report that on average only two in six secondary school subject departments make effective use of ICT; the remaining four use ICT little if at all. Few practitioners in any phase of education fully exploit the possibilities for learning and teaching that new technologies offer. Using technology for analysing information and problem solving is limited, especially in the secondary phase. Few teachers incorporate new technologies to support students to work together collaboratively or cooperatively; there is little evidence of ICTs used to support creativity.[6]

The challenge, then, is to make the best use of new technologies for the benefit of learners, to enable practitioners to incorporate ICT securely and effectively in their practice and to develop their pedagogic repertoire.

Why does this matter?

Policy documents refer to evidence that incorporating ICT to support learning has a positive impact on learning outcomes. 'Statistical links between the use of technology and learning outcomes have been identified in an increasing body of evidence . . . The impact is greatest where ICT is an integral and embedded part of the day-to-day learning experience'.[7] If this is so then, at the most basic level of social justice, we owe it to our students to engage with this issue.

Research evidence also suggests that young people exhibit a higher level of engagement and more positive attitudes to learning where technology is incorporated. A large majority of primary and secondary teachers surveyed in 2006 agreed or strongly agreed that ICT could have a positive impact on the motivation of all student groups listed. Three-quarters or more of primary teachers in the survey agreed or strongly agreed that ICT also can have a positive impact on attainment. Secondary teachers were less sure about the impact of ICT on attainment, but even so, two-thirds of them thought the impact could be positive.[8] In theory, at least, the climate among teachers appears to be favourable to incorporating ICT in teaching and learning.

The notional twenty-first-century learner and worker, in 'the knowledge economy', is at the centre of much current educational discussion. The competencies, skills and attitudes required by this person are inextricably involved with new (and yet to be developed) technologies. But the issue goes beyond technology to the need for changes in current educational practices. Rather than using technology to keep learners in a passive role (as some technologies make possible), where learners are on the receiving end of resources and requirements for activity determined by teachers, schools or other agencies, the idea is to utilise the potential of technologies for more learner-centred approaches, to give learners more autonomy and choice about how to engage with what is offered. Although recent surveys show that around 60 per cent of teachers say they need training in the use of ICT in their teaching,[9] the kinds of pedagogical change that new technologies make possible frequently challenge current practice; so this is dangerous country, an uncomfortable place to travel for many schools and teachers. Our research experienced this at first hand and this book does not play down the tensions and dilemmas that are a part of the change process.

There is, then, a general feeling that pedagogical change is needed, and that, to an extent, technology will drive. This is also bound up in a concern that young people's informal out-of-school experiences with and of technology are so at odds with their in-school experiences that they may lose enthusiasm for formal education. The concept of 'personalised learning'[10] has appeared, associated with new approaches to learner support and management and to closer links between formal and informal learning which are in the process of being articulated and exemplified.

While a main driver for these desired changes may be to encourage the range of competencies increasingly demanded by employers and the economy more generally or to 'benefit learners entering a rapidly changing knowledge economy',[11] many in education will associate them also with the creation of a more just, humane, inclusive society, where the development and transformation of teaching and learning serves social and emotional as well as economic ends.

The InterActive Education research project took up the challenge of expanding teachers' practice and empowering them in their uses of technology for teaching and learning. The Methodological Appendix sets out the details of how the research was carried out. The knowledge and understandings teachers and researchers acquired during this process are set out and developed in subsequent chapters of this book. This chapter provides an introduction: it sets out some of the central ideas that informed the work teachers and researchers did together and illustrates some of the processes by which knowledge was collectively constructed.

Achieving change

We know that to enhance learning using ICT, having the equipment and meeting the technical challenges is necessary but not sufficient. Truckloads of hardware (however shiny) arriving in school will not necessarily change much for the better. Teachers are key and effective; professional development is the crucial element.

Experience has taught us that teachers remain central to students' learning with ICT but, to fully exploit the potential of new technologies in transforming learning, there is much for them to learn. Incorporating ICT frequently challenges well-established ways of teaching and learning. This sometimes involves painful rethinking. Things do not always work as planned and hoped. Ambiguities and paradoxes emerge as new roles and new rules emerge. Technology alters the social relationships in the classroom between students and between the teacher and the students in ways that are challenging. The tension between freedom/autonomy and constraints in managing learning is a constant issue and is an important thread developed in other chapters. We have found that learning is enhanced when teachers analyse and understand the potentialities of different ICT tools as they relate to the practices and purposes of their subject teaching, and when these tools are deployed appropriately for their students. The teacher's role, at best, involves a complex shifting of perspectives from the 'more-knowledgeable-other' to the 'co-constructor of knowledge' to the 'vicarious participant'. Effective teachers orchestrate the use of ICT, the interactions around it, and their own interventions.

Developing professionals

If the aim is to have a lasting impact on the current situation quick-fix approaches are a waste of time and money. We believe that to change practice and achieve a long-term shift in conceptions of how

ICT can enhance teaching and learning, the traditional relationship between teachers and researchers has to be changed. Both groups should bring their distinctive and complementary perspectives to the project, and should see themselves as co-constructors in the knowledge-building process. This book is based on research partnerships between university researchers, teacher educators and teachers. This group of people collaborated in designing research-informed learning initiatives and then analysed the outcomes.

A model of professional development where researchers are seen as knowledge generators and teachers as knowledge translators or users is too limited to achieve what is needed. The process of creating researcher-practitioner communities as places where co-learning takes place is complex, but the outcomes can be substantial. The majority of teacher researchers in the InterActive project used ICT successfully to enhance student learning. They attributed this success to the support they received from the project team and to feeling they had permission to take risks and experiment with embedding ICT into their classroom practices. In many cases this was in the context of institutional constraints and conditions.

Putting a 'thought experiment' into practice is not always a comfortable process. The relationships established within a community of practice are crucial. And, of course, being a member of a community researching practice is only one of teachers' many concerns and priorities. In our experience, professional events such as inspections by Ofsted,[12] high stakes assessment periods, school reorganisation, staff changes and crises, as well as personal events such as getting married, having twins, accidents and illness, all had an impact. One effect is that teachers engage with their professional development in different ways and at different levels.

Video as a tool for investigating teaching and learning

Digital video can be crucial to teachers' development. As a means of capturing teachers in action and students' responses, video, for us, proved to be vital in understanding and evaluating practice.

Teachers and students quickly became used to the presence of cameras in class. Teachers adapted more slowly to the experience of seeing themselves in action, but in many cases the outcomes were very positive, as this vignette shows.

VIGNETTE 1
A teacher reflects on the use of video

Ian Thompson was acting head of English in a secondary school when he joined the InterActive project. Ian's design initiative involved 13–14-year-old students producing a magazine-style newsletter for their parents about the school. The initiative was developed jointly with ICT staff at his school. All the classes took place in the computer room where students worked individually with a PC each. Students had different roles on the magazine and there was some interaction and collaboration. There were also teacher-led class sessions reviewing progress and highlighting different aspects of ICT and English. However, the majority of the work was individual and the configuration of the space was very different from that of the English classroom. Although he could circulate and interact more with individuals because the others were all working on their PCs, Ian felt that he was less in touch with the thinking of the whole class. The video evidence gave him an additional perspective.

Ian   It was a bit unnerving at first having two cameras in the room. Of course you got the usual reaction – some of the kids made faces and played up to the camera; some of them begged to be filmed. But we told them no-one was going to appear on TV. After a while it was like everyone says – we just forgot it and got on. Ours was a long initiative and we had hours of tape to look at. It sounds strange but it was one of the most amazing professional experiences ever. I've been formally observed many times – sometimes it was uncomfortable – things like Ofsted – but no matter what anyone said to me I wouldn't believe a word of it. Watching yourself is a completely different experience. It's the best form of reflection I've found. It allows you to step back from your practice and ask yourself: what is going on here? What are the thought processes here – mine and the kids'? Why am I saying that? Why did I think that objective was so important? We've taken extracts from the tapes and shown them to other members of the department. If I want to make a point about teaching and learning it's easier to pick myself to pieces – it's a good tool for a head of department. It's particularly valuable because it allows you to see the outcomes of your interventions in a way that doesn't focus on written outcomes. To see process when you are in the thick of it is difficult. On video you can see yourself interacting one-to-one or with a group, more importantly you can see students working when you are not there. I've got insights into the way they think, what they are doing with what I said at the beginning of the lesson. To be able to see something of their thought processes is very unusual.

Most of us when we look at ICT we go for what's safe. We go to what we know. Whereas this sometimes is not particularly safe – I like that. Have a go and get it wrong. The video was the important thing – it's allowed me to sit and watch and be comfortable with it . . . It's an important process. I can now refine my teaching . . . sit back and reflect properly. I never had the chance and video made it happen.

Ian was one of the teacher researchers who became deeply engaged with the project. He was also one of the first to use a video recording of himself to promote discussion in his department. His story continues in Chapter 4. For other teacher researchers micro-analysis of video data enabled the development of ideas about the kinds of learning that were happening, and speculation about the range of factors that were having an impact on this. Chapter 2 provides detailed examples of this.

The use of video to focus issues and offer 'realistic portraits of practice' can be a powerful way of moving thinking on.[13]

Using theory and research to inform practice

The research that informs this book drew on socio-cultural theories of learning (Vygotsky 1978, Wertsch 1985, Wertsch 1991). For us, learning events in school have to be understood as embedded in institutions and linked to the historical and political dynamics of the classroom. Similarly, learning in the home both shapes and is shaped by the history and structures of family formation and family life.

A key aspect of socio-cultural theory is the claim that all human action is mediated by 'technical' and 'cognitive' tools. We interpret the idea of 'tool' to incorporate a wide range of technologies and artefacts such as pen, paper, book and computer, as well as semiotic systems and institutional structures. Within this broad conception of tools the master tool is language. We understand the computer as a technological tool where the culture and context of use shapes the potential and possibilities of the tool.

> A fundamental assumption in a socio-cultural understanding of human learning is precisely this: learning is always learning to do something with cultural tools (be they intellectual and/or theoretical). This has the important implication that when understanding learning we have to consider the unit that we are studying is people in action using tools of some kind.
>
> (Saljo 1999, p. 147)

From this basic assumption of 'tools' or a 'tool kit' as central to learning we use Wertsch's idea of 'person-acting-with-mediational-means', and Salomon's (1993) distinctions between the 'effects-with and the effects-of technology', to consider classroom activities and interactions.

We also draw on ideas of intelligence as distributed (Salomon 1993, Pea 1993) and learning as situated and socially constructed (Vygotsky 1978). Our interest is in learning communities and group practices, and in the ways these are dynamic and changing. The way in which individuals and groups draw on 'available resources' to create new resources (New London Group 1996) led us to expand ideas around the 'potential' of a tool (Gibson 1979, Norman 1983 and 1993) to consider the differences between the planned and actual use of the tool and to point to the crucial role of the teacher in considering and planning for the use of tools. The concept of 'appropriation' (Wertsch 1991) is important to the analysis of the variety of ways in which ICT tools are incorporated in different subject domains and the concept of 'instrumentation' (Verillon and Rabardel 1995) explains why different people appropriate the same tool in different ways.

To think about the processes and progress of change in the production, reception and use of ICT in teaching and learning, a holistic perspective is important. The national, local and institutional context within which teachers teach and students learn is salient. A whole range of school-related factors – teachers' experiences of ICT outside school, how schools are managed, the ways different school subjects mediate how ICTs are used, how learning with ICT might be theorised in different subject domains – inter-relate and have an impact on what happens in classrooms. What students bring into school from their out-of-school experiences of ICT and how this relates to their in-school learning provides another essential dimension.

Building knowledge about ICT

An important concept in this respect is the idea of communities of learners (Wenger 1998, Lave and Wenger 1991). Co-researchers and knowledge builders need to develop mutual understanding, confidence and trust. In our communities, group members explored beliefs about their subject and the ways in which it is best taught and learned. Key points about ICT and the subject were discussed and clarified. In general teachers make little use of research to think about or inform their practice. We set out to share research-based ideas about teaching and learning, and about embedding ICT in teaching and learning and to consider them in relation to teachers' practices and their institutional settings.

For example, in the English Subject Design Team (SDT)[14] an activity exploring poems using PowerPoint sparked a discussion in which the issue of the 'English bit' and the 'ICT bit' emerged strongly. (The team made a note to look at the work of Gunther Kress and of the New London Group in subsequent meetings.[15]) Also articulated were the tensions between current definitions of the school English curriculum and its approach to assessment (as in the Literacy Hour, the National Curriculum and GCSE courses[16]) and the kinds of activities learners engaged in and the work they produced in response to the incorporation of ICT in learning.

Questions like: 'Is English becoming a new subject, with new genres and new texts?' 'How do we understand and respond to terms like visual literacy, multimodality, multimedia?' became central to the English SDT as the project progressed. (This is considered more fully in Chapter 6.)

Most teachers liked engaging with research-based ideas and findings.

Dan   Working closely with my university partner and the whole team was without doubt the biggest influence on my learning. I was introduced to new subject knowledge and new theories of teaching and learning.

Maria   Sometimes research was introduced but not in a pushy way. It was more thoughtful. The university people would try to explain why things had been done a particular way by using their own knowledge of the area and sometimes they would quote key sources and back them up with references. Then it would move to us choosing one for discussion at our next meeting.

They also for the most part enjoyed the idea that they were involved in a research activity. Data collected in the classroom was considered first by teacher-researcher partnerships. Key points and issues that emerged from this collaborative analysis became the focus for the whole group. Extracts of data were presented and discussed. The larger group became for us the forum in which understandings developed and knowledge was co-constructed. In this context teachers achieved insights into their own practice and to ICT in teaching and learning generally.

Heidi   It's just another tool – and it's what you can do with it that counts, not the tool itself.
Simon   Researching work with ICT in my class reminded me that learning doesn't happen in straight lines but is a social and shared experience which at times can appear chaotic.

Two examples, from secondary mathematics and primary English, show how teacher researchers can work on data to extend the analysis and generalise from the specific. Both examples are shown in the 'comic strip' format we developed to share ideas with other interested teachers.

CASE STUDY 1
Learning about functions and graphs

Rachel Zewde worked with her Year 9 mathematics group (13–14-year-olds) to investigate the properties of linear functions.[17] She chose to use graphic calculators because they could be easily brought into the classroom, which meant that she didn't have to go into the alien surroundings of the computer suite. Many secondary teachers dislike taking students to a computer room and this was particularly marked for the mathematics teachers we worked with.

The class worked on functions for four lessons. Rachel's research partner from the university, Steve Godwin, used two cameras to collect video recordings of Rachel with the whole class and also of two boys (John and Mike) working together. Rachel and Steve looked closely at the video from the third lesson, and from their analysis selected one extract for discussion with the maths team (see Figure 1.1 below).

The team members were interested in how the two boys approached the task. John starts by ignoring the set task and trying out the function he suggested earlier. He shows the results to Mike and only then applies himself to the set task, quickly loading the examples Rachel has provided. He identifies a trend: 'The gradient gets steeper'. The video shows the way the boys use their calculators: sometimes they work separately, sometimes we

The story begins with a whole class session...

Rachel begins to investigate the properties of linear functions with the class

Rachel now moves on to other linear functions

Rachel records John's example but does not investigate it.

Later, Rachel directs the class to work on further examples of straight line graphs using their calculators. They have then to reconstruct the line accurately in their books. The students begin to work in pairs...

Ignoring the set task, John uses his calculator to try out the function he suggested earlier. He shows the results to his friend.

John helps Mike to see how the calculator can help them to reconstruct the line in their books.

John and Mike construct the graphs on paper.

Figure 1.1 Learning about functions and graphs

continued

see both hands on one calculator in close collaboration. The final section of the video shows the two boys transforming what they have learned from using the calculator. John shows Mike how they can use the trace facility of the calculator to identify the coordinates of two points along the line and thus reconstruct it on paper.

Analysis of the video suggests that both students, as well as following their own thinking, were learning the mathematical knowledge that was the intended focus of Rachel's lessons. Comparing assessments before and after the lessons, John's score went up by 57 per cent and Mike's by 71 per cent.

Discussion of the video extract produced ideas about how the potential of graphic calculators was helping John and Mike's learning.

- Investigating and trying out things – John was able to try out his suggestions for a non-parallel function, see what happened, show his friend and then apply himself to the set task. With pen and paper John would not have been able to pursue his idea AND follow Rachel's plan for the lesson.
- Constructing and viewing a large number of graphs quickly to develop an insight into the properties of related graphs (graph families). John constructed a series of graphs suggested by his teacher and was able to see how the gradient became steeper. The time taken to produce graphs with pen and paper places a limit on 'seeing' relationships and properties.
- Experimenting within liberating constraints[18] – Rachel was able to set up carefully chosen tasks to scaffold the learning.
- Supporting pen and paper forms of representation.

The idea of 'liberating constraints' became a useful one for the project. It is illustrated and discussed further in Chapter 4.

CASE STUDY 2
Using e-mail to develop understanding of how a sense of audience shapes writing

Emma Scott-Cook's class of eight-year-olds used e-mail as a source of information for their history work on Vikings. An associated aim of the design was to increase understanding of the role of audience and purpose in shaping writing. A university-based researcher took on the identities of Thor and Freya, Viking settlers in England in 880. In the history activity, information gained from 'e-mailing a Viking' was combined in group presentations. E-mails (with permission) were also shared with the whole class; in these plenary sessions the focus might be on the historical content or on the style of the children's writing and the effect this might have on a reader.

It was the writing development aspect that was foregrounded when the English team looked at the data. In this case the data was in the form of copies of the e-mails written over several weeks, and evidence from six children who were recorded as they read through the whole e-mail exchange with an interviewer and recalled whatever aspects of the reading and writing were prompted by this activity.

Presented below is the group's commentary on the e-mail exchange between one of the students, Annette, and the Viking Freya.

The group commented on the way in which all the children had entered the 'fiction'. The interview data showed that although they 'knew' that they could not really be 'e-mailing a Viking' they were very happy to sustain the idea that they were. This 'willing suspension of disbelief' appeared to create a strong sense of authenticity which enabled useful work around 'audience'. Looking at the data and the analysis of Annette's writing the team thought that Annette had learned a lot about writing from the activity. The 'authenticity' of the communication seems to have sharpened her sense of audience as a controlling factor. The ongoing feedback provided by e-mail was encouraging. Being given access to a computer and time to write, the supportive frame of the e-mail and little expectation about length were also identified as

continued

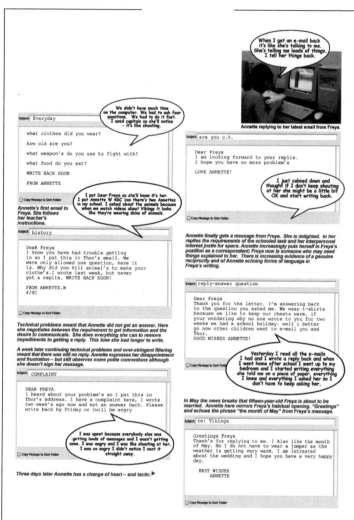

Figure 1.2 E-mailing a Viking

contributory factors in Annette's writing development. The team also thought that the more 'public' discussion of the exchanges in plenary sessions had been useful in enabling a specific focus on language and 'audience'. Gaining the e-mail recipient's permission for the messages to be shared was seen as important as a clear acknowledgement of the interpersonal nature of the format.

The group discussed e-mail as a genre and the many conventions assumed to be associated with it. The feeling was that this was a valuable form for the discussion of the range of 'appropriate' styles and the negotiation of a relationship between writer and reader. The group also considered the effects of the research method by which a sample of students had been encouraged to reread, reflect on and reconstruct the process of composing their e-mails. Team members felt this was a strategy that might be incorporated in the teaching and learning as it was valuable for writers to be given an opportunity to reflect on, review and be articulate about a writing sequence captured in this way.

We end this chapter with a teacher's story. It illustrates how working as part of a research community of practice had both a personal and professional impact, and how the various strands evident in this book interweave in one teacher's experience.

A teacher's perspective on researching ICT and learning

CASE STUDY 3
A personal account by Simon Mills

The school where I work is on an estate in South Bristol. Built in the post-war housing boom of the 1950s it now suffers from many areas of deprivation. We have over 450 students aged from 3–11 but the school population is constantly in flux. On average 30 per cent of a year group can change during a Key Stage. A very high proportion of our students enter school with significant learning delays, emotional and social difficulties and very low self-esteem. The development of speaking and listening remains a high priority. In a typical Key Stage 2 classroom attainment ranges from children 'working towards level 1' to those achieving well above the nationally expected average for their age.

I have worked at the school for 16 years, which has been rewarding, exhausting and high stress in turn and simultaneously. In 2002, my head teacher asked me, as ICT co-ordinator, to evaluate how the use of the interactive whiteboard in my classroom was influencing student learning. I heard about the InterActive project, made contact and was invited to join the mathematics team. Looking back over the past six years I can see how much my involvement has meant to me personally and professionally. Most importantly, I think, it meant that I came again to see teaching as a research-informed practice, something I had lost sight of since my undergraduate days.

During one of our team meetings we were discussing how and perhaps why some children found the interpretation of graphs and charts to be problematic. One of us suggested that one of the barriers to developing understanding of graphs and charts was that young children could not distinguish between the roles that various charts fulfilled. As the discussion unfolded I began to think that perhaps the reason for this was not embedded in children's understanding but in the way the teaching of mathematics in this area was limited by the paper-based activities we use to develop it, and perhaps by the way in which charts and graphs were perceived as mathematical tools by their users.

I decided that this was an area I would like to explore and develop further. Data handling and graphical interpretation were areas of the curriculum which my colleagues in school were concerned about. It was becoming a common vehicle for engaging children with 'using and applying work' within science. The National Curriculum docu-mentation links data handling, with the mathematics and science curriculum, and with areas as diverse as geography (exploring land use, climate and change over time) and design and technology (surveying and supporting the identification of needs). There is also the everyday use of charts and graphs in non-fiction texts, newspapers and on TV.

I was also aware that the data-handling units, within the Qualifications and Curriculum Authority (QCA) scheme of work we were using, were frequently taught in isolation from the rest of the curriculum. As a curriculum leader I wanted to be able to offer an alternative, more integrated approach.

I could see the limitations of paper-based work. It is very difficult to teach young children to draw, for example, pie charts. They may be limited in the accurate use of instruments, and also in their conceptual understanding of how to divide a circle using trigonometry or proportion. The time it takes to generate charts and graphs on paper has been pointed out by Ainley, Nardi and Pratt (2000) as a reason why children rarely engage with charts and graphs beyond their drawing and simple interpretation, and why charts were rarely used for problem solving or the identification of trends and patterns within the primary school. ICT offers a solution to these limitations. I decided that for my design initiative I would work with my class of eight-year-olds to look at charts and graphs not as things we draw, but as meaning-making objects. The focus would not be on drawing charts, but on collecting data and using ICT to help us generate graphical representations. We could then concentrate on reading the charts and understanding what they were able to tell us.

In class the sessions began within a structure very much like a literacy hour. The children were given a number of chart types, and asked to discuss these, framed by the following questions:

- what was the chart about?
- who might have made the chart and why?
- who might find it useful?
- how useful was the chart?
- what features of the charts enabled you to make these decisions?

They also sorted the charts into the ones they thought were more and less useful; in doing this they had to discuss and present reasons for their decisions. In the sessions which followed, we used a range of interactive approaches including Smart Board Notebooks and PowerPoint presentations to discuss ideas and support the continued exploration of charts as meaning-making structures, and to identify and establish the features of 'good' charts that enable us to interpret what they represent. It was apparent from these sessions that the children had fewer problems in understanding how to extract the stories that common chart types told than we had conjectured during our discussions in the mathematics team.

Moving from the classroom to the ICT suite, children were introduced to the software environment Microsoft Excel, as a tool to support the evaluation of a real-life problem. The problem was 'borrowed' from the work of Janet Ainley (2000) but I had no problems presenting it to the children as an authentic one. I really, really like Smarties, but I had noticed that there never seemed to be the same number of my favourite orange flavour in every tube. And it had also struck me that there were more of some colours than others in the tubes I bought. I asked the children to investigate whether my impressions were correct. Each child was given a tube of the sweets, and asked to count them, and input the frequency of each colour to the spreadsheet. I emphasised the need for titles and labels which would help the readers of our data.

What was interesting from the start was the existence of two distinct ways of organising the Smarties for counting. Some children sorted colours into groups while others sorted and arranged their beans into columns, making a pictogram-type presentation before inputting their data to the spreadsheet. This observation became a key feature and teaching point since it represented to me and the children a powerful way of linking the frequency table to the bar chart representation they eventually made.

Having completed the frequency table, one of the children began playing within the spreadsheet environment with the chart wizards. (We had used wizards in other Microsoft packages.) He quickly and independently began generating pie charts and bar charts from the data he and his partner had collected. Later when the researchers interviewed children on their out-of-school uses of ICT we learned that some of them had used spreadsheets at home, and this experience must also have impacted on what the children produced in the classroom.

For the following lesson I decided to have this student model his learning for the class, and to use his actions to help teach what I wanted the other children to learn about presenting data in chart form. With the student modelling and me talking, the students were shown how to create charts using the wizard. He also modelled how to change the colours of bars or segments, giving clear reasons why he was doing so: he wanted to match the chart colours to the sweets as this would make it easier for people to understand. We discussed how to add axis labels and titles to the chart and began to draw on previous work to think about how we could use these to further help users to understand the charts.

Aside from learning about presentation, we also concluded from our work that my impressions about the frequency of different coloured Smarties were right. I asked the group in the final session to suggest ways that I might be able to investigate how many tubes I would have to buy, in order to get a fair share. One of the girls suggested that we could combine the class data sets in a pie chart; we could watch the segments in the chart until they were about the same size, and then we could count the number of tubes we had used, and this would tell us.

This whole sequence of lessons took eight hours. The children followed these up by desk-top publishing their results, and together we e-mailed our findings to Nestlé and asked for some explanations. To judge from their reply (an acknowledgement and a fact sheet) they didn't seem to understand we were a group of eight-year-old investigators.

The conversations with my university research partners, the video data and discussion in the maths team all made me more aware of what was happening in my classroom and in the ICT suite. I noticed myself being a 'scaffold' and a facilitator: picking up on what the children had done, encouraging them to be explicit and share their thinking, helping groups identify next steps, focusing them on the ideas and skills they were developing and constantly referring them to the questions they were investigating. I was interested in the number of bits of unplanned and opportunistic teaching and learning that had happened because of the technology: the missed opportunities I might have developed. It was clear to me that I needed and wanted to think more about the relationship between my pedagogy, the ICT and the children's learning, in mathematics and all the rest.

Recent years have provided many exciting and fascinating opportunities for me. In order to engage further with the data I had collected I applied for and was awarded a DfES Best Practice Research scholarship.[19] I then began a part-time MSc degree in Education Technology and Society at the University of Bristol's Graduate School of Education. I am gripped by the things my students can teach me about what it means to learn. For my

Master's dissertation, I am using video data collected in my classroom as a 'way of seeing' and understanding what learning looks like, and exploring how the range of classroom tools helps me achieve my planned outcomes. I have been involved in other university-based researcher-practitioner partnerships around new technologies. I have had opportunities to share my emerging classroom-based findings and practices with other practitioners, researchers and a wider educational audience. This has been through workshops, conference presentations, teachers' TV and publications. I feel I have also been a contributory voice in local, national and international debates on policy, practice and curriculum development, involving the role ICTs might perform as tools to support teaching and learning. This year my school has acknowledged this by providing the opportunity for me to take on a non-classroom-based role to review our use of ICT and develop it as a learning tool across the curriculum.

In school currently we have examples of children blogging in Year 6, multimedia authoring in Year 2, staff multimedia authoring to tell holiday stories from the point of view of our travelling teddy bear, geotagging, stories developed within digital writing frames and a host of other things, some of which have been sought out for use by the Local Authority as examples of good practice for the development of writing. I was recently asked to lead two sessions for ICT subject leaders on the roles and potential uses of blogs in the primary school. Web 2.0 is a really exciting place to be.[20]

I have started thinking out loud on my own blog (http://two whizzy.blogspot.com). Reflections on the new framework for primary literacy and numeracy are helping me analyse and come to grips at long last with what multimodality seems to mean, and supporting my thinking around the use of video. Having avoided semiotics for so long, it has now become an inevitability, not just because of my dissertation, but in terms of its practical application to the emerging literacy curriculum in school. Interactive white-boards, the new numeracy framework and our ongoing work on data handling within social contexts, have all encouraged me to push hard for our literacy and numeracy subject leaders to begin broadening their views of what 'literacy' might mean and look like from the perspective of some of our students. I am confident that none of this would have happened without the experiences and the impetus to think about my practice and the children's learning that my involvement with the InterActive project gave me.

Simon's story shows the development of an enabled and proactive practitioner; he exemplifies the kind of Masters level teacher the profession is looking towards. Ideas around how we achieve this are explored more fully in Chapter 4. Simon's experience also provides a practical illustration of how classroom experiences must be seen as embedded in the wider context of home and school. Simon worked effectively within existing local and national constraints on curriculum and pedagogy. He was also already very aware of much of the social background of the children in his class. However, as a result of reflecting on data collected in his classroom and with the support of his co-researchers he began to find out much more about the experiences of ICTs as tools that the children were bringing to school, and to think about how these might relate to their in-school learning. We consider the out-of-school dimension more broadly in Chapter 8.

Summary and conclusions

This chapter has identified the challenges, issues and questions which this book addresses. These are located firmly in the current context and stage of development in embedding new technologies in the processes of learning and teaching for the benefit of students in school. Arguments about why it is important to address the issues and questions associated with the challenge of incorporating ICTs in learning have been set out.

The chapter explains briefly some of the central ideas that inform the book: the theories we draw on and the principles that underpin the processes of the work teachers and researchers did together. The three case studies illustrate some of the processes by which teachers and university researchers worked together to build knowledge. They show how teachers' 'designs' are informed in an ongoing and iterative way by theory, research-based evidence, teacher's craft knowledge and the expertise of the whole community. Reciprocity characterised the processes by which knowledge was constructed.

Each of the following chapters in the book develops and adds to these ideas, drawing on research experience to engage in depth with the issues and questions surrounding improving learning with ICT which we have outlined and begun to raise here. Chapters 2, 3, 5 and 7 provide more detailed examples of this process in action. Chapter 7, for example, uses the instinctively negative response of a teacher to moving from his own classroom to the computer area (the same instinct that in part prompted Rachel, in this chapter, to use graphic calculators) as a starting point for discussing ideas about the ways in which ICTs constitute a challenge to assumptions about how people learn and how teachers should teach. Chapters 6 and 7 look also at the epistemological challenges the InterActive project has highlighted in relation to 'subjects', the tensions around subject definitions and subject cultures that technology produces, and the associated challenge to articulate these changing understandings in defining a school curriculum and approaches to assessment. Chapters 10 and 11 are concerned with the way in which our own thinking has moved on as we deal with a very fast-moving technological environment.

The vignettes and case studies in this chapter give a voice to some of the teachers who have been active collaborators in the quest to find ways to make the most effective use of the potential of new technologies for learning and teaching. We hear these voices consistently throughout the book. Not all those who were part of the community moved as far as Simon or Ian. For others, their steps on the road towards the 'enabled practitioner' described in Chapter 4 were smaller, more hesitant, less secure. But it is important also to hear their voices and their experiences if we are to understand how to face the professional development challenge.

The book constitutes our response to the issues we identified and the questions we posed at the start of this chapter. It also, we hope, demonstrates our commitment to the most effective incorporation of new technologies in learning and teaching for the benefit of all those involved. We believe this is an issue that matters. We also know that improving learning with ICTs is a complex, many-layered and subtle process; this book aims to contribute to the development of better understanding of how this can be achieved, and to bring some important issues into sharper focus.

Notes

1 Prior, G. and Hall, L. (2004), DfES (2007).
2 Kitchen, Finch and Sinclair (2007).
3 See Goldstein (1997), DfEE (1997), Becta (2007).
4 Kitchen, Finch and Sinclair (2007).
5 This is a concept developed by Butt and Cebulla (2006) to indicate the extent to which the use of ICT is integral to teaching and planning in a school, and the extent of students' access to ICT in and out of the classroom.
6 Kitchen, Finch and Sinclair (2007).
7 Becta (2007).
8 Kitchen, Finch and Sinclair (2007).
9 Ashby (2007).
10 This concept first appeared under this name in a pamphlet 'A National Conversation about Personalised Learning' DfES (2004). It is supported in the report of the DfES 'Teaching and Learning in 2020' Review Group. For more detail see the government websites www.standards.dfes. gov.uk/personalisedlearning and www.teachernet.gov.uk/management/ newrelationships/personalisedlearning.
11 Becta (2007).
12 The Office for Standards in Education, a governmental agency charged with inspecting and assessing standards of student attainment, teaching quality, effectiveness and value for money of schools in England.
13 The InterActive project has incorporated video data in materials developed to disseminate project outcomes. These include video papers and CPD resources on the project website: www.interactiveeducation.ac.uk. See also Olivero et al. (2004).
14 For an explanation of the role and operation of Subject Design Teams (SDT) in the InterActive Education project see the Methodological Appendix (p. 217).
15 See New London Group (1996). Gunther Kress is a member of the New London Group. He has written widely on multimodality, representation and new media in relation to education and learning.
16 Since 1986 the national curriculum in the UK has provided a structured and assessed education through Key Stages for students aged 5–14. At the time of the InterActive project students took standardised assessment tests at the end of each Key Stage, at ages 7, 11 and 14. Post-14 students generally followed two-year courses, including those for the GCSE (General Certificate of Secondary Education) which are available in all subjects. The National Curriculum and GCSE are administered by the government's Qualifications and Curriculum Authority (QCA). From September 1998 all primary schools in England have been expected to teach the literacy hour as laid down in the National Literacy Strategy. The structure

and content of the daily hour-long lesson is prescribed. From 2000 this initiative to raise literacy standards was extended to English lessons in secondary schools for students in Key Stage 3 (see www.standards.dfes. gov.uk).

17 For a fuller discussion of Rachel's work see Godwin and Sutherland (2004).

18 For further discussion of the concept of liberating constraints see Chapter 5.

19 Best Practice Research Scholarships were awarded to teachers by the government Department for Education and Skills (DfES) on a competitive basis. Several teachers working in the InterActive project gained scholarships which enabled them to pursue their research in more depth. University researchers acted as mentors. These scholarships have now been discontinued.

20 Web 2.0 is a phrase coined in 2003 and since popularised. It refers to a perceived second generation of web-based communities and hosted services – such as social-networking sites, blogs and wikis – which facilitate collaboration and sharing between users.

Part 2

What does the research tell us?

In this part we enter into the detail of the InterActive Education project. We introduce a range of theoretical ideas that can be used to help understand the challenges involved in introducing ICT into the classroom. We present arguments and case studies to illustrate the results from the project, which include:

- the teacher remains key to the successful use of ICT for learning;
- learning is distributed between the technology, the learner and the social and cultural context;
- effective teaching and learning with ICT involves building bridges between 'incidental' and 'intended' learning;
- there is nothing inherent in technology that guarantees the intended learning;
- there is a two-way exchange of knowledge between home and school use of ICT that impacts on learning in school;
- professional development needs to enable teachers to take risks with ICT and learning;
- teachers can work within the constraints of available technology to enhance learning;
- language remains the keystone of literate practices.

Chapter 2

Integrating ICT in teaching and learning

Research in the area of ICT and classroom learning is now virtually unanimous in claiming that while new technologies can be used to enhance learning, they are not sufficient in themselves to produce effective learning. This chapter builds on this proposition and shows that the teacher is key to 'improving learning with ICT'. The chapter further highlights the processes by which a teacher can act as a lever to reorientate learning so that there is a convergence towards the development of common knowledge. Much of the chapter's argument is based on the idea of the classroom as a collective experience where learning is not seen as an isolated endeavour but one which is both mutual and collaborative.

One clear observation to be taken from the chapter is that classroom learning with ICT requires teachers to exploit the sense of familiarity with new technologies that is now widespread among young people. However, this also means that teachers themselves need time to gain an intimate knowledge of the technology and that this can sometimes be best achieved through 'playfulness' and experimentation. The chapter has three aims at its core:

- to discuss the ways in which ICT can be integrated into classroom practices to enhance learning;
- to highlight the ways in which students bring out-of-school experiences of using ICT into the classroom;
- to emphasise that effective teaching and learning with ICT involves building bridges between 'idiosyncratic' and 'intended' learning.

* This chapter was authored by Rosamund Sutherland and Dan Sutch.

Exploiting available technology

We know that merely introducing ICT into schools will not in itself lead to enhanced learning nor will devolving the responsibility for teaching to the technology. But we also know that it is possible to find ways of incorporating ICT into classroom practices to improve learning. However, beginning the process of integrating ICT into teaching and learning is not straightforward and involves being able to imagine the potential of particular technologies for learning within the contexts in which it will take place. It also involves taking the risk of experimenting with ICT in the classroom. This process has to be concerned with the here and now of available technologies, as opposed to looking to the future for the next big technological development that will somehow solve the problem of integrating ICT into teaching and learning. Those of us who have been around since the early days of the introduction of computers into schools have observed how each new technological development, from Logo to multimedia, to the Internet, to mobile technology to Web 2.0, has been heralded as being the final breakthrough that will make the difference to education. We have also observed that riding the wave of each new technological breakthrough never begins to address the issues that face education. Rather, we believe that we need to focus on understanding the inter-related factors that come together when technology is being used to enhance learning.

Within the InterActive project we developed a way of working that enabled teachers to work together with teacher educators and researchers in order to start the process of using ICT in the classroom. Each teacher developed a subject design initiative (SDI) and this process involved:

- *deciding on a focused area of the curriculum* that students normally find difficult to learn and choosing ICTs that could potentially enhance learning in this area;
- *out-of-the-classroom design as a thought experiment.* This involves thinking about the area to be taught, considering relevant research, developing activities and experimenting with the chosen ICTs, while at the same time imagining how students would engage with these activities from the point of view of the intended learning. It also involves taking into account the background knowledge and experience of the students;

- *into-the-classroom contingent teaching* which draws on all the prepared activities while at the same time opportunistically using what the students bring to the lesson to extend their learning;
- *out-of-the-classroom reflection* on and analysis of the design initiative using video data collected from the classroom experimentation.

In this approach learning initiatives usually started out as simple ideas which exploited the use of available technology in schools. Over time and with iteration they were transformed into powerful new uses of ICT for learning. As discussed in Chapter 1 the InterActive Education project was organised around subject design teams (SDTs) in English, mathematics, science, modern foreign languages, music, history and geography. Within each team a partnership of teachers, teacher educators and researchers supported teachers to take the risk of experimenting with ICT in the classroom.

Throughout the book we have incorporated case studies that highlight the ways in which ICT can be used to enhance learning. We start this chapter with an example from the work of one of the teachers, Dan Sutch, from the English design team. Dan's starting point was a desire to help his 10–11-year-old students learn about spelling in the English language. He worked with students, using WordRoot,[1] a multimedia sound and word package to analyse the structure and etymology of 'hard words', and through this work students' spelling improved.

Throughout the book we present the work of other teachers from the InterActive project. In Chapter 5 we discuss how Elisabeth Lazarus and Ruth Cole used ICT with 13–14-year-olds to support their writing in German. They designed a drop-down menu template in Word that enabled students to write more in the foreign language and take more risks with grammar. Students' writing on paper was also enhanced after this initiative.

In Chapter 1 Simon Mills describes how he incorporated the use of spreadsheets and an interactive whiteboard to teach 8–9-year-old students statistical ideas. This initiative centred on a whole-class investigation of the distribution of the colours of Smarties in a tube.

Later in this chapter we discuss how Marnie Weeden used dynamic geometry software with 13–14-year-old students to learn about geometrical proof. Students worked in groups and presented their work to the class for feedback on the validity of the proofs they had produced.

In Chapter 5 we discuss how primary and secondary students used software to learn about composing in music.[2] Also in Chapter 5 we present the evolution of an SDI for geography in which the teacher used ICT to support geographical inquiry.

Incidental, idiosyncratic and intentional learning

Analysis of the video data from the InterActive project showed that students often work with ICT for extended periods of time, investigating their own questions and experimenting with ideas in an interactive and iterative way. This relates to the power and potential of ICT for learning, and through this process students inevitably learn and construct new knowledge. However, there is a tension inherent in this potential of ICT. Extended individual engagement often leads to the construction of idiosyncratic or incidental learning which is at odds or is only part of the intended learning. For example, as we discuss in Chapter 3, when primary students were using simulation software to learn about the ecology of the sea they treated the simulation as a game and became engaged in winning. The language they used as they interacted with the software was about winning: *'Don't die . . . we gotta beat people . . . we need to beat 5 minutes'*. In this situation the students were not entering the world of science, as the designers of the simulation had intended: 'The Fishtank draws on research from the new field of "artificial life", which focuses on computer modeling of animal behavior. The VirtualFishtank adopts a constructionist approach, enabling visitors to design (and not merely observe) the behaviors of fish.'[3] It was not until the teacher began to analyse video data from classroom interactions that she became aware that students were interacting with the software as a computer game, and that unknowingly she had supported this practice through her own use of language.

Learning is an inevitable part of living. We learn from interacting with the people and things which surround us, through language and play. We call this sort of learning 'incidental' because it is not normally planned as learning, and can take place in settings which have not been specifically designed for learning. For example, we can learn how to sing, how to play chess and how to throw a ball through interacting with family and friends.

By contrast schools have been developed as institutions to foster particular kinds of learning, and whatever the country or culture there is always some kind of 'intended' learning associated with schooling which relates to a curriculum. Such a curriculum is not fixed and changes over time and between cultures. In fact, as we discuss in Chapter 9, ICTs are challenging what should or could be in the curriculum, challenging knowledge domains, such as mathematics, science and geography. And, as we discuss in Chapter 6, ICT is also challenging what is important in the school subject of English.

It is important to emphasise that in school there is not a simple relationship between what students learn and what a teacher intends them to learn: in other words there can be no simple transmission from the teacher to students. Students will always learn much that is incidental to what is intended. All that teachers can achieve is a sort of convergence towards a 'common knowledge'. Introducing ICTs into the classroom does not necessarily help this process of convergence and in fact can actually work against it. This is because students can work with ICTs to develop idiosyncratic knowledge that is actually at odds with what the teacher wants to teach, as illustrated by the VirtualFishtank case study discussed more fully in Chapter 3. Students also bring to the classroom a history of learning which can also be 'different' from that which the teacher wants them to learn, as illustrated by the vignette on geometry and proof discussed later in this chapter. Students can also construct knowledge that is 'correct' for a particular situation, but is not generalisable to a wide range of situations, as illustrated by the vignette on learning language, discussed in the next section of this chapter. This is not a new phenomenon, but can be exacerbated by the introduction of ICTs into schools, and also by the more informal use of ICTs out of school, as discussed more fully in Chapter 8.

Throughout the InterActive project we struggled with the ideas of 'incidental' and 'intended' learning. Whereas the mathematics and science subject teams were comfortable with discussing these concepts, members of the music and English teams were less so, sometimes seeming to adopt a position in which they wanted to value all learning which takes place within music or English classrooms. However, as we worked together throughout the project it became clear that within each subject area teachers have strong views about what they consider to be appropriate learning. This is evident in Chapter 6 in which Sasha Matthewman argues for the importance of retaining a focus on spoken and written language within the English curriculum. This argument for maintaining an emphasis on language in school occurs at a time when students are likely (if given the

freedom) to privilege other modes, such as the visual, when constructing texts in the English classroom. We are not suggesting that all
teachers agree on what is to be valued within a particular subject
area, but that they have views about what they want students to
learn: views that are, of course, influenced by the curriculum. The
'intended learning' is what the teacher wants students to learn, which
is not the same as what they actually learn.

We now present two case studies taken from the work of the
English and mathematics SDTs in order to illustrate the creative
tensions inherent in integrating ICT into classroom practices, and
the crucial role of the teacher in focusing students' attention on the
'intended' learning.

CASE STUDY 1
Learning language in the primary school

Introduction

This case study is taken from the work of Dan Sutch who was a
member of the English design team. It is used to illustrate three
important aspects of learning with ICT. The first is that students
inevitably bring to the classroom experiences of using ICT out of
school and that it is important for the teacher to value this learning.
The second is that when students are constructing knowledge for
themselves it is likely to work for a particular situation but is not
always generalisable to a wider range of situations. The third is
that an effective way of confronting students with their ongoing
knowledge construction is through whole-class discussion.

Dan worked over a period of two years to develop an inquiry-
based approach to learning spelling which incorporated the use
of the software WordRoot and PowerPoint. Students aged 10–11
years worked on a series of investigations of the English language
that centred around the idea of providing them with a 'speller's
toolkit'. In general lessons consisted of a mixture of whole-class,
group and independent work supported by extensive homework
investigations. The vignette we present here relates to two lessons
in which students were investigating how to select the appropriate
grapheme to represent an irregular phoneme.[4] For example, recognising when the phoneme /e/ should be spelt 'e', 'ei', ie', 'ey', etc.

Into the classroom – Investigating spelling rules for the sound /e/

At the beginning of the lesson students were asked to consider whether there are any spelling rules to help them build the sound /e/. For example, if they were writing the word 'bossy', and they had no visual memory of the word, how would they choose to spell it? The teacher prepared a presentation in PowerPoint so that all students could read and recognise the phoneme /e/ as an introduction to their investigation. The slides were hyperlinked so that the student would only move to the next screen when they had selected the letter strand that represented the phoneme /e/. This design took advantage of the potential of hyperlinks in order to make the teaching point visually 'jump out' at the learner. The on-screen action was activated by the learner and the final screen (screen 4) would present words with particular letter strands (in this case the phoneme /e/) highlighted in an exaggerated manner.

Using synthetic phonics the students presented the possibility that the word could be spelt: bossee, bossy, bossey, bossie, bossea,

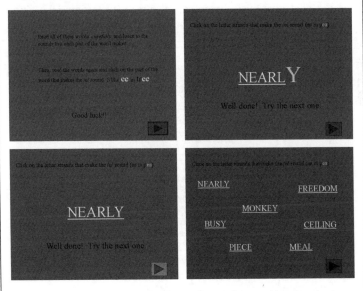

Figure 2.1 Teacher-made 'activity' for reading and recognising the phoneme /e/

continued

bossei or even bosseigh. Students then collected words that included an /e/ sound and categorised these into groups according to letter strands. They compared and contrasted their own data with that collected by other students in the class. They were then again asked by the teacher to suggest methods for spelling new words that included the /e/ sound. Towards the end of the lesson one student Joe put forward the conjecture that:

> The spelling strand ey only makes the sound /e/ when at the end of a word.

Homework – ongoing inquiry

For homework the students were asked to continue their investigational work. Interestingly, while working at home Joe tested his conjecture by using the 'Ask Jeeves' website[5] to support his investigation. This strategy had not been suggested by the teacher and seems to have drawn on Joe's out-of-school knowledge of ICT. In the query field in Ask Jeeves he entered 'dictionary' and in the next query field he entered five tests, each time recording the results through cut and paste methods, printing and pen and paper marking (see Figure 2.2).

	Text entered into query field	Reason for test
1st test	????ey	Search revealed list of words with ey letter strand at end of word.
2nd test	???ey?	Ey letter strand towards end of word.
3rd test	??ey??	Ey letter strand in middle of word.
4th test	?ey???	Ey letter strand towards beginning of word.
5th test	ey???	Ey letter strand at beginning of word.

Figure 2.2 Overview of data collected by Joe

In the classroom – discussing Joe's conjecture

When Joe presented the results of his investigation to the class the following day, his use of Ask Jeeves was greeted with excitement. Joe spent nearly ten minutes explaining his research methods to the class and the teacher, explaining how he used a question mark to represent an unknown quantity. Joe was only interested in searching for words with the letter strand /ey/ and was not interested in what other letters were in the words he found. Using this method of investigation, Joe found words from 'abomey' to 'winey' in a matter of seconds, creating a vast data bank for analysis.

Joe then cross-referenced his investigation data with his own knowledge of phonics to see if he could prove his spelling rule. *The spelling strand ey only makes the sound /e/ when at the end of a word.* When he presented his 'theory' to the class (and the teacher) other students came up with counter-examples to his espoused theory. Below is a short extract of the discussion in class.

			Analysis
1	Joe	My spelling rule is that if you spell [the sound] /e/ at the end of a word it will be spelt ey.	*Joe presents a spelling rule that is not generalisable to all English words*
2	Ben	What about eye? That's not at the end of a word.	*Ben provides a counter-example which he suggests does not follow Joe's rule (not an appropriate counter-example as eye is an /i/ sound, not an /e/ sound)*
3	Joe	Oh yeah.	*Joe accepts Ben's suggestion even though it is not an appropriate counter-example*
4	Ben	Oh no, that's not an /e/ sound.	*Ben realises for himself that his example is not an /e/ sound*
5	Joe	Yeah, so I'm right. My rule's right.	*Joe then assumes his rule is correct*
6	Claire	What about sea or bee?	*Claire finds two valid words that counter Joe's claim*

continued

7	Joe	Oh yeah.	*Counter-examples accepted by Joe*
8	Claire	Or she.	*Claire offers another exception to Joe's rule*
9	Joe	OK, so if you use ey at the end of a word it will say /e/.	*Using the new data, Joe alters his rule so that it includes Claire's new words (changes the logic, still to explain)*
10	Claire	That's like a reading rule isn't it?	*Claire highlights that Joe has presented a reading rule and not a spelling rule – a rule for decoding words for pronunciation, rather than for encoding words in spelling*
11	Joe	Yeah.	*Joe accepts the new version of his rule*

Summary – the phenomenom of over-generalisation

This interaction and discussion was typical of the way in which students in Dan's class engaged with spelling rules. They had been motivated to discover new spelling rules by the challenge that if they could find a new rule it would be sent to the editors of the Oxford English Dictionary in order to make it known. The excerpt shows how Joe creatively came up with a 'new' spelling rule that he backed up with an investigation of the spelling of a large number of words. However, the rule he 'discovered' was not actually 'correct' and he came to realise this through discussion with other students in the class. Here the teacher played a crucial role in orchestrating discussion with the class community to reason about the structure of the English language in a detailed and knowledgeable way. The excerpt also illustrates the tenacity with which people stick to their espoused theories. Joe was using the examples he found to confirm his own spelling rule and he only changed his view when the whole class discussed and confronted his findings by putting forward counter-examples to this rule.

Interestingly, this is very much how 'scientific' communities work, and it may very well be that because the introduction of ICTs into the classroom is often accompanied by empirical investigation, there is a need to balance this empirical work with 'scientific' debate, which relates to the development of a classroom-based 'community of inquiry'. This idea is developed further within the next case study.

CASE STUDY 2
Geometry and proof in the secondary school

Introduction

This case study draws on the work of the mathematics teacher Marnie Weeden who developed an SDI to introduce 13–14-year-old secondary school students to the idea of mathematical proof, using the dynamic geometry software Geometers Sketchpad.[6] The case study illustrates several important aspects of using ICT to enhance learning. The first (similar to the case of language above) is to illustrate the ways in which students bring to the classroom previous knowledge that is valuable in previous work, but potentially gets in the way of the intended learning. The second is that mathematical proof can be considered to be a particular type of mathematical discourse, which the vast majority of students in the class had no knowledge about, and which, interestingly, was removed from the mathematics curriculum in the UK for many years because it was considered to be both irrelevant and not accessible to the vast majority of students. Thirdly, similar to the language case study, this example illustrates the importance of whole-class discussion orchestrated by the teacher in order to bring the students to a common understanding of mathematical proof.

Taking into account students' prior knowledge

The students were in the top set of an inner city multi-ethnic comprehensive school. Before starting the work most of the

continued

students had a range of informal ideas about mathematical proof, as illustrated by their responses to the question 'what is proof?':

> Is it kind of like a survey?
> Is it just like testing?
> When you get school photographs you get those little ones that say 'proof' on them. Is it like a sample or something?
> Show your workings.

Only one student's response showed a beginning understanding of the idea of mathematical proof:

> It's how to make sure ... to prove it, to say that is right because ...

Marnie knew that students were likely to find the difference between proof (which relates to mathematics and logical deduction) and demonstration (which is more related to science and empirical evidence) difficult. Interestingly, the introduction of ICT into the mathematics classroom in the UK has led to a more empirical approach to constructing mathematical knowledge,[7] and some people argue that such an emphasis on inductive aspects of mathematics can make it difficult for students to learn to construct mathematical proofs through a process of mathematical deduction.

From the beginning of the design initiative Marnie explicitly discussed with students the difference between proof and demonstration.

Marnie   If I say proof, what do I mean?
Rob   Gathering evidence ... in order to back ...
Sarah   Exploration.
Marnie   Gathering evidence to support a theory, conjecture? In science we repeat an experiment loads of times. Is that mathematics proof as we know it? There is a difference between proof and demonstration ... are your eyes and the way your brain works enough for you ...

Measurement or proof?

In the third lesson students were asked to construct a mathematical proof of the property that the angles of a triangle add up to 180 degrees. They used dynamic software to first construct a triangle and then to make conjectures about the sum of the angles. As discussed already, from the beginning of the design initiative Marnie emphasised that measurement is not mathematical proof. Despite this emphasis many of the students started to use the measurement tools in the dynamic geometry software. This is likely to relate to their previous experiences of measurement in geometry and the types of empirical proofs[8] which they were likely to have been introduced to in primary and early secondary school. The following excerpt illustrates how Rachel and Joanna started to explore the possibility of measuring.

Rachel   Is there some way we can calculate what J, K, L and M add up to?

Rachel   We'll just have to look around [they start to look through the menus].

Joanna   Oh . . . angle bisector . . . that looks fun.

Rachel   So I guess we'll have to highlight an angle.

By experimenting they discovered how to measure an angle. They then discovered the calculator tool and started to sum the angle measures. At this point Marnie, becoming aware of their activity, intervened to the whole class.

Marnie   . . . before you go off on a tangent, which is where you seem to be going . . . [ ] . . . you need construction, but the other important thing is don't get het up and caught up in the measuring . . . measuring is not proof . . . you've already said that . . . measuring is not proof . . . for a start computers can make mistakes . . . also for the particular computer program it tends to measure to the nearest point. Zero point something . . . so what you'll end up with is something which doesn't equal 180 degrees . . . when you've measured it will add up to 181. So you cannot rely on that software. And the reason we

continued

> are here doing this now is proof . . . so don't get muddled up with the measuring . . . measuring is not proof . . . it is being able to apply what we know about our angle laws to a situation in order to come out with some kind of reasoning, mathematical reasoning as to why that may add up to 180 and I know some of you are nearly there . . .

Analysis of the video data showed that Joanna and Rachel eventually stopped using the measuring tool and started to construct proof statements on the screen.

> Angles A, B, C and D are all right angles: they are 90 degrees and are all in rectangle so all the angles in the rectangles add up to 360 degrees.

> Angles J, K, L and m are an average of 45 degrees each.

Whereas these 'proof statements' are rather empirical and descriptive, they provided a starting point in terms of supporting students to enter the world of mathematical proof. Marnie continued to emphasise the idea of mathematical proof by asking groups of students to present their embryonic proofs to the whole class at the end of each lesson. When one group of students decided to use PowerPoint to present proofs this idea was taken up by all of the other students. This idea of using PowerPoint (which had not previously been used in mathematics classes) is likely to have come from experiences in other school classes or experiences from out of school.

An analysis of the final proof produced by Joanna and Rachel (Figure 2.3) shows that they had moved from a focus on measurement to the production of a proof which contains logical justifications for what they observed on the figure.

Summary

Within this design initiative students brought to the classroom ideas about proof that related to their out-of-school uses of the

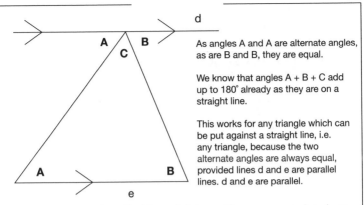

Figure 2.3 Excerpt from final PowerPoint proof for one group of students

word, for example a 'photographic proof'. They also initially wanted to use measurement and not mathematical proof as a way of justifying a conjecture. The teacher's role was key in supporting students to shift from these initial ways of thinking into the world of mathematical proof. Her interventions drew on observations of students' activity in the class, her own analysis and understanding of what constitutes mathematical proof and her engagement with the research literature. She created a collaborative classroom community which enabled students to share and progressively refine their ideas about what constitutes a mathematical proof.

Marnie   Remember that there is no wrong or right here there is just ideas. There is just us coming together with ideas and that is us learning from each other about what we're doing and this is to do with working collaboratively together. OK learning to work together and come together with our ideas (*Session 1*).

Students' collaborative presentations to the whole class were also important in the class convergence towards the new practice of mathematical proof as explained below:

If I was just doing it, I probably wouldn't have got anywhere, but knowing that we had to present made me do it.

continued

The fact that we were sharing, put a competition element into the investigation, plus we were able to compare what we had found out. It was a group effort so when a group found out about something another group could continue from there.

It kinda made you work more because you knew you had to show something at the end of it. If you don't have to show it, what's the point of working hard at it?

Understanding and exploiting the potential of ICTs

These case studies raise the question: what is the teacher's role when ICT is being used successfully to enhance learning? We suggest that one important capability which the teacher (and students) need to develop to obtain maximum benefits from ICT is awareness of the potential of particular ICTs with respect to particular learning outcomes. This means that they need to play and experiment with the ICT for themselves. Both Dan Sutch and Marnie Weeden had developed an intimate knowledge of the software tools that they used in the classroom, and this related to their knowledge of the subject area to be taught, what we have called the intended learning. It also related to their intimate knowledge of the students they were teaching. In Chapter 3 we continue to discuss the issues surrounding developing an understanding of the potential of ICTs, and how this cannot be separated from a consideration of the cultural and social context of use, together with the design of the particular ICTs to be used. As Wertsch says:

> looking at action in isolation, without concern for the mediational means employed, loses sight of one of my most fundamental points and what is perhaps the most central contribution Vygotsky, Bahktin and many of their colleagues made to the study of mind; mediated action is an irreducible unit of analysis, and the person(s)-acting-with-mediational-means is the irreducible agent involved.
>
> (Wertsch 1991, p. 120)

These ideas are taken up again in other chapters of the book. In Chapter 5 we discuss the ways in which different digital composition software environments can be used for composing music. We emphasise that how the potential of such environments is realised in the classroom relates to both the software itself and the context of use. In Chapter 5 we also discuss the case of a geography design initiative in which the teacher did not anticipate that students would spend time on 'presentation aspects' when using a graphing package, detracting from the 'intended' emphasis on geographical inquiry. In Chapter 7 we present the case of a history teacher who found that his language shifted from an emphasis on history to an emphasis on technical aspects of ICT when he moved from his normal 'history' classroom to teaching history in a computer room. All these case studies highlight various aspects of the complexity of improving learning with ICT.

It is important to emphasise that learning how to use a new digital tool cannot be separated from learning about the knowledge domain (the intended learning) and thinking about the background experiences of the students to be taught. Through working within the English design team Dan Sutch developed an understanding of the etymology of the English language, while at the same time developing an understanding of how WordRoot and PowerPoint could be used to investigate language rules. In a similar way Marnie Weeden developed an understanding of how dynamic geometry could be used to introduce students to the idea of mathematical proof, through working in partnership with a researcher before realising the design in the classroom. In both cases the thought experiments related to this pre-planning also took into account research on learning language and spelling and mathematical proof.[9]

In Chapter 3 we introduce the idea of the 'instrumental process' in order to further develop our argument that simply making a technological system available to students and teachers does not imply that they will take up the potential it offers to enhance learning. This concept helps us to understand that the way in which a technology is used in the classroom emerges from an inter-relationship of the designer's and the teacher's intentions, the teacher and students' perceptions and constructions of how the technology can be used, and the cultural context into which the new technology has been placed (including the subject domain and its culture). Teachers bring a much needed perspective to the process of understanding this complexity. We would argue that it is only when teachers and researchers work together to study the ways in which digital technologies are being used in the classroom that we can begin to understand these complex interactions. Arguably students should also be given a voice in this research process and in Chapter 7 we pay more attention to young people's perspectives on how ICT could be used in schools to enhance learning.

Developing common understandings and knowledge

As we have discussed above, effective teaching and learning with ICT involves finding ways of building bridges between incidental (and often idiosyncratic) and intended learning. Within successful design initiatives teachers became aware of incidental learning and worked with the whole class to share, challenge and confront knowledge-building. This sometimes involved students presenting their work to a critical audience, with the teacher commenting and directing. Here the interactive whiteboard or a projected computer image could be used, although non-digital tools were also used productively for such purposes.[10] Teachers themselves often underplayed their role in directing learning, influenced by the dominant rhetoric of 'teacher as facilitator'. It was only through micro-analysis of video data that their crucial role in orchestrating a knowledge construction community became apparent.[11] In many unsuccessful SDIs (from the perspective of the intended learning) the teacher did not orchestrate a knowledge community, seemingly believing that knowledge was embedded within the software and that ICT would somehow replace the teacher. Analysis of video data also indicated that students themselves often confronted and supported each other with the process of knowledge construction. Superficially this could appear chaotic, but close analysis of the video data highlighted the productive nature of this informal networking in the classroom, although teachers themselves were often unaware of the resourcefulness of students in this respect.

Which tools should be privileged?

In the example on mathematical proof discussed above we discuss the difference between measurement and proof. Both are mathematical tools which have evolved over centuries for particular (and different) purposes. Within any discussion of the similarities and differences between proof and measurement we do not want to suggest that one is in any way better or more important than the other. But we do suggest that students should become aware that different tools can be more or less efficacious for particular purposes, that they can be used to do different things. A similar discussion might arise when discussing whether composing with digital software is better or worse than composing with traditional music notation together with an acoustic instrument (for example a piano). We return to these ideas in Chapter 10 when we introduce the idea of 'privileging', which refers to the idea that a particular tool might be more appropriate than other tools for particular purposes. Whereas such a discussion is always relevant when considering how a person might choose a particular tool for a particular purpose (whether for work or for leisure) it is even more critical within educational contexts where, as discussed above, there is always a focus on intended learning.

So, for example, if we want students in school to learn the long multiplication algorithm (and this is a good example of a tool which was developed within a particular book-keeping culture to expand what a person can do) then we might not want them to use a calculator to multiply. This argument might be different if the context was the work place and the objective was not to learn how to multiply, but to accurately perform a calculation. In this example we contrast the digital tool of 'calculator' with the non-digital tool of the long multiplication algorithm. As we shall see in other chapters of the book a digital tool is not always more appropriate than a non-digital one; there is, we would argue, still a place for paper and pencil, both in schools and in the workplace.

Summary and conclusions

As we have discussed throughout this chapter ICT can be used to transform and enhance learning in schools. However, such learning will not happen spontaneously by merely inserting it into the classroom. Teachers are key to the transformation process. Also, there are huge risks associated with integrating ICT in school learning, because when not used appropriately students' learning can be diminished and not augmented (as discussed more fully in Chapter 7). We believe that because of these risks teachers are not likely to start a process of integrating ICT into classroom practices unless they are supported through a professional development process. Within the InterActive project we developed a particular approach to professional development (discussed more fully in Chapter 4) which we believe worked because of an emphasis on knowing and under-standing the complexities of working with ICT in the classroom. Such an understanding was developed through working collaboratively on analysing ongoing experiments with ICT, through viewing and interpreting video data. This interpretive process enabled us to see that 'successful' uses of ICT entailed a collective pedagogy in which each student's learning narrative blends with the collective community of individuals, knowledge and learning that makes up the dynamic of a classroom. As we discuss in Chapter 10, such viewing of video data is always framed by our (often implicit) theories of teaching and learning and this is why throughout the book we aim to make our theoretical perspectives as transparent as possible.

Notes

1 For more information about the software WordRoot see www.wordroot. co.uk.
2 See Gall and Breeze (2005).
3 www.virtualfishtank.com/main.html.
4 A grapheme is a unit of the writing system. In the English language writing system a grapheme represents a unit of sound – a phoneme. A grapheme can be a letter or a combination of letters. The word 'book' for instance is made up of three graphemes – b,oo,k. The 'oo' grapheme is called a 'digraph' – in this case a 'vowel digraph'. There are also consonant digraphs such as ch, sh, th, etc. The units of sound (phonemes) which a grapheme represents are not consistent – the English writing system is not phonem-ically consistent. See George Bernard Shaw's famous example of ghoti representing 'fish': gh (as in enough), o (as in women), ti (as in nation).
5 www.ask.co.uk.
6 This case study is discussed more fully in Weeden (2002) and Sutherland (2007).
7 See Gibbs (2007).
8 For a discussion of what is meant by empirical proof see Balacheff (1988).
9 For example Bell (2004); Carney (1994); Olivero (2006).
10 See Godwin and Sutherland (2004).
11 See Sutherland *et al.* (2004); Sutch (2004).

Chapter 3*

Learning and technology

This chapter focuses on the ways in which interaction with ICTs in the classroom can lead to novel and sometime unplanned outcomes. In so doing it draws together ideas from human computer interaction (HCI) theory, and focuses on the critical and often overlooked relationship between the designer and the user through the concept of instrumentation. From this perspective learning and technology are viewed as part of a rich fabric of relationships between people, technologies, institutions, tools and practices of all kinds. Here learning through interaction can be thought of as a form of mediated communication where the tool or artefact is structured so it can be both understood and then appropriated by students in particular ways. These ideas are explored through a concrete classroom case in which primary school students are using simulation software to learn science. In summary, the chapter:

- highlights how theoretical perspectives can help to probe more deeply into classrooms and thereby reinterpret uses of both new and old technologies for learning;
- introduces the idea of instrumentation that explains how learning is always distributed in some form between the technology, the learner and the social and cultural context and there is nothing inherent in technology that automatically guarantees learning;
- emphasises the importance of a variety of interactions that operate during learning.

Introduction – the finger-tip effect

Educational innovations with technology often take on a deterministic character in popular thinking. This has been called the finger-tip effect,

---

* This chapter was authored by Federica Olivero, Rosamund Sutherland and Peter John.

that is a belief that simply by making a technological system available, people will more or less automatically take advantage of the opportunities that it offers.[1] Drawing on this idea policymakers tend to advocate the educational use of new technology as if it were both invariant and determinate, even though observation and research show that this is not the case.

As we discussed in Chapter 2 technologies do not work by themselves and just 'throwing' ICT in the classroom is not enough to change and transform learning. Adults and young people do not automatically take on board a new technology; in fact on the contrary, new technologies are expressive media that attract different people in different ways and for different reasons.[2] We believe it is important to recognise that ICTs are often taken up by people (which includes teachers and students) in unintended and unpredictable ways.

In this chapter we introduce a range of theoretical ideas that can help our understanding of what happens when ICT is used in classroom settings, in particular when 'things don't go to plan'. The chapter starts with a case study taken from a primary science lesson in which the students interpreted the available software in ways that had not been planned or intended by the teacher. A range of theoretical ideas are then introduced to help us make sense of what was happening from the perspective of the role of ICT in teaching and learning. Further analysis of the case study reveals how the teacher had 'redesigned' the chosen software to support her teaching objectives in a way that had not been envisaged by the designer. In Chapter 10 we expand on the ideas introduced in this chapter by discussing more generally the ways in which theory can be used as a lens to support us to interpret teaching and learning in the classroom.

CASE STUDY
The use of VirtualFishtank in a primary science lesson[3]

This case study centres around a lesson in which the software VirtualFishtank was used as part of a primary science class (students aged 10–11) investigation. The lesson was part of a sequence of lessons which focused on learning scientific investigation. Within each lesson students were asked to carry out a different scientific investigation using web-based software. The lessons included both whole-class work around the interactive whiteboard and group-work at the computer (Figure 3.1 and Figure 3.2). The software VirtualFishtank was chosen by the teacher from a package that came with the interactive whiteboard installed in her classroom, and is available to download for free from the website www.virtualfishtank.com/main.html.

Figure 3.1 Whole class around the interactive whiteboard

Figure 3.2 Pupils using VirtualFishtank in groups at the computer

continued

Part 1. The teacher's aim and introduction to the lesson

The teacher, Sarah Curran, started the lesson by showing students how to use the software VirtualFishtank.com on the interactive whiteboard (Figure 3.1 and Figure 3.3). This environment enables the design of fish with different characteristics (e.g. size of mouth, position in the tank, likes/dislikes), which is then placed in a Virtual Fishtank where its survival time before it is eaten by a shark can be timed. Sarah stated that the objective of the lesson was for the students to design a number of fish with different characteristics and then compare how the characteristics of each fish contributed to their ability to survive in this virtual environment before being eaten by the shark.

Below is an extract from the beginning of the lesson which shows how the software and the activity were introduced by the teacher.

Teacher   What we're going to do now is to think about your fish. You are going to design your own fish that you can try and get to live in a particular ... We haven't got an ocean, it's a fish tank, OK? What do I mean by the word virtual?

James   It's not real.

Figure 3.3 Student designing a fish using the interactive whiteboard

Teacher It's not real, it's like a simulation. So it's a bit of a . . .
James   It's a bit like a game.
Teacher It *is* a bit like a game.
[. . .]
Teacher So you can spend as long as you want building your fish.
         . . . So what we're going to do now is to time – you'll
         need to have one of these, a stopwatch. You need to
         time how long your fish survives.
[. . .]
Mark   How long is it going for?
Teacher That's it. If I tell you that in the other group . . . their
         fish varied from living from thirty seconds to living for
         five minutes and five minutes was the most they got their
         fish to live for.
[. . .]
Teacher [*fish died*] So that particular design lasted two minutes
         and one second. I want you to investigate what are the
         best different types of design to make the best fish to
         last the longest time.
[. . .]
Jenni   If it's friendly it might go up to the shark.
Teacher Well this is it, you can investigate, that's it.
[. . .]
Teacher So all these predictions that you are making, you've got
         to change your design and see if those predictions then
         are true and whether the life expectancy of your fish is
         actually then increased.

Part 2. Students working in pairs

After the whole class demonstration, the students were asked to
work in pairs and design their fish (Figure 3.2). Below are extracts
from the discussion of one group of students that was video
recorded.

Jessica I bet you mine isn't gonna last five minutes. Oh, what's
         going on? Where's he gone?
Liam   Give him food, he's going crazy. He is going crazy. He's
         getting really thin.

continued

Teacher	[in background] One minute thirty seconds. Well done Marcus. Fantastic.
Sunita	Give him some food!
Liam	No let him go. When our fish dies . . .
Sunita	. . . Don't die! **We gotta beat people.**
[. . .]	
Sunita	It's going, it's going for two minutes. Two minutes Miss.
Teacher	Fantastic.
Jessica	I know I am.
Teacher	What do you think is very good about this fish?
Liam	This is Sabah's fish.
Teacher	What do you think is good about your fish?
Jessica	It's because, I can't remember. I think it's shy.
Liam	It's at the top of the tank . . .
Sunita	. . . so he gets more food.
Teacher	So if you can't remember what should you have done?
[. . .]	
Teacher	I've given you a piece of paper because lots of you have created fantastic fish and you've got over four minutes. But you're not recording, first of all what was your prediction – what did you think was going to make a good fish and also then what type of fish you've created. Was it shy, was it fierce? And more importantly now, what are the conditions you are giving to your fish to try and make sure it's got a long life. So I want you to jot down some of your learning that is happening. OK?
[. . .]	
Sunita	. . . 4 minutes 30.
Jessica	Oh no. Mine's trying to eat a shark. What's wrong with it.
Pete	I'd laugh if it did.
Sunita	Give it food.
Jessica	I have.
Sunita	We're still going.
Jessica	**We need to beat five minutes.** [. . .] This is really boring.
[. . .]	
Liam	I wonder if anything happens to the castle if you click on it.
Jessica	No, nothing.
Jessica	See, this is actually fun when you're building it and other stuff is quite fun as well but it's just like . . .

Liam	I just want him to eat it.
Jessica	It's taking ages.
Jessica	Oh don't eat mine, eat him. Oh it'll be really stupid if we spent the whole lesson just doing this, just waiting for it to die. It's still not dead.
Jessica	Oh my gosh. 14 minutes.
Liam	I wanna see Tom's get eaten.
Jessica	Yeah that would be really funny.
Liam	[*writing on a sheet on paper – properties of fish*] Is it shiny or not shiny?
Jessica	It's shiny but being shiny means it attracts more attention which is kind of stupid. I shouldn't have made it shiny. Imagine if I didn't make it shiny it would be even longer than this.
Liam	20 minutes. Tom what are you on?
Tom	21:35. I just got killed!
Liam	You just got killed? Yes! **Tom got killed!**
Jessica	We have to beat Tom. Tom's an idiot! Eat that one, don't eat me. It's called competitiveness . . . died on 21:30 or something.
[. . .]	
Teacher	Can I just say, I don't know what you did but your fish lasted an awful lot longer than the other group's fish did. What was it that you think you did to your fish that the other group obviously didn't?

Part 3. Reflecting back on the lesson

As part of the research project, the teacher analysed the video recording of the lesson. The first time Sarah viewed it she became aware that the way in which she and the students had engaged with this software in the lesson was at-odds with her intended lesson objectives.[4] Although the students had been asked to design a number of fish, time their survival time and compare their different characteristics, this was not possible because most of the fish survived from twenty to thirty-five minutes, making it impossible to carry out the investigation in the way it had been envisaged. The question behind this brief analysis is: did the technology cause the discrepancy between the declared lesson objectives and the actual process of the lesson? Or was it part of a wider pedagogical question?

Interpreting what happened in the classroom – a complex mix of people, culture and technology

To understand what happened in Sarah's lesson, and more generally to interpret situations in which the planned learning objectives (in this case comparing survival time according to the characteristics of different fish) are not achieved, we need to delve deeper into the case study and explore the complex mix of people, culture and technology that comprised the lesson. This might help us to shift away from 'criticising' the lesson to a more subtle process of interpretation. This in turn might help us think about the redesign of the lesson with a more explicit awareness of the role of the technology and its interaction with a range of classroom issues.

A starting point for this exploration is a range of theoretical ideas that helped frame the InterActive project. One conceptual tool we found useful was the notion of person-acting-with-mediating-means. This recognises that people learn with much more than their apparent reliance on cognitive power, and instead sees all learning as mediated by tools. Put simply, this was in many ways Vygotsky's 'big idea'.[5] These mediating-means or tools, it is proposed, can be both material (for example, paper and pencil) and symbolic (for instance, language). Furthermore, the idea that human action is inextricably linked to tools is particularly important when considering the ways in which ICT can be used to enhance learning. This idea has become more prominent in recent decades alongside the rapid development of new technologies.

Although software was first introduced into schools for teaching and learning purposes in the early 1980s, the Internet is a relatively recent phenomenon, while what has been called 'social software' or 'digital tools' are a very recent and continuously evolving phenomenon.[6] In this respect digital tools include such possibilities as the word processor, dynamic geometry software, wikis, blogs, the interactive whiteboard, online information systems and virtual learning environments. It is also important to take into account that such digital tools have not replaced more recognisable tools, such as dictionaries, books, paper, pencils and pens. Above all, language, which is regarded as the 'master tool', permeates all our activities and behaviour and everything we do is supported by the use of language (this idea is discussed more fully in Chapter 6) from the mundane to the hypercomplex.

However, when considering the potential of ICTs for enhancing learning there is still a tendency to take an optimistic view, predicated on the view that ICTs are in themselves a positional good and will somehow automatically extend young people's capabilities. This relates to an uncritical interpretation of the 'person-plus' idea which does not take into account the fact that the ways in which technology is taken up relates to both the social and cultural context of use as well as to the design of the particular technology. This is illustrated by the VirtualFishtank case study where the teacher and students brought to their use of the software a background of game-playing which influenced how they interpreted and used the software in a way that had not been planned by the designer.

In drawing attention to the importance of the social and cultural context of use we do not want to swing too much in this direction and not take into account the 'designed' technology and the intention of the designers. In this respect the range of potentials offered by ICT tools inevitably shapes, urges and constrains particular uses. Also, the way in which technology is designed is only one of a range of factors in the complex mix of potential new technology offers teachers and learners in classrooms. These factors came to the fore in the analysis of the VirtualFishtank lesson. For instance, the ways in which the students engaged with the software appeared to be at odds with both the teacher's intended lesson objectives and the original designer's intentions for the software. VirtualFishtank.com was originally constructed to be used as a museum-based interactive exhibit to teach about emergent animal behaviour, as explained on the website:

> Built by Nearlife, Inc. (www.nearlife.com) for the Museum of Science, Boston (www.mos.org), VirtualFishtank.com represents the dawn of a new era in educational entertainment. Until now, most museum exhibit websites have merely contained static descriptions of the exhibits. They have not included an interactive element. And they certainly have not been dynamically linked to the actual museum exhibit. VirtualFishtank.com changes all that and enables the highly successful Virtual Fish Tank™ exhibit at the Museum to transcend its walls to be experienced in homes and schools anywhere in the world.
>
> Virtual Fish Tank™ at MoS is all about building your own fish, releasing it into the gigantic 24,000 'gallon' virtual tank and watching YOUR fish interact with the others. VirtualFishtank.com lets you build your own fish online and release them directly into

the Museum tank! You also can release your fish into an online simulated tank, or save your fish and go to the Museum to retrieve and release your fish there.

The Virtual Fish Tank™ exhibit teaches lessons about emergent behaviour, group behaviour and modeling. The rich functionality of VirtualFishtank.com will enable parents and educators to enhance the educational experience by planning pre and post Museum visit online exercises.

The teacher decided to use this software to conduct a scientific investigation. The students were asked to design a fish which lived for the longest possible time, but without being asked to send it to the Museum tank, in which it would have interacted with other fish (as intended by the software designers). Therefore the students were only paying attention to the survival time within their own individual fishtank, in which there were no interactions, and the scope of the software was lost in the transformation of VirtualFishtank.com to fit the teacher's aims for that lesson. Another transformation of the software also took place, in which the students appeared to use VirtualFishtank as a 'gaming' tool. Moreover we can observe that there is no direct causal relationship between the fish design and survival time, and there is no mention of survival time in the designer's brief on the website.

We suggest that whereas it is never possible to predict in advance how an ICT will be taken up in the classroom, it is possible to carry out a thought-experiment[7] in advance of using it in the classroom: an experiment that might help make the technology work more effectively for both teacher and students. Such a thought-experiment must take into account the complex mix of people, culture and technology that will come together in the classroom context. But such an experiment will not be sufficient to understand or predict what will actually happen in the teaching and learning situation. Here, as in the case study of Sarah Curran's lesson, video data can play an important role in helping the teacher to both see and distil the complexity of the teaching and learning situation through continuous analysis.

What we are emphasising here is that learning is always distributed in some form between the technology, the learner and the social and cultural context and there is nothing inherent in technology that automatically guarantees learning. This is a relatively difficult idea to grasp and in the next section we introduce a theoretical framework that might help explain the idea further.

The instrumentation framework

In the previous section we discussed how ICT is a new type of tool that can potentially be used in the classroom to enhance learning. Over the course of the InterActive project we found that we needed to find a means of distinguishing between the different ways in which young people start to use and appropriate such digital tools. This is based on the idea that a tool is not neutral but instead has particular potentials or capabilities that can make it easier to achieve some activities and harder to do others. Using a tool for doing mathematics (science, English, etc.), for instance, not only changes the way to do it but also requires a specific appropriation of the tool. This, essentially, is what is called the 'instrumentation framework'.[8] This conceptual approach allowed us to understand more about the ways in which learners and teachers interact differently with the same tool, and over time learn how to use it in different ways. This framework distinguishes between two aspects of a tool – the artefact and the instrument. As Mariotti (2002) explains, the word *artefact* is used to describe 'the particular object with its intrinsic characteristics, designed and realised for purpose of accomplishing a particular task' (p. 702). When such an artefact is taken up by a user, this person brings to its use a complex set of previous experiences and knowledge, which relate to the individual's social and cultural history. With greater familiarity and use the artefact is then transformed into an *instrument*, which is defined as 'the artefact and the modalities of its use, as elaborated by a particular user in accomplishing different tasks' (p. 702) and built through activity and appropriation. By appropriation we mean 'the process of taking something that belongs to others and making it one's own'.[9] This development, called the instrumentation process, is presented in Figure 3.4.

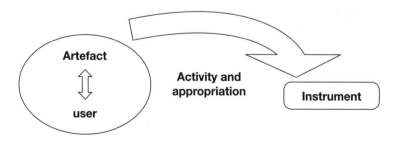

Figure 3.4 The instrumentation process

The instrumentation process takes place over a long period of time and is linked both to the characteristics of the artefact (its potentials and constraints) and to those of the people using the artefact (their previous experience, knowledge and ways of working). According to this perspective, an instrument does not exist in itself, but is constructed as and when a person appropriates the artefact for himself/herself and has integrated it with his/her activity. This has a number of consequences. First, an instrument is not a fixed thing but is always evolving through use and activity. Second, a particular artefact may serve as several instruments in different situations. Third, a range of artefacts may be available but no instruments are elicited, for example when a person is unable to operate an unfamiliar device or when a tool cannot be incorporated in a given activity (see example in relation to music software later in the chapter). Finally, it is quite possible that the developing instrument is not consistent with the original purpose for which the artefact was designed – as illustrated by the VirtualFishtank case study.

Another important point to bear in mind is that the instrumentation process works in two ways: from the user to the artefact and from the artefact to the user. This highlights the inextricable link between person and tool: the person acts on the tool and the tool acts on the person. Looking more closely at the instrumentation process in a classroom where ICT is being used, the situation is as follows:[10]

- The students have at their disposal a tool (artefact), for instance VirtualFishtank.com.
- This tool will provide a given student the potential for several instruments, related to several types of tasks that are set by the teacher. In other words, the tool-artefact can be transformed into several instruments according to what activity is set and to what interpretation the students bring to the activity and the artefact itself.
- The development and articulation of these instruments is not an easy process and may require the support of the learning environment, which includes the support of the teacher.

Given this complex situation, a key challenge for the integration of ICTs into classrooms is to find ways to support the instrumentation process, towards the construction of an appropriate instrument for particular intended learning. For example, in the case study in Chapter 2 built around the work of Marnie Weeden, at some point we see the students using measuring in the dynamic geometry environment in the context of an activity around proving. The teacher interrupts the students' work, highlighting the fact that measuring is not proving. This can be seen as an attempt to support the students in shifting from using the software as a measuring tool in an activity in which another instrument needs to be constructed. In other words in this activity the software needs to be used as a tool for discovering mathematical relationships and properties (which relate to the process of proving).

This example and other examples in the book highlight the central role of the teacher in creating, appropriating and designing lessons taking into account the process of instrumentation. This implies that the social dimension is central to the process of instrumentation. This is because different meanings and uses are produced in the classroom starting from the same tool/artefact, and the teacher plays a crucial role in directing the students' attention towards the construction of the appropriate instruments for the given activity, starting from the same artefact. This has been called 'instrumental orchestration'[11] (Figure 3.5).

To summarise, the instrumentation framework shows that the integration of ICT into the classroom is not a straightforward process but requires a careful analysis of the process of instrumentation. Given that students develop different instruments, and therefore meanings, starting from the same artefact, understanding how different

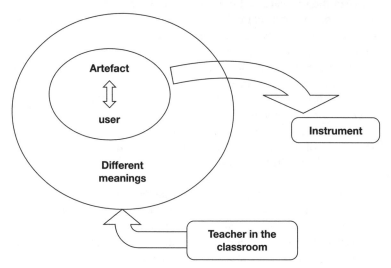

Figure 3.5 Instrumental orchestration

instruments are constructed is important because the construction of the instrument ultimately affects the development of the learning activity. In particular, the instrumentation framework makes it possible to analyse and interpret the difficulties encountered by students when interacting with complex technologies. The complexity of the instrumentation process may also help explain discrepancies between teachers' expectations and students' performances, as in the case of the VirtualFishtank lesson. Moreover, the potentials and limitations related to the different uses of an artefact, as elaborated by the students in classroom activities, can be effective in pedagogical terms as long as attention is paid to the instrumentation process and to the meanings that may emerge.

How can instrumentation explain what happened in the VirtualFishtank lesson?

Within this section we consider how the idea of instrumentation can help explain what happened in the VirtualFishtank lesson. This is an example of theory being used to illuminate practice with ICT, which is a key theme of the book.

To consider ICT from an instrumentation perspective means focusing on the design of the tool, the sorts of choices offered by it and those which are not. It also means exploring the relationship between the software and the learning process as well as uncovering the sorts of pedagogical implications attendant upon that relationship. We also need to know how the designer of the technology anticipated who the users would be and what they would be likely to do as well as taking into account the character of the ontological assumptions represented in the software.

In Sarah Curran's lesson, the students had at their disposal the software VirtualFishtank (artefact) to be used within the activity that Sarah had prepared (a scientific investigation). Looking back at the description of the lesson, can we identify the instruments constructed by the students? In particular:

- what are the different uses of VirtualFishtank the students and the teacher show in the context of the prepared activity?
- how do students make VirtualFishtank *their own Virtual Fishtank*? How do they appropriate the software and construct their instrument, within the set activity?
- what elements play a role in the instrumentation process?

The artefact – VirtualFishtank

The artefact used in Sarah Curran's lesson is the software Virtual-Fishtank (Figure 3.6).

The website from which the software can be downloaded states that:

> The VirtualFishtank.com draws on scientific research in complex systems, and makes these ideas accessible to a broad public audience. The Fishtank draws on research from the new field of 'artificial life', which focuses on computer modeling of animal behavior. The VirtualFishtank.com adopts a constructionist approach, enabling visitors to design (and not merely observe) the behaviors of fish. What makes VirtualFishtank.com different from any other website is the ability to Build-Your-Own-Fish online and release them into the Virtual Fish Tank™ exhibits at the Museum Of Science, Boston, and the St. Louis Science Center. You can create your own fish, save them, go to the Museum and use an interactive kiosk to retrieve and release them into the Museum tank. This represents a new dimension for museum exhibits, where

Figure 3.6 Interface of VirtualFishtank.com

traditional walls disappear and the experience is available in homes and schools everywhere. We could explain to you for days about how simple rules can lead to complex behaviors, but, really, isn't just experiencing that here online a lot more fun?' Statistics related to the fish life in the tank can also be obtained and compared for different fish.

From this description we can see that the software was designed to teach about emergent behaviour and complex systems, through observing interactions among designed fish in the Museum tank. The website seems to suggest there is no scope for using the software on individual machines if they are not connected to the Museum. It is interesting that this particular software was recommended for use by the company selling the interactive whiteboards to teach about science investigations in the classroom and that the teacher chose it just because it was available, without reading the description on the website. She chose the software to fit with an activity she had already planned. We suggest that at this stage the artefact has already been transformed into something that does not concur with the original designer's intention – it has been transformed into an instrument for the teacher.

Instruments constructed by students

Starting from the artefact VirtualFishtank, what instruments were constructed by the students and how/why?

The activities the teacher wanted the students to engage with were to design different fish, record the characteristics of the fish and make predictions about how these characteristics may affect their life expectancy. They were also asked to investigate if their predictions were accurate by creating their fish, sending them to the fishtank and timing their survival time. The teacher introduced the task in the following way:

> So that particular design lasted two minutes and one second. I want you to investigate what are the best different types of design to make the best fish last the longest time.

The particular formulation of the task, which was couched in language drawn from the genre of gaming ('the best' . . . 'the longest time'), and not the language of science, may help explain some of the issues that emerged in the lesson. Furthermore, the fact that the children brought to the activity their previous experience and knowledge – also possibly drawn from a knowledge of computer gaming – may have directed the students towards the construction of a particular instrument for VirtualFishtank.com, one which had not been previously envisaged. Moreover, the design of the software included a visual interface that resembles that of commercial gaming packages, and this too may have contributed to the particular instrumentation process emerging in the lesson. What happened for the students, as shown by subsequent viewings and analysis of the classroom interaction, was that the students did indeed begin to view and use the software as a game, thus creating an instrument 'gaming software' from VirtualFishtank. com. This is evidenced by the dialogue between students in the group work – often containing exclamations such as:

> Don't die! We gotta beat people and we need to beat five minutes!

When one boy announced that his fish had been killed after twenty-one minutes, his neighbour jumped up exclaiming:

> You just got killed? Yes! You got killed!

So we have a process in which the instrument constructed from the VirtualFishtank.com artefact is not an appropriate instrument for the particular learning that the teacher had in mind. The process of instrumentation in this particular case is represented in Figure 3.7.

What affected the instrumentation process for these students was:

- in terms of the artefact, the way in which the software had been designed, resembling gaming software, which also influenced Sarah's use of language in presenting the activity to the class;
- in terms of the users, the particular socio-cultural context in which the majority of students play computer games out of school, as further elaborated in Chapter 8.

Some other examples of instrumentation

The instrumentation framework is a useful lens through which to view a range of uses of ICT in classrooms and also a way of viewing other practices at work in the forthcoming chapters in this volume.

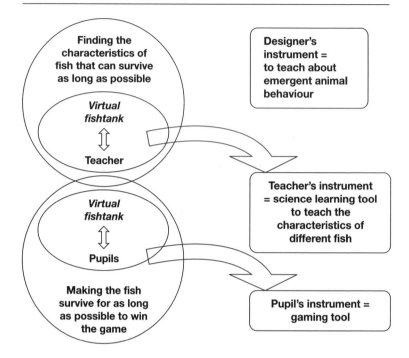

Figure 3.7 The instrumentation processes in the VirtualFishtank case study

For example, the case study around the use of drop-down menus in modern foreign languages in Chapter 5 shows a process of instrumentation through which the students gradually appropriate the tool (drop-down menus) and transform it into an instrument. During this process they become designers both manipulating and designing their own menus. The second case study on the use of music in Chapter 5 is a further example of how the instrumentation process is affected by students' previous knowledge and experience. In particular, this case study shows that students with a background experience of learning to play acoustic instruments (for example piano, trumpet) were not able to make use of these skills when composing with the software package Dance eJay. These students could not use the software to realise their composition ideas. With their experience of acoustic instruments they did not need the composition package for melodic and harmonic purposes and they struggled to make use of it. They also pointed out that the software did not do what they wanted it to do.

Put simply, they failed to transform the tool/artefact (Dance eJay) into an instrument that could support the further development of their composition skills. This situation is similar to other examples of the use of ICT in other subjects, as for example dynamic geometry software in mathematics.[12] However, we should bear in mind that students whose musical skills have not been developed with acoustic instruments can be immersed in the environment and 'play' within its constraints, transforming it into an instrument that supports the development of their composition skills. Finally, the case studies around the use of ICT and English discussed in Chapter 6 can also be interpreted from an instrumentation point of view. It can be seen that the students create their own instrument starting from artefacts such as Word or PowerPoint, which may incorporate elements from 'traditional' writing practices as well as multimodal practices.

Summary and conclusions

The VirtualFishtank lesson discussed in this chapter clearly shows that simply making a technological system available to teachers and students does not imply that they will automatically take advantage of the potential that it offers related to the intended learning. Therefore this is an example of how the technological determinism often advocated by policy makers does not work at the classroom level, as further elaborated in Chapter 7.

The first thoughts of the teacher Sarah Curran after watching the video from the lesson using VirtualFishtank.com focused on how 'bad' the lesson had been in terms of achieving the planned lesson objectives and how unsuccessful the use of the software VirtualFishtank had turned out to be. She also thought she would never use this particular software again. However, a more detailed analysis of the video data enabled Sarah to begin to 'see' what had happened in the lesson in terms of the use of VirtualFishtank.com. Theoretical frameworks like the one discussed in this chapter are needed in order to go beyond 'criticising' the teaching towards understanding and interpreting how ICT tools are or could be used in the classroom to mediate and transform learning. This will be further elaborated in Chapter 10.

The fact that students may construct different instruments starting from the same artefact shows that the integration of ICT tools in classroom practice is not a straightforward process but requires careful analysis. One of the key challenges for the integration of technology into classrooms and curricula is to understand and to devise ways to foster the process of instrumental development towards the construction of an appropriate instrument for the intended learning. This implies taking into account the experience and knowledge that young people are likely to bring to the classroom from out-of-school use of ICT. The instrumentation framework allows us to 'see', and bring into the analysis of classroom learning with ICT, what important and influential roles these experiences have in the transformation of artefacts into instruments within a given activity. The role and relevance of out-of-school experiences with ICT is taken up again in Chapter 8.

The role of the teacher emerges as important, showing that the software *per se* does not guarantee a successful achievement of the learning objectives and a transformation of learning. The teacher also constructs different instruments, which influence the instrumentation process developed by the students and their appropriation of the software. The teacher should orchestrate the teaching/learning process so that the given artefact is transformed into an appropriate instrument for the intended learning. This would also require a more extensive reorganisation of pedagogical practices, developing new forms of pedagogy which involve 'doing different things' with ICT rather than 'doing the same things differently', as further discussed in Chapter 7. The process of development of the teacher as 'enabled practitioner' within a community of practice, as discussed in Chapter 4, may allow this transformation and reorganisation to take place.

More broadly, the VirtualFishtank case study also raises questions in relation to the official policy discourse on learning with ICT, which promoted the use of the VirtualFishtank software through its inclusion in the package distributed in the school by the interactive whiteboard company, with probably no suggestions for meaningful use in the classroom. The teacher simply accepted this particular software as useful because of where it had come from, and only when analysing the video data did she start to reflect on the software itself. The role of official policies and social discourse is further elaborated in Chapter 7.

Notes

1   For further discussion of the finger-tip effect see Perkins (1985).
2   See Turkle and Papert (1990).
3   This example comes from a spin-off project from the InterActive project, funded by the ESRC Research Equipment for the Social Sciences (REISS) initiative, and predicated on the same principles. See Armstrong *et al.* (2005) and Armstrong and Curran (2006).

4 As discussed more fully in Armstrong and Curran (2006).

5 Vygotsky defined the notion of *mediated act*, saying that mediation is the characteristic that allows humans to go beyond simple stimulus-response reflexes (Vygotsky 1978, p. 40).

6 See Chapter 9 for further discussion of social software.

7 For further discussion of the idea of thought-experiment see Davis *et al.* (2000). It is also discussed in Chapter 1 and Chapter 2.

8 This framework was initially elaborated by Verillion and Rabardel (1995) in the field of human-computer interaction (HCI) and has then been taken up in different ways and further elaborated to take into account social interactions (see for example Artigue 2002, Mariotti 2002, Trouche 2003). In this chapter we present a simplified version of the framework that, however, maintains its key elements, drawing in particular on Mariotti (2002).

9 See Wertsch (1998, p. 53).

10 See Trouche (2003).

11 See Mariotti (2002).

12 See for example Olivero (2006).

Chapter 4*

The enabled practitioner

This chapter provides an account of the emergence of a professional learning community around a number of subject design initiatives (SDIs). The account begins with a brief discussion of the concept of community and its semantic and etymological origins. Building on this, the second section focuses on the 'two communities' question in education, in particular the cultural gap that appears to separate teachers and researchers. The third section explores a range of ideas surrounding teachers' professional knowledge and the sort of communities in which it is best fostered and developed. The chapter concludes with an exemplification of the 'enabled practitioner' and how the idea might form the basis to a new view of professional development and its relationship to ICT. In summary, the chapter concentrates on:

- the growth of a professional community around various strands of the InterActive project;
- the ways in which individuals worked within the different layers of community that emerged – in particular the micro, the meso and the macro;
- how engagement with these communities led to the creation of 'enabled practitioners'.

Introduction

One of the distinctive features of the InterActive project was the way in which teachers, teacher educators and researchers worked together to create a professional learning community. The focus of this community was the development and dissemination of emerging

* This chapter was authored by Peter John and Pat Triggs.

professional knowledge as it relates to teaching and learning with ICT. Our concept of a learning community, however, was neither monolithic nor static. In this chapter we show how members of the whole project team came together in varying sized groups and for different purposes, and how individuals had membership of a number of overlapping and inter-connected communities of learning. To discuss how all this worked we use a hybrid concept of 'layers of community'. We describe how the layers operated at the 'micro', 'meso' and 'macro' levels to create the settings and arenas for professional growth. At the core of the analysis is the idea of the 'enabled practitioner'; this means viewing teachers as professionals who see their practice as a self-determined, dynamic and critically valued process.

The interlocking and overlapping communities that constituted the InterActive project provide the context for a range of stories of how learning changes who we are. This, in Wenger's (1998) evocative phrase is 'the personal history of becoming'. The following vignette illustrates how a single teacher moved through the different layers of community and in so doing became 'professionally enabled', developing new and varied perspectives on the teaching of English.

VIGNETTE 1
Ian Thompson

Ian is a confident and experienced teacher, who at the start of the project was the acting head of English in a secondary school. The school was embarking on an experiment in team teaching of ICT and literacy in Year 9 and becoming involved in the InterActive research seemed a good way to evaluate this initiative.

Ian's relaxed approach disguises a thoughtful radicalism that is grounded in a profound commitment to providing opportunities for all young people to learn and attain. The meso-community that was the English subject design team (SDT) quickly built a basis of common experiences and shared stories. The fact that the membership included primary and secondary teachers was a definite plus for Ian, who valued the extra dimension this gave to the team's thinking. The subject culture of English, even in a disparate group, produced some commonality around ideals. Attitudes to ICT ranged from the enthusiastic embrace of teachers from a City Technology College[1] to the doubting Thomases and Thomasinas whose experiences so far had induced scepticism and technophobia. Ian was somewhere in the middle, with a sense of the potential and the challenges of new technologies in teaching and learning English. As a group the English team slowly identified individual and collective expectations and a sense of agreed goals.

In the micro-community of the SDI, Ian worked with a university researcher, his junior colleague and colleagues from the ICT department at this school. The design involved one lesson a week for a term. Video data was collected on selected students as well as the whole class. Work produced each week was printed out; students and ICT staff were interviewed. The challenge of 'integrating' English and ICT as 'subjects', each with their own culture, curriculum and assessment provoked much discussion. But it was the video data that had a powerful impact on Ian, as we saw in Chapter 1. The amount of time allowed to teachers for analysis by the project was augmented in Ian's case in the second year by a scholarship.[2] This enabled him to use the experience of the first SDI to rethink the iteration and be more involved as a partner in considering the outcomes.

Ian was active in the meso-community of the SDT in that he was interested in other teachers' data and experiences. He valued contact with other teachers and with all the university-based members, not just his SDI partner. This was a characteristic of all the teachers who moved furthest in their professional development during the InterActive project. He also involved the meso-community of his department by feeding back some of what was emerging, and contributed to the thinking of another macro-community, his school.

Ian's understanding of the potentialities of ICT increased as a consequence of his involvement in the various layers of community. His professional knowledge grew and his understanding and use of an ICT-related language of practice increased. His existing attributes of reflection and self-awareness were honed through inquiry and collaboration. In the final phase of the project he was appointed head of English in a school which was looking for leadership in the incorporation of ICT in teaching and learning. Ian's view was that the professional development he had gained from being involved in the project had equipped him for this post. By the end of the project, Ian, a clearly 'enabled practitioner', was in his new post and registered for a PhD, researching ICT in English.[3]

This vignette not only describes Ian's 'history of becoming' but also illustrates the ways in which the different layers of community interacted during the course of the project. This idea of community was central to many of the strands of the InterActive project and provided much of the conceptual apparatus that allowed the strands to cohere. In the next section the concept of community is discussed in more detail.

The concept of community

In recent years, the discourse of professional learning and development has become suffused with the language of 'community'. The term has become attached to a wide range of human groupings and settings. It is used rhetorically with reference to a range of structures including the 'academic community', the 'research community' and the 'professional community'. In addition we have, for example, the more specialised 'communities of practice' and the 'online' or 'virtual community'.

Despite this abundance, some basic agreements have emerged which have been best categorised by Keller (2003). She sees community in terms of dimensions: (1) as turf, place or territory; (2) as shared ideals and expectations; (3) as a network of social ties and allegiances and (4) as a collective framework. The first focuses on the ideas of community as a bounded, identifiable territory best represented geographically. The second sees community as 'habit of mind' where collective coherence and relationships are formed out of common experiences; the third identifies community as a union of common elements directed towards agreed goals, while the fourth has a more legalistic bent focusing on rules, activities, projects, structures and governance to maintain collective configurations. These groupings, argues Keller, make community a chameleon term but the standard dimensions outlined above are the 'bedrock' of any discussion of the concept.

It is interesting also to look at the semantic provenance of the term. The *Oxford English Dictionary* indicates that communication, communion and community have their origins in the Latin verb *communicare* (to make common or many) and the associated Latin noun *communion* (mutual participation, fellowship). To communicate literally means to 'give to another as a partaker'. Saville-Troike (2003) claims that all social science definitions of the term include the dimension of shared knowledge, possessions or behaviours – all derived from the Latin *communitae*, 'held in common'. Ideas about communities as essentially collections of individuals, and the more contemporary notion of a deeper more communicative community linked by ideas, social relations and learning, have been influenced by the theoretical work of Jurgen Habermas (1987) *The Theory of Communicative Action* and Lave and Wenger's *Situated Learning: Legitimate Peripheral Participation* (1991).

The concept of 'community of practice' has been used freely and widely in many different contexts and the version used in the InterActive project emerged from the needs and nature of the chosen activities. It is important to note, however, that our use of the term community did not emerge by accident; on the contrary, the idea of community that lies at the heart of the project was a deliberate attempt to fuse the language, rituals, norms and values of a range of educationists. This range included practising teachers, teacher educators and researchers. In many ways our idea of community was akin to what the French sociologist Pierre Bourdieu (1980) calls an enabling context or *habitus*, where different traditions, ideas, backgrounds and expertise intersect to generate new knowledge.

Allied to our idea of community is the view of knowledge as being produced by an engagement with and in practice. This helps us to see why professional 'enablement' is more than simply the ability to change procedures and patterns according to the demands of the external environment. Rather, it demands that practice be guided and legitimated by a blend of practitioner wisdom and researcher knowledge and credibility. We therefore see the idea of creating and linking up three interlocking layers of community – micro, meso and macro – as holding the key to rethinking the currently dominant model of professional development.

This dominant model is predicated on the idea that there are general rules underpinning 'best practice' (however defined) that can be communicated and applied through a process of engagement. This engagement is assumed to involve attendance at workshops, presentations and gatherings where teachers are 'professionally developed'. In this model teachers' professional learning is assumed to be an 'additive' de contextualised process based on the accumulation of knowledge (both craft and research informed) to an existing pedagogic repertoire.[4] In InterActive we chose to develop a more iterative approach. The ideas of Nonaka and Takeuchi (1995) are useful here. They describe knowledge creation and transfer in terms of a cycle that involves the individual, the group and the community. In this iterative process tacit and explicit knowledge are kneaded together. From this perspective, innovation becomes the process by which individuals and groups create and define mutual problems and then actively develop new knowledge to solve them.

Such iterative, collaborative processes wrestle continually with key questions: what levels of practitioner engagement are possible and acceptable to them? How might the voices of research subjects be represented in accounts of research? In what ways might practitioners become more involved in the design, process, and findings of research? Also, what factors – individual, institutional and professional – inhibit long-term engagement? The next section of this chapter shows how the InterActive project engaged empirically with these questions and how the project participants interacted in various 'layers of community'.

Layers of community

As already discussed in Chapter 1 our research into learning with new technologies was organised around five interwoven strands: teaching and learning, management and policy, subject cultures, professional development and learners' out-of-school uses of technology. In our analysis the *macro-community* consists of the whole project and its many varied participants and partners including four primary schools, five secondary schools and one college of further education. At the heart of the project was the teaching and learning research strand, which in this analysis was made up of a number of *meso-communities*, each formed around a curriculum subject and consisting of teachers from partner schools, researchers and teacher educators from the university. These communities were designated subject design teams (SDTs). From these teams came the SDIs which were designed, carried out and researched individually in teachers' classes. Developing and researching each SDI was the focus for a *micro-community*. A teacher and a researcher from the SDT formed the core membership around which a variety of relationships formed.

Outside the core project but linked to it by the teacher members were other micro, meso and macro communities such as subject departments in secondary schools and subject groups in primary schools, year groups, whole school staffs and professional associations of teachers. As the project progressed it was possible to trace the flow and development of ideas and practices around these settings and through the project.

The SDTs met for the first time in June 2001.[5] There was no pre-scribed model for when meetings would take place or what happened in them, although ways of working were discussed at whole-project level meetings. Notes of planning meetings with the subject coordinators, accounts and reports of the work of the teams, audio and video recordings of meetings and interviews with participants allowed us to consider the development of these meso-communities and the ways in which issues of hierarchy, relative power, discourse, roles, identity and knowledge transacting and transformation were addressed.

The focus from the start was on the curriculum subject. In the first whole-day meeting the mathematics group, for instance, worked with mathematical transformations using a dynamic geometry software and played with the interactive whiteboard. The English group became involved with a story-writing activity using pencil and paper alongside the computer, and read and discussed a seminal paper on writing on the computer. Modern language teachers looked at different ways that writing frames could be used and discussed both commercially available software and a home-grown version. The music group discussed technology in the music classroom; they shared their ideas about and past experiences of using music computer software for composing and thoughts on different music programs.

Reflection on and discussion of the activities led to the telling of professional and personal learning stories thus enabling members of the team to share beliefs about teaching and learning, and to understand something of the contexts within which they all lived and worked.

During the activities some members acted as observers while others worked together. This opened the way to interrogating the activity of 'research', as experiences, perceptions and reservations were recounted and aired. At the end of the first meeting teacher members agreed to undertake a 'mini-design' initiative with ICT and to report back on this at the next meeting.

This opening tactic for engagement was recalled with approval by teachers when interviewed about the process. Ellie, Pam and Rachel (members of the SDI mathematics and English team) spoke for their colleagues in both teams when they claimed that:

Ellie   Training at school, a lot of it can be kind of sitting listening to someone else, not really getting into the nitty gritty yourself. In InterActive, straight away you're involved and then you're off doing something. So it never felt a waste of time, you know.

Pam   The fact that it immediately involved children – a plus for me.

Rachel   It was encouraging everyone who hasn't got it sorted yet – we're all trying to work it through together. If you had a lot of experts going 'this, this, this and this and English and ICT works well in this particular way', I think this would be daunting to the rest of us.

Subsequent whole team meetings combined the introduction of new ideas with the sharing of experience, ideas and expertise. Teachers were encouraged to demonstrate and lead sessions. There were also opportunities to play with software, and experiment with equipment such as digital cameras and interactive boards; the research literature was also introduced carefully and discussed widely, as illustrated in Chapter 1. As video data from the SDIs became available extracts were shown to the whole team and again rich discussions ensued (for further discussion see Chapter 5). During the second phase of the project, as teachers collaborated with their university partners on conference papers and presentations, new ideas were shared. In this way the insights gained from the research-oriented micro-communities, which were focused on the SDIs, fed into the meso-community of the whole team and led to a greater sharing of practice and research knowledge. Out of this process, the teams began to define and engage with a whole range of issues and questions related to subject teaching and learning and the incorporation of ICT.[6]

In both the meso-community of the SDT, and the macro-community of the whole project there was also evidence of the boundaries between the two communities of research and practice beginning to blur. One teacher member summed this up thus:

Ian   People from an academic focus tend to look at things with a theoretical background. Teachers are always concerned with the practical. But we should be looking at teaching and learning more than we are able. You [the three university

> partners] are all teachers but you each have a different pers-
> pective. It's been enjoyable – the different ways of working.
> It makes me think a lot . . . I think it's in my mind all the
> time.

The key here is the recognition of difference and an acceptance
of plurality within the project. There was also an acknowledgement
that teachers, teacher educators and researchers have different yet
complementary roles to play in terms of the development of professional knowledge and practice.

Micro-communities and the investigation of practice

As the project moved into its main classroom research phase, members
of each *meso-community* began to form themselves into a new layer –
or *micro-community*. The process of fusing members from different
perspectives into a micro-community of practice focused on an SDI
was an important aspect of the project. At this stage each teacher
worked closely with one university colleague – either a researcher or
an experienced teacher educator. In some cases where there were two
teachers from the same school in a subject team there was further
collaboration. The complexity of identities within these relationships
had to be worked through, however. For instance, issues surrounding role shifts and conflicts came under discussion. The fact that in
some cases teachers were both researchers and research subjects,
and university colleagues were co-designers, data collectors and co-
teachers, was articulated and sometimes contested. Perceptions and
assumptions about hierarchies and power relationships were addressed
so that, for example, teachers who began by asking 'What do you
want me to do?' were later more likely to ask 'How can we do it?'
Furthermore, the university researchers, initially conceptualised as
consultants and non-participant observers, also redefined their research
positions as their relationship with the teachers and their more regular
presence in the classroom drew them into a co-teaching role.

The process and location of SDI planning was also pertinent to
the investigation of practice within the community. Work on the
preparation of the SDI took place both in the university and in school;
this was augmented by frequent e-mail exchanges. The combination
of involvement in 'research' and the support of partners from the
university encouraged many teachers to take risks they would other-

wise not contemplate. In playing the role of catalysts, the researchers and teacher educators in the project were mindful of Ricoeur's (1992) admonition that when talking about initiatives we must also remember our responsibility to support those taking steps forward often into the unknown.

University partners also went into school to capture lessons on digital video, the nature of these depending on the agreed focus of the SDI. In some classes, for instance, six sample students from across the range of attainment were identified as a focus for data collection. Their interactions with the technology were prioritised for video capture along with digital videotaping the whole class or the teacher as appropriate. Two cameras were routinely used occasionally, but not regularly, there was a brief discussion with the teacher after each lesson. Digital video data was then transferred to VHS and offered to teachers for validation and reflection. Diagnostic tests were likewise devised and evidence of attainment collected before and after each initiative. In most, but not all cases, other work pressures prevented teachers from being involved in video analysis before the end of the SDI. In general, however, the analysis and review of each SDI was undertaken at a time when teachers felt they had some time and space for this. This iterative design of the research meant that the findings from the first SDI were the basis for a redesign in the following school year. In what follows, a number of teachers give a flavour of how they experienced this process. Their comments are indicative and resonate across the SDIs:

Marnie   Working together always felt quite valuable. That relationship was definitely important in things I designed and how I went about it. Things grow, ideas flourish. I wasn't worried about getting things wrong because I could – because I actually had an excuse to, without messing up.

Elisabeth It's been very exciting to do some of the background work and the research work and the reading that the project allowed me. The time to actually get into reading about language use and what's happening in other countries. I enjoy that hugely. I've had a really enjoyable collaboration with Ruth, the other teacher. We've designed our first writing frames and we've used them. And that's really exciting. You can actually try something out, although we were following a recipe. And initially we didn't get the recipe right. So things didn't work to start with. And I had a very frustrated night, trying to work out why for example in the writing frames I couldn't actually type anything into my word box. And it was purely that we had jumped a step too quickly.

Becca   Having meetings to discuss how other schools were doing things differently . . . was very good, as well as for evaluating your own work. I mean it's nice to know that you're not the only one in this sort of situation . . . being the only teacher in this school . . . it was really good to speak to other people about what was going on in their department as far as ICT was concerned . . . and having a researcher partner worked really well, especially since the researcher had quite recent, relevant experience in the classroom.

Ellie   Not having the attention on me but on my lessons and my planning was just really nice. I've never had another teacher sit down with me for like an hour and just talk about one lesson that I was going to teach . . . with another teacher we'd probably have kind of muddled through and just not had as many ideas. It gave me a lot of confidence to just do different things and you were just so kind of 'Yeah go ahead and just do it on your own.' The project kind of slowed me down and made me think.

Heidi   [Being observed by the LEA consultant] I've felt pretty intimidated – this was wrong, this was wrong, this was wrong – and he wasn't helping me to make things better really. In InterActive there's never been any criticism – far more positive.

The importance of community is exemplified in the above commentaries. They highlight how community structures helped the teachers develop personally and professionally by providing zones of support and wisdom. When well structured these communities helped members form a strong bond that contributed to a climate of openness – to each other and to new ideas. The motivational influence was also strongly represented in the comments – a process which was developed through the creation of a strong identity with fellow professionals and with the project team as a whole. The following section explores these ideas further, with a more detailed case study of the learning that can accrue from being a member of such a community.

An illustration of community learning

The vignette described below illustrates something of the essences that emerged from the interactions in the various 'layers of community'. It is a story of one English teacher. Rachel had just started her second year of teaching. The case illustrates a noticeable shift away from viewing teachers as 'constrained deliverers' to what we term 'enabled professionals' whose knowledge and practice have moved according to their collective volition.

VIGNETTE 2
Rachel Yates – 'Thinking it through'

For her first SDI, Rachel, an English teacher, worked with a mixed-ability class of 13–14-year-olds on the language of film. It was not as successful as she had hoped. Later she reflected on this stage in the research:

Rachel   With the first project I spent, yeah, a long time writing the scheme of work and trying to do it and it was a bit demoralising when things didn't work out the way I wanted them to.

The support within her community meant that Rachel was not defeated by this. In her micro-community she was able to stand back and, with her university-based partners, look at the evidence from the video, from the diagnostic tests and from the student interviews. Together they identified a tension between Rachel's need to control the learning and the students' need to have ownership of the activity. Rachel acknowledged a sense of the pressure within her school to speed up delivery and cover content when she commented: 'I think it's my habit to try and pack everything into a scheme of work and try and do too much . . . and by trying to do a lot of things perhaps I was missing a focus for the learning'. She also described her feeling of vulnerability and loss of control when teaching with computers in the library or computer room. Rachel took account of this analysis when planning a repeat of the lesson with another year group. She started with activity-based work on digital images in her classroom using a data projector. This was followed by a move to the school's computer room where the students worked collaboratively on their own story sequences using digital cameras and PowerPoint.

Rachel   With the first project I had the idea . . . and they followed that story. [This time] I gave them the option of thinking up their own story . . . and they had, I guess, more ownership over the task, which I think was a very positive thing.

Rachel was more satisfied with this second sequence of lessons and the evidence indicated that her students had developed further their abilities in critical and visual literacy. However, Rachel's learning went beyond the single SDI; she had begun to develop confidence and ideas about teaching and learning. She declared:

Rachel   Thinking through it from a learner-centred perspective rather than a teacher-based perspective – I think is something that the SDI has helped me with quite a lot.

Interestingly, the change in her approach, attitude and aspirations brought her closer to her espoused views about teaching and learning articulated at the start of the project. In her initial interview Rachel said she thought that learning was best achieved by students 'having ownership, being collaborative, not being lectured at . . .' However, her sense of what was expected in the school, combined with her unease around learners with technology, meant that she was not carrying this through in practice. The evidence of the first design initiative and the supported analysis enabled her to see this. Through participation in the community, Rachel also learned to feel comfortable with new learning contexts and situations produced by ICT. She continued:

Rachel   I think it's partly a case of being comfortable with using the ICT personally and feeling that you can handle the equipment or you feel that you know what to do with the class. But I think it's maybe relaxing into what you're doing too, that you have a sense that this is purposeful and it's getting somewhere and the children are enjoying it.

For Rachel the initial activities and discussions in the meso-community were interesting and started her thinking, but it was her experiences in the micro-community which were central to her professional development. Time away from school for collaborative analysis of the data, which the project made possible, combined with the opportunity for iteration and reflection, were key in enabling her to confront issues and engage with ideas which had been suppressed in the pressure of day-to-day practice. As the project progressed she was able to place her experiences in the wider context of the shared understandings developing in the meso-community of the SDT. Among Rachel's departmental colleagues in school there was little interest in incorporating technology in teaching and learning. In this context Rachel's experiences on the InterActive project made her neither evangelical nor overtly revolutionary. But she did return to school a more thoughtful and confident teacher, an enabled practitioner with a sound foundation for continuing professional development.

Towards the 'enabled practitioner'

In order to exemplify the ways in which the 'layers of community' idea contributed to the creation of what we term 'enabled practitioners', we first highlight the importance of context. This relates to the various layers of community growing out of each SDI where we attempted to challenge the traditional focus on what the user does with new technology and instead explore who the user is, why they are using the technology, what are the most appropriate sites for teaching with technology and when is the best moment to engage learners.

The creation of this enabling arena helped the participants blend their professional experience with more formal research-informed knowledge, as Ian's story shows. Not only did he engage with research and scholarship of different types, he was also actively writing by the time the project was complete and was also planning his PhD. We also discovered that although craft insights are important starting points, most participants had to bridge their understandings between what was known and what they wanted to learn. This meant being reflective and analytic about their practice, their underlying implicit theories about teaching, learning and new technologies, and above all it meant being explicit about what they wanted to get out of the SDI. Again Rachel's story is instructive where interacting with her community allowed her to gain new confidence that came from confronting the tension between her espoused theories and her beginning practices with ICT. The bridging metaphor also helped us to think about the ways in which research-based knowledge might be connected to practice and the ways in which it might inform the process of knowledge-building within individuals and teams. The 'layers of community' therefore had a catalysing function which helped the participants frame their transition from one of constrained professional to that of enabled practitioner. In many ways this relates to the idea of liberating constraints highlighted in Chapter 5, although in this sense the liberation came as a result of careful nurturing and a recognition that both pedagogic process and practice had to be addressed simultaneously.

In the micro-community the teacher educators and researchers often acted as brokers working in conjunction with the teachers, helping them to fuse different forms of knowledge with their emergent understandings, working within the constraints of their local contexts. This fusing process involved the following activities:

- direct observation of practice through video analysis;
- narration of pedagogic processes through the description and explanation of practice;
- imitation and comparison of ideas and practices observed;
- experimentation through iterative analysis;
- joint execution.

Within the meso-community teachers tested their emergent and evidence-based knowledge and understanding by presenting their evidence to their SDT. In this setting, ideas were affirmed, challenged and refined. The larger group began to develop generalised theories from the experiences of the micro-communities; these contributed to the thinking of the macro-community. Teachers gained in confidence:

some simply in their approach to incorporating ICT into teaching and learning; others in a sense of themselves as critical and analytic practitioners who would engage with colleagues in school and with the wider professional community.

The concept of the 'enabled practitioner' that emerged within this context had four essential attributes. These attributes relate to both the personal and collaborative domains:

Personal attributes
- Professional knowledge growth
- Reflection and self-awareness

Cooperative attributes
- Language of practice
- Inquiry, collaboration and community

In terms of the first, the participants exhibited considerable knowledge growth within their various communities (macro, meso and micro). This knowledge included both the formal theories often derived from empirical research of various types (often described as *knowledge for practice*) as well as the craft knowledge embedded in each teacher's professional practice and repertoires. This craft knowledge when made explicit (which happened continuously throughout the project) is termed *knowledge of practice* while that which remains implicit is termed *knowledge in practice*. The second attribute emphasises *reflection and self-awareness* and was vital in challenging existing practices and the tacit interpretations and perceptions that underpinned many of the teachers' pedagogic understandings. The 'enabled' perspective therefore rehabilitates the idea of uncertainty and stresses the need for teachers and others to theorise the contemporary complexities of practice through creative pedagogy. This notion also invites practitioners and researchers to think more creatively about the relationship between theory and practice, and to consider models and processes of 'professional development'.

The third attribute focuses on the importance of the development of an appropriate *language of practice*. Here the project highlighted the need to integrate concepts, ideas, knowledge and skill that emerged from all the communities involved in the project. A comparison with other professions is instructive. Architects and medical practitioners, for instance, have developed a way of thinking and expression that enables them to take ownership of their professional practice that teachers have, as yet, been unable to do. Teachers' language, for instance, is mundane in that it uses a recognisable and unspecialised lexicon. Perhaps the most complex term in education is 'curriculum', although pedagogy (which is rarely used and has multiple definitions) is also more specialised. Medics, on the other hand, have used both the language of science and their own professional vocabulary to create a high-status, respected and enabled profession.

If this language is to develop it will, in part, be dependent on the need for all educationalists (teachers, teacher educators, researchers, theorists, consultants, etc.) to engage in *inquiry, collaboration and community*. Here the distributed nature of the knowledge which is context dependent is more likely to lead to diversified understandings and perspectives where communication and collaboration – where they occur – lead to increased opportunities for professional creativity.

Summary and conclusions

To summarise, our evidence suggests that various layers of community emerged within the InterActive project which contributed significantly to bridging the gap or blurring the boundaries between the research and practice communities. Using the idea of 'layers of community' we were able to understand how different levels of activity were structured into the project, how from these structures 'communities' emerged, developed and supported professional growth. The process also helped give granularity to the idea of the 'enabled practitioner', which we believe affords the teaching community promise of a real way forward in terms of its professional project. Ultimately, three features underpinned the professional development process; all of which had a major impact on the emergence of the 'enabled practitioners'. These features include:

- *mutuality*: a reduction of a sense of isolation, and contact with others who share professional interests and concerns;
- *interaction*: involving knowledge exchange and generation as a basis of professional transformation;
- *encouragement*: to take supportive risks combined with help and guidance in analysing practice.

All, we contend, are sustainable if the idea of the 'layered community' is taken up in ways that are nested within the realm of practice.

Notes

1   In England the City Technology College (CTC) programme was established in 1988 – many CTCs are converting to City Academies.
2   Throughout the InterActive project Best Practice Research Scholarships were awarded to teachers by the Department for Education and Skills (DfES) on a competitive basis.
3   The title of Ian Thompson's PhD is 'The Process of Students' Writing Using ICT'. It will be submitted to the University of Bristol in 2008.
4   See Day (1999).
5   See methodological appendix for an overview of the number of teachers and researchers working within each SDT.
6   For further discussion of this, see the methodological appendix (p. 217).

Chapter 5*

Creative designs for learning

In this chapter we consider ways in which ICT can enhance learning in a variety of subject domains, through a focus on subject design initiatives (SDIs) in modern foreign languages (MFL), music and geography. Through the use of detailed case studies we explore teachers' considerations when integrating ICT into learning situations and the decisions that were made, particularly in relation to notions of freedom and constraint within the classroom. The chapter aims to:

- explore ways in which technology can liberate and constrain learning;
- explore issues surrounding the teachers' consideration of freedom and constraints within classroom settings;
- compare work within the three subject areas in relation to 'liberating constraints'.

Liberating constraints

From the beginning of the InterActive project we were interested in the ways in which teachers' choices of ICT resources and design of classroom activities relate to their beliefs about their subject and the way it is best learned. Such choices are partly influenced by the available technology, the subject knowledge domain, the pedagogic practices associated with a subject domain and the phase of schooling (for example primary or secondary). They are also influenced by top-down factors such as the curriculum and assessment systems, and more bottom-up factors such as young people's out-of-school learning with ICT. Our theoretical perspective has given us the capacity to reconceptualise these 'choices' as mediating tools that can either constrain or enhance a teacher's way of working.

* This chapter was authored by Marina Gall, Elisabeth Lazarus, Celia Tidmarsh and Nick Breeze.

From this perspective we view the process of designing a learning initiative as a creative process that is framed by a balance of freedoms and constraints, or what Davis, Sumara and Luce-Keplar (2000) call 'liberating constraints'. They suggest that 'well-crafted learning activities are ones that maintain a balance between enough organisation to orient students' actions and sufficient openness to allow for the varieties of experience, ability and interest that are represented in every classroom' (p. 87). When developing lessons, whether or not they intend to use ICT, all teachers make decisions about how open-ended activities should be and how much and what type of support to provide for students. But are there new or different issues arising from the introduction of ICT into the classroom?

Within this chapter, through a consideration of a series of case studies, we discuss the ways in which MFL, music and geography teachers used ICT to enhance learning. The case studies illustrate the choices teachers made about software, the curriculum focus, the types of activities and their associated pedagogies; they also exemplify the ways in which choices made by teachers impacted upon students' learning. Within the discussion that follows each case study, we explore further the issues of freedoms and constraints and, in particular, the implications for teachers when planning for the use of computers in the classroom. At the end of the chapter we return again to the idea of 'liberating constraints' and discuss the ways in which teachers can experiment with freedoms and constraints when designing new ways of using ICT to enhance learning.

CASE STUDY 1
Writing in a foreign language

Context and aims

From the beginning as teacher members of the MFL design team, Elisabeth Lazarus and Ruth Cole, along with other members of the team, expressed the view that whereas students make good progress in listening and reading, they often experience difficulties in writing and speaking a foreign language.[1] We are both German teachers and were colleagues at the same school during the project, a school which is technology rich, with language learners

---

continued

having fortnightly access to a specialised computer room, with a wide range of software available to improve reading, listening and speaking. Having decided to focus on writing in German we explored the potential of language software and found that this was only available for writing in French.[2] While this available technology incorporated prompts to support writing, we were critical of these because they were in English and we believed that this would impede the teachers' attempts to maximise the use of the target language in lessons. Furthermore, we wanted to be able to personalise the texts and tasks to suit our learners and the context within which we were working.

The design process

Our aim was to create writing frames to model extended and accurate writing in German. Although initially influenced by the 'French' writing frames, we discovered that it was possible to use a simple function in Word which mirrored some features that were available in this commercial language learning software. In this way we were able to personalise software commonly available in schools and homes. By activating 'Forms' in the Word toolbar menu, we were able to insert drop-down menus in the model texts we were creating (see Figure 5.1). The drop-down menus could contain single words, shorter or longer phrases.

Our approach differed from that of the French language learning software since it provided more grammatical structure for the students and also encouraged writing based on a model sentence, a series of sentences or longer texts. We wanted students to be able to choose from a range of possible prepositions or synonyms in German, hence the single word was important. At other times we were concerned about word order and inversions which, for example, a 'weil' clause necessitates; thus the ability

Figure 5.1 The 'Forms' toolbar in Word

for the drop-down menu to contain a series of words was valuable. Another feature of the design was that students had the choice whether or not to access prompts: these were not on display by default. As a result, this left the screen relatively free from 'clutter' and allowed the students to concentrate on the drop-down 'foreign language' choices and the implications of these for their developing writing in the target language.

These first writing frames were developed collaboratively with the whole MFL team. We also discussed how we would integrate these ICT resources into our overall teaching approach in order to ensure we provided appropriate learner challenge. Initially we trialled the writing frames with 14–15-year-old students and over time developed these for all our classes, sharing them on the school's intranet with other language teachers. We became proficient in creating these electronic writing frames in very short periods of time, and modifying them to suit different groups of students and the different topics they were learning. We also liked the fact that students were not given 'correct answers': they had

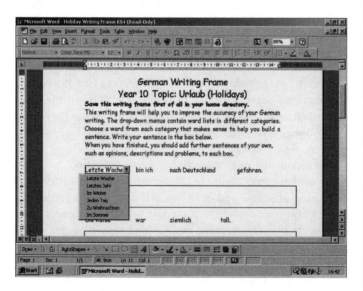

Figure 5.2 Section of an early design of a Year 10 writing frame showing a drop-down menu

continued

to work out the written language for themselves, together with their peers, with support from the teacher or other available reference materials, such as dictionaries and student files. Eventually we incorporated sound and images into the design of the writing frames and these brought them to life in a way that we had not originally anticipated.

Students' work

When the writing frames were used in the classroom we constantly encouraged students to question their choices and to extend their writing by including additional materials. Even in its earliest design format, there was room for a variety of approaches in the way the students worked. Some students, instead of scrolling up to the original model to retrieve information, minimised the original text and created a Word document for their free writing, toggling between the two; others used a split screen to the same end. From working with students we found that our early design of writing frames (see Figure 5.2) which contained a box for writing underneath each sentence was met with a certain amount of criticism; students wanted the potential to write longer texts. In this sense they were requesting more challenge for their writing in German. We started to incorporate colour, symbols and pictures and comments to help students in their choices (see Figure 5.3). Students very soon began to 'unlock' the drop-down menus to insert their own choices of words; these new versions they could save in their home directories. A spin-off from the project was the creation of such writing frames by students for others.

We found that over time students who had used our tailor-made writing frames performed better in both written course work completed at school and at home, and also in tasks carried out under exam conditions.[3] The drop-down writing frames appeared to support them in recalling and re-using new language in the classroom or in homework tasks or examinations some time later. However, it must be noted that at all times students were still encouraged to use other more traditional writing tools such as pen and paper, paper-based dictionaries and class files.

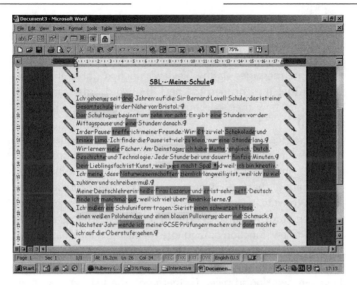

Figure 5.3 Longer writing model adapted using student feedback – grey
boxes contain standard drop-down menus with choices, placing
the cursor over the yellow boxes shows a comment to help the
learners. This disappears once the cursor is moved somewhere
else on the screen.

Discussion

Within this MFL SDI, we see that a change in the balance between
freedom and constraint came about through the iterative process
of developing the writing frames over a period of time. The
teachers' initial intention was to design a framework to enable
the students to practise sentence building with varied lexical
items (for example, a wide range of adjectives or past participles)
before using the structures in a freer way, also allowing for the
incorporation of new ideas. This involved imposing considerable
constraints on the students' writings. The teachers started by asking
students to deconstruct individual sentences, making choices and
considering alternatives. However, quite quickly, the students
seemed to want more of a challenge: they asked for models of
longer texts where they could see how sentences and paragraphs

continued

interlinked and how descriptions and arguments could be built up. Responding to the request of students, who were also keen for additional pointers and reminders, the MFL teachers began to incorporate messages via the 'Review' function (for example, the message that they needed to check the word order carefully or be aware of how their selection of words could affect tone and meaning).

Here we see what Davis *et al.* (2000) refer to as teachers taking 'a flexible approach to events that unfold in the classroom . . .' (p. 144) involving 'responsive attunement to the learners'. Incorporating these additional tools gave the students more freedom to write in German without needing to request help from a teacher: students could choose to read the messages provided via the 'Review' function or to ignore them. The additional support provided within the writing frame also freed the teachers from constantly repeating similar comments to various students while they were working in pairs. Furthermore, the teachers had been developing the use of the school's intranet for student access at home and it became clear that messages incorporated into texts would also be helpful during completion of homework.

Despite certain freedoms associated with this work, a design of this kind also places many constraints upon the learner – this was the intention. Here, the ICT template contributed to scaffolding the students' learning and was a key element in this process.[4] Furthermore, its use inevitably involved a considerable amount of repetition and copying. Davis *et al.* (2000) suggest that 'copying and repetition are valuable and important techniques in the development of complex competencies . . .' (p. 204). This is supported by other research which considers young people's use of computers[5] and seems to be important when students are learning the complexities of writing in a foreign language.

Despite the recognition of the importance of repetitive procedures, Davis *et al.* (2000) suggest that teachers should avoid the possibility 'that the form be reduced to mere mechanics – to rules, procedures and exercises aimed at proficiency rather than creative possibility' (p. 199). This was a concern for the MFL team in its development and use of the drop-down menus. While the most important aim within the MFL lessons was to develop proficiency in writing, the teachers also wanted lessons to be enjoyable and to open up possibilities for creativity in the writing process. As such, teachers responded to student initiatives and experimentation with the 'writing-frame' tool was encouraged.

Overall this SDI in MFL was characterised by a creative use of available software (Word), designed to meet the learning objectives of the teachers and redesigned over time in response to student feedback.

Composing in music

From the beginning, all the music teachers involved in the InterActive project decided that they wanted to consider the use of ICT to support practical music-making rather than, for example, to encourage the development of notation or listening skills. As such, they all agreed to create SDIs in which the main focus of work was the development of composition skills. In the following two sections we introduce two music SDIs, one of which took place in a primary school and the other in a secondary school. The reason we consider work in both phases is because the types of software used within primary and secondary music classrooms tend to be very different.

CASE STUDY 2
Dance eJay in the primary school

Context and aims

Natalie Butterworth and Jo Heppinstall, non-specialist primary school teachers, were new to the use of ICT for music-making purposes. Selecting from a variety of composition packages they were concerned that the software should be relatively simple to

continued

use, exciting for the students who had never used ICT for music before and not too costly. They were animated about Dance eJay:

Natalie   It's [Dance eJay's] built on things that kids would already know about, like fast forward and rewind buttons . . . I just wanted them to be able to access it quickly so that the software wasn't a problem.

Jo   . . . you get instant achievement in that sounds can be arranged and rearranged easily if you don't like them . . . and it's at 'a press of a button' . . . it makes it so much more accessible.

Natalie and Jo taught in an inner-city primary school, where networked computers were situated in a room separate from their normal classroom, bookable for only one hour a week and where Dance eJay was loaded onto all the machines.

The software

Dance eJay is a sample sequencing package that provides the user with a variety of short musical samples that they can organise to create their own piece of music (see Figure 5.4). Each sample is represented as a coloured box containing its name; these boxes vary in length, according to the length of the sample itself. Samples with a similar musical purpose have the same colour and are placed together in sound groups. Using the computer mouse, sounds are selected and dragged onto the 'Play Window' which consists of a number of audio tracks that can be filled or left empty, depending on the number of samples that the user wishes to place together. The 'Play Window' can be saved as a file for future work. The available recorded samples are selected by the software developer so that they all sound 'good' together. Each eJay package allows the user to compose within a single musical style. The package gives access to a range of sophisticated sounds that are included in contemporary music listened to by many young people outside school, including drum and electric guitar sounds.

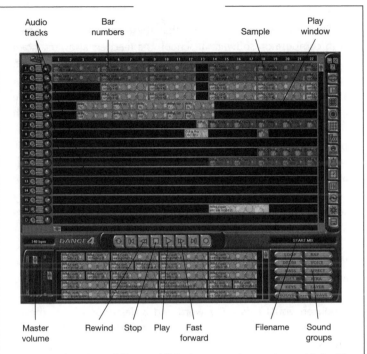

Figure 5.4 Opening of 'Dream Mix': demonstration track provided with the software

The design process

Jo and Natalie decided to develop a music SDI for 10–11-year-old students using Dance eJay because it offered the students the opportunity to compose within a 'popular' style. Working with the music specialists within the subject design team (SDT) they decided that they wanted pairs of students to learn to compose through creating a piece of music within a simple structure. They decided upon ternary form ('ABA form' where section B is a contrast to A and section A has to be repeated after B) with an introduction of sixteen bars. Within the composition brief the students were also to be asked to include three 'intended effects': the sixteen bar introduction had to include one continuous sample ('*Myth*') throughout and had to build up to a small climax in preparation for section A. Section A had to have an 'ambient' feel.

continued

Since this was the first time that these students had worked with composition software at school, the teachers also prescribed the approach to the composing and the composition process itself: within each lesson students were to be asked to work upon a specific section. However, Jo and Natalie planned to encourage informal talk between pairs of students and individuals, which might involve movement from their allocated computer to other parts of the room.

Recognising that listening and analysis skills are also important when composing, the teachers planned the SDI so that the beginning and/or the end of each lesson would include a plenary session which would provide the opportunity for students to share and discuss work in progress. In order to support the development of the students' 'music' vocabulary – which would aid their ability to appraise their work and that of their peers – Natalie and Jo introduced new musical language each lesson, deciding exactly when to introduce the different 'music' words.[6] They also produced visual aids – the word and a description of its meaning – to place on the board as an aide-memoire for plenary discussions.

Despite the relative simplicity of the program, the teachers recognised the need to overcome certain common difficulties experienced by the students, such as saving work accurately.

Students' work

All pairs of students produced completed pieces of music which fulfilled the requirements of the brief. The teachers felt that this was in contrast to 'acoustic' group music composition where the success of a creative piece often relied upon the input of an instrumentalist or one or two students with considerable experience of music-making outside of school. Throughout the project, the motivation and full engagement of the students was evident, with almost no off-task talk. In part, the teachers felt that the simplicity of the software helped; as one student described:

Sarah It's a lot easier than learning to play an instrument. It takes years to manage to actually sound good.

Furthermore, since work could be saved on the computer, students did not have to worry about notating their music and the teacher did not have to spend what would have been considerable time recording each pair's work onto disc or tape.

Jo and Natalie also became aware that the visual representation of the music (see for example Figure 5.4) was helpful in enabling students to 'see' what they were producing and in acting as a focal point for discussion; this was particularly supportive for those students who had difficulty with musical vocabulary since they were able to point to areas of work on the screen and refer to the colours of the samples and sections of music.[7]

The students themselves were excited by what they were able to achieve:

Andy It is much more interesting [than other composing work] and there is more range of sounds.

Prior to the commencement of the SDI, some students – mainly boys – had criticised the fact that they rarely had the chance to compose music in a style that appealed to them. After the work, many students remarked that this software gave access to a contemporary style of music that they really enjoyed and often listened to outside school but were unable to replicate without computer software.[8]

CASE STUDY 3
Music for film in the secondary school

Context and aims

Teachers of music are aware that by the time students reach Year 9 (aged 13–14 years) many have decided not to carry on with the subject and motivation can be low. Paul, teacher of music in

continued

a secondary school, decided that he wanted to create an SDI to enthuse the students, offering them their first opportunity in school music lessons to work with visual as well as audio material. The music department in his school has a subject-specific computer classroom with enough workstations for students to work in pairs. At the time, Cubase VST 5.1 software was installed on all computers and was used within this work.

The software – Cubase

Cubase is a MIDI and audio sequencer, originally developed for professional musicians for composition purposes. With this software, students input their own ideas either through the music keyboard, sound mixer or the mouse. It also offers the ability to include 'virtual' software-based instruments, allowing composers to employ western orchestral instrumental sounds, synthesised sounds and sounds from popular music as well as those from a wide range of cultures. MIDI and audio sequencers, like sample sequencers, also provide a visual representation of the music which does not rely upon an understanding of conventional music notation. However, they also incorporate various editing facilities including a traditional music score editor, thus offering a variety of ways to view the music on the computer screen and to change the sound. In this SDI, most of the students worked within the 'Key Editor' where, similarly to eJay, the notes are displayed as horizontal lines in the window and the length of a line indicates the note length (or in eJay, the length of the sample). Within Cubase, the vertical height of a line, referenced to a vertical keyboard, indicates the pitch.

The design process

Paul worked with the composer-in-residence[9] to devise their own Cubase template which contained prepared musical clichés (composed by the composer-in-residence); students were to synchronise these with the film already loaded as part of the template and available in a small auxiliary window on the screen. In pairs, students were asked not only to simply arrange the fragments of music but also to cut, copy and paste them appropriately so that they provided a suitable soundtrack to the film. In addition, those who had completed all the work and higher-attaining students were required to compose their own sections to fit the 'action' film which had many dramatic moments.

Students' work

Paul was delighted with how well all students completed this multimedia project. They enjoyed matching the sounds to action within the film, including using descending repeated string motifs to illustrate the falling of a lift in a tower block and adding a 'danger' musical cliché to match the realisation on film that someone was trapped in the building. The structure of the template provided allowed the students to work in pairs at their own pace. The motivation was high: all students were observed to be fully engaged in the work with virtually no off-task activity and Paul noted that many students were more successful than they had been in previous projects.

Many of the students who did not normally do well in music also appreciated the new approach, which did not rely on their knowledge of musical notation, and enjoyed the creative aspects of the work:

Steve   ... quite a lot of the computer stuff that we've done before we were given the music on the sheet and we had to play it into the computer. But now we've just been given the music and then we can compose our own bits as well.

Interestingly, some students experimented with the software and came across the 'score editor' which illustrates the music in traditional musical score form; they preferred to work for at least some of the time with this more 'traditional' representation. Students were aware that the software environment opened up new possibilities for working:

Fran   ... you can like hear them [the sounds] together and you can try out different instruments together and see what they sound like.

Working with Dance eJay and Cubase

The various software packages used within the music designs have different potentials which affect the potential freedoms and constraints within teaching and learning. As might be expected, the software package chosen for work with primary school children, Dance eJay, was less complex than that for the secondary school work and thus easier to use. Dance eJay allows students to sequence prerecorded extracts of music; sounds are placed together in layers through the use of the mouse and the computer keyboard. In comparison, sequencing software such as Cubase enables the user to create his or her own music either by inputting ideas from the music keyboard or through writing music as traditional notation, via the software or the computer keyboard (however, although this possibility was available, precomposed scripts were used in the design initiative discussed above). As opposed to the single style dictated by the Dance eJay software, students using Cubase have an 'open canvas' to decide upon exactly what type of music they wish to create. Furthermore, depending on the available MIDI equipment, Cubase offers a wide variety of musical sounds to select from and there are possibilities to manipulate almost all parameters of these sounds, whereas within eJay opportunities are relatively limited.

Dance eJay could be considered as a template in itself, in that it provides a very structured environment in which the students can experiment with 'Dance' music sounds in a necessarily constrained way. Conversely, many music educationalists have commented upon the freedom that is provided by such packages which make composition accessible to young people whether or not they have 'traditional' instrumental, notational or theoretical music skills.[10]

While the majority of the students in the primary class commented on the positive aspects of Dance eJay some of the students, mainly those who were also instrumentalists, were aware of its limitations:

Martin   The basics of getting it to sound OK, that was easy ... fine tuning it so it sounded really good was a bit tricky because you might want to cut one bit and add another but then you realise that doesn't work.

Lesley   ... it [eJay] sounds very techno and everything and also you can't really get notes to harmonise.

Here, the student in the first quote raised a concern about the absence of a way to shorten or lengthen the samples in this program. The student in the second quote not only wanted to deviate from the style that the software package prescribes but also wanted to change the harmonies as he does when using the piano for composing – a function not possible within eJay. So we see that some of the students in this primary school class who had experience of 'traditional' musical skills, perhaps through taking instrumental lessons, were critical of Dance eJay because it did not allow them to manipulate the music at an elemental level (for example, to edit the rhythms or individual notes). This was not only a loss to them in their individual work but also to the class who might have learned from hearing how students could change certain harmonies from those provided by the software.

Producing music which largely evolves from manipulating sound samples produced by other people is still a major concern for some music educationalists.[11] These concerns centre around how original a composed piece can be when using sample sequencing such as eJay. Even if we consider originality to mean producing something that is original to the students themselves and not *completely* original,[12] the Dance eJay software *in itself* could be seen to provide limited opportunities for creativity, since all sounds fit together well so that, as in the words of Cole Porter, 'anything goes'.

Within the second iteration of the primary SDI, to enable students to create their own original ideas rather than just 'arranging' prerecorded sounds, the two music teachers decided to build in time for vocal experimentation and the inclusion of acoustic instrumental parts. While this offered new musical opportunities, a further set of constraints were placed upon this extension to the creative process, as a result of the classroom situation. Since all the students were working in one computer room, they were not able to add their own ideas to their music produced on Dance eJay, even though there is a record function within the music software; to do this would have required all other groups to stop working to avoid the spill-over of the sound of the other groups practising.

Another teaching approach that Jo and Natalie used to avoid what might have been quite a simple task of 'arranging' the musical samples and to ensure that the software was being used 'musically' – that is, the students were making careful selection of sounds within their pieces – was to prescribe the structure of the piece together with certain musical techniques that had to be considered and/or utilised within the compositions. While this might appear to place limits upon students' work it is interesting to note that the composer Igor Stravinsky (1947, p. 68) was aware of the positive impact of constraints within composition: 'my freedom consists in my moving about within the narrow frame that I have designed myself . . . the more constraints one imposes, the more one frees oneself of the chains that shackle the spirit'.

If we now move to consider the secondary SDI work we see that a very different liberating constraint – this time for the teachers – is inherent when considering the use of Cubase sequencing software for composing. MIDI and audio sequencing software such as Cubase and Logic is necessarily complex, being the same as that used by professionals, where a mastery of a wide set of technological skills is required in order to use it creatively. In England, where this software is used for classroom music, the curriculum rarely allows more than an hour a week for music lessons, so the technological skills need to be developed gradually through musical activities, over a number of years. This can constrain the music activity but is essential to enable students to become capable of utilising all the functions of the software without the need for constant teacher support.

Paul's SDI itself provides a clear example of a focus upon technological skills. From the start of the music for film project, the constraint provided by the template enabled the students to begin their creative process with the use of prepared sounds and this provided the 'space' for the students to acquire a new technical skill – aligning the musical snippets with the film – before they composed their 'own' music. Here the development of technological skills took precedence over creativity, yet the series of lessons was structured such that higher-attaining students had the freedom to create original ideas within the structure provided by the template. As a result, there were more opportunities for generating 'something original' than within Dance eJay.

Having considered the freedoms and constraints potentially available within two software composition packages we now move to a rather different situation in which ICT is used to enhance geographical enquiry.

CASE STUDY 4
Enhancing geographical enquiry

Aims and context

This design was developed by a geography teacher, Sally Leeming, at an inner-city comprehensive school and focused on the question: 'Can ICT enhance geographical enquiry?' Sally decided to incorporate the use of various forms of ICT into an existing unit of work for 11–12-year-old students, with a focus on geographical enquiry, to investigate the question: 'Is the area around the school a good place to live?' Both the focus of the study (the local area) and the approach to the study (geographical enquiry)[13] are requirements within the geography curriculum for this age group. Sally envisaged that the use of ICT would allow students to explore, analyse and then present their findings in different ways, for example through e-mind-mapping software, PowerPoint presentations and leaflets produced using MS Publisher. Sally had to book the school's computer room a number of weeks in advance and, as such, was predisposed to maximise the use of ICT during these lessons. She planned for each of the seven lessons, except for the one involving fieldwork, to be carried out in the computer room (where there were sufficient computers for each student to work individually).

The design process

Recognising that this was the first time the class would be experiencing the process of geographical enquiry, Sally structured the students' work with a set of key questions:

- what do we already know about our local area?
- how could we find out about our local area?
- how do we present our results and what do they show about our local area?
- is the area around our school a good place to live?

continued

The ordering of these questions reflects a particular approach to geographical enquiry which involves students working through a sequence of questions which structure the investigation.[14] In this case the teacher provided the questions herself rather than inviting the students to generate their own. The class was divided into groups of three to work on the task collaboratively. Each group was expected to produce a presentation in which the enquiry questions were addressed and in which students demonstrated how the gathered data had influenced their response.

The first lesson started with all the students involved in (sitting away from the computers) a brain-storming session on the issue of what physical and human features of their locality should be considered, before they moved to carry out work at the computer. The main activity planned for this and the next lesson was for students to use an e-mind-mapping package to identify the key features of their local area. The students were encouraged to draw on their own perceptions and to use websites provided by the teacher that gave details of the local area. The third lesson was spent walking around the local area completing environmental assessment sheets and drawing field sketches. In the next lesson, photographs of the local area, taken previously by the teacher, were made available to the students on the network. The following three lessons involved students working in their groups writing up and analysing the results, and putting together a presentation of findings in order to answer the enquiry questions. At this stage they were provided with a handout suggesting how to structure their findings, although they were encouraged to decide how they organised and presented their work within their groups. During the final lesson each group presented their findings.

Students' work

Reflecting on this sequence of lessons Sally expressed pleasure about the quality of work from some of the students, but was concerned that only five of the ten groups actually completed the activity, three using PowerPoint and two using MS Publisher. This seemed to be because students spent too much time considering the detail of the presentation rather than engaging with the 'geographical' data itself and ran out of time to produce a final product. Furthermore, the groups had divided their labour according to their perception of who had the 'best' ICT skills rather than who might best engage with the geography enquiry. Sally was also concerned that when working in the computer room students worked individually and not in groups; another concern was that the use of ICT had resulted in much information from the websites being cut and pasted by some and there was no sense of informed selection and critiquing of the material.

Reworking the geography SDI

The SDI was reviewed in the light of these issues and some aspects were redesigned. Generally the structure of the enquiry was tightened up with a reduction in the level of student autonomy and a corresponding increase in teacher control and direction of the activities. The outcome of the activity became more prescribed: each student had to complete a writing frame provided on the computer by the teacher. Students were instructed to use the data collected through fieldwork to complete the frame but the form of the outcome had been decided for them. The teacher was pleased that this new approach resulted in all the students completing their work. In this respect the teacher was experimenting with the available freedoms and constraints.

Discussion

In this geography SDI, the teacher had imagined that one of the potentials of various ICT tools would be to 'save time' on the construction of graphs so that more time could be spent on the geographical skills of analysis and evaluation. Instead she observed, in the first SDI, that:

Sally   . . . they spent absolutely ages deciding what font and colour looked best. So whereas I'd envisaged the computerised graph construction making things far quicker

continued

than if they'd done it by hand, I don't think it was any quicker at all. In fact it might have taken even longer.

This concern has also been raised in relation to work within subjects other than geography: research suggests that students can spend considerable time selecting font style, size and colour when producing final products for assessment.[15] In response to the problem, when reworking the SDI for the second time, Sally introduced the writing frames that included graphs *she* had constructed from the collected data. In doing this she felt that:

Sally   ... time wasn't lost in creating the graphs. There was more focus on interpreting the data with the end result that every single student ... unlike in the first design initiative ... managed to reach a conclusion based on the data that had been collected about whether or not they thought the area around Fairfield was a good place to live.

Here we see that the teacher concern about how to structure the lesson in relation to freedom and constraints resulted in two quite different iterations of the SDI. Sally's second approach to the SDI illustrates the advantages and disadvantages of a tight structure for this work: a tangible outcome was produced by the majority of students, but it was at the cost of freedom for individual and group creativity in terms of presentation.

Durbin explains that geographical enquiry is central to increasing 'creative activity in learning processes' and suggests that a key feature of creativity is 'an openness to ideas and ways of representing but which remain within parameters'.[16] In her final reflections on both the SDIs Sally commented on how her approach to using ICT had changed as a result of the InterActive project:

Sally   ... it's made me more aware that you can't just expect students to be told 'Okay, here's ICT, go away and do what you want'.

Freedoms and constraints

Having considered work within the modern foreign languages, music and geography teams separately, we will now draw together what we have learned about the issues of freedoms and constraints within the SDIs of all three subjects and suggest some implications for practice. The issues fall into four main categories:

- choice of tools
- time
- choice of student activities
- choice of student grouping.

While the first two categories relate more to choices made by the teacher, the latter two present areas wherein the teacher is required to make decisions about how much freedom to give to the students.

Choice of tools

Within each of the case studies discussed above different types of tools were chosen which related to the particular aims of the design initiatives. The MFL teachers reported that the customising and constraining of Word using drop-down menus for writing in a foreign language opened up more creative possibilities for students' writing than the use of more commercially available software. This possibly relates to the students' familiarity with Word and their confidence in experimenting with the provided templates in order to give expression to their writing. The MFL teachers recognised that allowing students to experiment with the provided template supported their learning of a foreign language and thus encouraged and supported the experimentation.

By contrast, in the geography SDI it appears that students experimenting with the presentation of graphs detracted from a focus on geographical enquiry and so was not encouraged by the teacher. In the second iteration of the geography SDI the teacher placed more constraints on the students' use of the graphing software which led to more students completing the work. However, it is also important to consider the quality of students' geographical work in both iterations. If, for example, the quality of geographical work produced in the first iteration was better than that in the second, then another possibility would have been for the teacher to have allowed more time for the work, as opposed to providing constraints in the form of teacher direction.

In the cases discussed above, teachers had considerable control over which ICT tool they chose to use, often informed by the potentials that it offered, as seen in the two music case studies. In all the design initiatives, once the teacher had decided on which ICT tool to use to support teaching and learning, there were still many decisions to be made about how to constrain its use in the classroom. For example, the comparison between the two music case studies illustrates that what emerges in terms of learning music relates to the software chosen, the teachers' structuring and the students' own experiences (see Chaper 3 for a more extensive discussion of this). Some software allows teachers to customise it for the particular learners, or to meet specific learning objectives (for example, Word) and other software does not readily allow this possibility (for example, Dance eJay). We suggest that when making decisions about which software to use in the classroom it is important to consider whether there is potential for both teachers and students to be able to personalise the software and to what extent this is appropriate.

Another choice that teachers have to make is when to use digital tools and when to use non-digital tools. This was seen within the geography SDI where, at first, the teacher made use of ICT whenever possible but later decided that, within the context of the particular learning objectives, the use of other tools such as pen and paper might have been just as suitable, for example, for the mind-mapping activities. In the MFL initiative students were encouraged to make use of paper dictionaries and other paper workbooks alongside the use of ICT, when it suited them.[17] In contrast, the primary music teachers provided constraints in relation to the students' use of digital and non-digital tools, specifying when students were to use the computers and when students were allowed to use acoustic instruments. Many teachers commented on the need to reflect upon the relationship between work with ICT and work with other tools; when first using digital technology it was something they had not fully considered, since their main concern was to ensure that they had thought through issues related to the use of just the digital tools themselves.

Time

Time is a constraint within schools but 'new' time issues arise when ICT is incorporated into teaching and learning. Within music, generally, the main concern for secondary teachers is the need for a consideration of the time required for students to develop music-specific ICT skills because of the complexity of software such as Cubase.[18] This was not such an issue within the MFL and geography SDIs discussed above, since the software was relatively straightforward to use or familiar to students. Although the geography teacher initially thought that the use of ICT would save students' time within data presentation activities, this was not the case. Within the primary music SDI, the teachers' concern that the students used time effectively led them to organise a very structured approach to the composition task: they prescribed the sections of music that were to be worked on each lesson and the point at which other instruments could be added to work with the computers.

Building time into lessons for play and experimentation with the ICT tools was not something initially considered by many teachers. However, our research suggests that, within all of the SDIs, even with simple tools, *some* freedom for students to experiment with the ICT tools, in the initial stages of use, is important. This process of experimentation is an important part of students beginning to appropriate the tool for themselves, and (as discussed in Chapter 3) an important part of the instrumentation process. As such, in all subjects it is important that teachers consider building time for such play and experimentation into their design initiatives.

In all the SDIs the teachers worked within the conventional constraints of 'one' lesson, which in most cases was just under an hour. This is the way in which time in schools has traditionally been divided up. However, we think that it is important to ask questions such as: would the geography enquiry have been better organised around one whole day of work, with mobile hand-held and digital cameras that students could take into the field? Would the challenges of synchronising music with film within Cubase be better managed through a more intensive whole day's work on music? We take this issue up again in Chapter 7, when we discuss the 'grammar' of schooling, and the main obstacles to the development of the potential of ICT in schools.

Choice of student activities

Within the work discussed in this chapter, teachers had to make decisions about the design of the activities which incorporated the use of both digital and non-digital tools. For example, the primary music teachers decided to be relatively prescriptive about how they presented their students with music composition, whereas, in the first iteration of the geography initiative, the teacher gave students a relatively open-ended set of activities and then, within the second iteration, considerably closed these down, choosing to be more prescriptive. In this latter case, the geography teacher provided the students with a template within which to write. The secondary music teacher also chose to create templates within the software and since this was the first opportunity for students to work with film, he decided to somewhat constrain the learners by creating a framework for all students. Interestingly, template use in the MFL SDI differs from its use in music. Within the MFL design initiative students were expected to learn to write in a foreign language (either with paper and pencil or with a word processor) without the use of the drop-down menu template, whereas within the music design initiative composing within the software environment was considered to be an end in itself. This relates to Salomon's idea of the 'effects of' and the 'effects with' technology, where the 'effects of' can be considered to be the residue left behind when a technology is no longer present (Salomon 1993). This idea is discussed more fully in Chapter 10.

Choice of student groupings

Within schools teachers can choose whether students work together as a whole class, or whether they work individually or in groups. Teachers may vary the way of working within one lesson or between lessons. When organising group work, teachers can prescribe the composition of the groups or leave this decision to students themselves. The design of the room and the furniture available also presents constraints on what is possible. For example, the geography teacher became aware that students were not likely to work in groups within a computer room where there were enough computers for each student to work individually unless, as a teacher, she arranged the furniture differently (something that can be difficult to do in a computer room).

When students work together at one computer teachers may also need to decide whether a particular student is taking more of a lead in various aspects of the activity. For example, the primary teachers decided that when students were working in pairs to compose music, the student using the mouse seemed to have more control over the composition process. For this reason they explicitly asked students to swap the role of using the mouse so that each student had the opportunity to be in a position of more control.

Within the MFL design initiative, the role of peers in supporting each other's learning was considered to be of great importance. The MFL teachers planned for pair work to encourage discussion, aware of research suggesting that students who enlist the help of others are more likely to check the endings of words, enjoy writing in the foreign language, check that what they have written makes sense and continuously check for mistakes.[19] Similarly, within the primary music SDI, although the teachers decided upon the pairings, they allowed students complete freedom to move around the computer suite, listening to and discussing other's work, such that, when speaking about the process of composing, the majority of students explained that they felt they had learned a lot from partners and their peers. In music classrooms, composing with computers within a networked space generally supports collaboration since students can easily access each others' work whenever they please, whereas when working without computers the ephemeral nature of music means that it can only be explored fully after it has been performed live.

Summary and conclusions

The case studies presented in this chapter have been used to illustrate particular freedoms and constraints that exist when using technology in the classroom. We have shown that within constraints related to the available technologies such as 'computers in a computer room', or 'a set of portable computers', there are always choices to be made, and these choices impact on learning. Our framework does not suggest that, for example, group work is better than whole-class work, or that digital tools are better than non-digital tools. Rather it asks the teacher to consider the range of possibilities available, since the technologies or the ways in which they are used within the classroom can act as 'liberating constraints', such that students are supported in their learning but are also given 'space' to extend their own ideas or practices or develop their work in personal ways.

Notes

1 This concern is also shared by Ofsted (2003).
2 See for example Adams (2000).
3 For further discussion, see Taylor *et al.* (2005, pp. 448–9).
4 Bransford *et al.* (2000, p. 213) in their chapter 'Technology to Support Learning' suggest that many technologies function as scaffolds.
5 See Facer *et al.* (2003, pp. 197–8).
6 'Sample' and 'texture' were introduced in lesson 1; 'timbre', 'introduction', 'drone', 'ostinato', 'repetition' and 'climax' in lesson 2; 'melody', 'hook', 'harmony' and 'ternary form' in lesson 3 and 'coda' in lesson 5.
7 See Gall and Breeze (2005) and Gall and Breeze (2007).
8 Dillon (2005) explains how this can make 'school' music more relevant and engaging.
9 The post of composer-in-residence was created prior to the work of the InterActive project to enable examination students studying composition to benefit from the support of a professional composer. The composer also supported the music staff in their development of classroom work.
10 See Airy and Parr (2001); Mills and Murray (2000); Folkestad *et al.* (1998); Durant (1990).
11 See Cain (2004).
12 Keith Sawyer *et al.* propose a delineation between 'creativity', everyday 'cleverness' as exhibited by children and 'Creativity', 'the creation of culture-transforming products' which they suggest is only possible by adults: see Sawyer *et al.* (2003, p. 24). See also The National Advisory Committee on Creative and Cultural Education (NACCCE) which posits the notion of three different categories of originality (1999, p. 29).
13 See Battersby (1995).
14 See Slater (1973) and Butt (2002, p. 124).
15 See Matthewman and Triggs (2004).
16 See Durbin (2003, pp. 64–9).
17 The development of writing in MFL lessons was just one aspect of the SDI. Four out of five lessons focused on other aspects, e.g. developing listening skills, reading strategies, spoken competencies such as pronunciation and intonation, etc. and those activities contained much pair and group work, self and peer assessment and were supported by the ICT work.
18 This is discussed more fully in Breeze (2008).
19 See Macaro (2001, p. 137).

Chapter 6

Discerning literacy

The focus of this chapter is on the meaning of literacy in the digital age. The author argues that the difficulties faced in terms of definition and use are not technological but social and cultural. Taking as a starting point the idea that technologies are not neutral, the chapter uses Green's three dimensions of literacy – the operational, the cultural and the critical – as a framework for analysis. The chapter examines the idea of multimodality and stresses the need for language to be viewed as the 'metamode' which provides access to the critical consideration of the cultural meanings of texts. In this sense the chapter is making a case for teachers to teach students discernment when they encounter a range of texts, images, sounds and information so they can reflect on meanings and be critical about the purposes and values of new media texts. The chapter thus aims to:

- highlight the need to blend operational, cultural and critical approaches in literacy teaching;
- challenge the idea that all literacies are of equal value and instead highlight the importance of language as the mode through which students can be taught to be critical and reflective;
- draw attention to a range of teaching approaches that will allow students to articulate the critical complexities of a variety of texts and images.

What does it mean to be literate?

What does it mean to be literate if almost any skill or practice can be termed a literacy?[1] Do we need a pick-and-mix approach to literacy teaching to reflect the diverse range of cultural forms and practices of the 'digital age'? In this chapter I examine the arguments

* This chapter was authored by Sasha Matthewman.

for shifting the definition of literacy away from the dominance of traditional reading and writing skills. My experience as a teacher of English, teacher educator and researcher over the last sixteen years makes me wary of an expanding English curriculum and multiplying demands on teachers and students. The approach to literacy in school should not involve piling on more objectives but could involve a qualitative shift, a discerning[2] approach that is able to account for important questions of cultural value.

In order to further consider the question of cultural value in relation to school English I would like to revisit a founding text for English teaching. First published in 1957, Richard Hoggart's *The Uses of Literacy* describes in moving and intimate detail the experience of working-class life with all its anecdotes, memories and gleanings of sayings, comments and aphorisms. In relation to this deeply felt, partly autobiographical cultural study, Hoggart explores the variety of literate practices and purposes of this social group. What is conveyed most powerfully from this account is that literacy is not just about functional skills; it is rooted in cultural experience and social relations. A rich cultural life enjoyed by a social group is reflected through innovative, personal and social literate expression.

However, Hoggart suggests in the second half of the book that not all forms of literacy are life enhancing. He shows how literate practices can also be limiting and intellectually narrow and enervating. He details how the rise of mass entertainment aimed at the working class can be anti-intellectual, inward looking and uncritical of received opinions. Literacy in this characterisation is not simply about the forms and mediums of representation but is a means for the sharing and expression of cultural and social values for good or ill. It is about how we express who we are and what we believe. Andrew Stables (2003) writes about the tensions between two views of literacy: the necessary functional ability to decode and encode sign systems (the forms of literacy) and the way that to be literate is to be valued in a world that values the literary (a form of artistic expression). What is valued in a society is not a constant and what is valued in terms of literacy is dependent on the particular social context involved. Thinking about literacy entails thinking about the cultural forms of literacy, both popular and elite.

Bill Green (1988, 2004), an Australian educator, has developed a view of literacy which takes account of this cultural dimension. His model identifies three dimensions of literacy: the operational, the cultural and the critical, and he argues that these dimensions should be interlinked in pedagogical practice. The operational dimension focuses on competence in the technical production of a variety of forms of writing in a range of contexts. The cultural dimension refers to competence in relation to real situations with the focus on knowing how to apply and to select from the different options and practices available to communicate effectively in any given situation.

However, reaching the critical dimension involves knowing how these literacy practices are themselves selective, ideological and constrained. So in some senses the 'correct' way to write a newspaper report is already defined by established conventions, and to ignore these in the pursuit of an original style may mean a rejected article. One of the dangers of teaching a rigid definition of literacy forms is that it can ignore the real world examples where writers have successfully flouted conventions for rhetorical or political effect. (Think about the challenge to the conventions of the novel posed by Virginia Woolf and James Joyce.) So in integrating this critical dimension of literacy, educators recognise that students should not just be inducted into a literate culture but should be empowered to critique, adapt and change the literacy practices that they encounter.[3]

Hoggart's analysis of working-class literacy in the 1950s argues passionately that the transformative and individual power of literacy was submerged in the passive consumption of poor quality mass entertainment. He makes an argument for the discernment of value in cultural forms and practices. Green's three-dimensional model suggests that this is still a crucial argument, raising important questions for literacy in the twenty-first century. What do we think of as valuable cultural texts worth sharing as part of a common heritage? How can we move discussion of literacy pedagogy in schools beyond a narrow focus on the operational dimension of literacy which can be as limiting on screen as on paper? How can students have the confidence to experiment with changing the literacy forms and practices that they are given?

One response to the perception of changing social and working lives in the twenty-first century comes from an influential body of academics and researchers who argue that communication and representation is turning multimodal and that literacy pedagogy should adapt to take account of the new communication resources offered by digital technologies.[4] The 'multimodal' refers to communication through different modes such as visual representation, sound, movement, gesture and language. (This multimodal turn is illustrated in the increasingly visual qualities of printed texts – such as school text books – and the growing sophistication of multimodal design features in web-based texts.) In these cases writing as verbal expression cannot be separated out from the visual or other modes without losing meaning. Meaning is made through complex interactions between the different modes.

At the same time as this shift in the representational nature of how texts work there is also a social shift in the way that texts are produced, circulated and consumed. In the digital age stable communities in defined geographical areas (such as the community set in the North East of England that Hoggart describes) are replaced by networks of interest and purpose which can be linked by rapid communication systems. Such networks require a more flexible, diverse and evolving range of literate practices to make communication possible. Users of the Internet can develop rapid networking with others who share their concerns; they have instant access to information in a range of forms; and can easily publish their ideas, images and video on the web.

This explosion of publication has implications for users of the web, who need to know how to negotiate a vast array of information and to use reading strategies and ICT tools to filter out that which is irrelevant. Publication on the web will make your work accessible to others but the major challenge is to gain the attention of a readership in a complex and competitive context. Knobel and Lankshear (2003) have described this as the 'attention economy'. How can we get your attention as producers in a web of information? And, as readers, what is worthy of our attention? One solution is for users to form networks of interest which can filter and sort the information. Consider the example of Wikipedia – an online encyclopaedia to which anyone can contribute but which is moderated by a majority ethos of responsibility, or MySpace where friends can share their tastes in music and be linked to others with similar enthusiasms.

Such major shifts in the conditions of literacy certainly seem to require a change in the literacy teaching of young people. The calls for a movement in literacy towards a conception of literacy as multimodal is in effect the movement from the paradigm of the essay towards the paradigm of the webpage.[5] The problem is that there is limited evidence of what this would mean in terms of classroom practice. Some theorists of multimodality may give the impression that all modes are equally important and equally difficult to manage. Literacies are in danger of being lumped together as if they all mattered equally and all had equal status in the world. In this chapter I want to stress that language is the mode in which we can be critical and reflect on meaning-making practices and in this respect it is the most subtle and sophisticated of the different modes. It is the overarching 'metamode' which allows critical access to the cultural meanings of texts. It is the only mode where the potential for transformation of literacy practices can be rooted. The view developed in this chapter is that use of language should remain the central mode and focus of literacy teaching. This is developed in relation to what happens when literacy is taught in classrooms within an awareness of the multimodal resources of technology. The aim is not simply to see how English could incorporate multimodal technology but to consider what might be at stake in a turn to multimodal literacy pedagogy.

Research context

The focus in the InterActive team for English was for teachers, teacher educators and researchers to work together using readily available technology such as word processing, presentation and web design software and CD-ROMs for English such as Storymaker and WordRoot. According to availability, some work took place in computer suites and some in the classroom with laptops. Most schools had Internet access and some had projectors or interactive whiteboards. The work took place within the curriculum and the constraints of current assessment practices and was designed to find ways of using ICT to enhance learning in English. Some explanation of the dominant model of English in schools during this period will indicate the parameters for the work in classrooms. The literacy strategy in primary and secondary education in the UK has focused on traditional literacy skills of reading and writing. This emphasis has meant that literacy teaching has become focused on the operational dimension of literacy. The concept of new literacies or multiliteracies[6] has had little impact on literacy policy and pedagogy in the UK. Literary texts can be reduced to vehicles for teaching literacy skills in relation to sharply defined objectives or specific coursework or examination tasks. Writing is generally controlled and delimited within elaborate writing frames and strict rules of genre. The pressure of high stakes assessment is felt by teachers who are held strictly accountable for their results. The pressure to measure performance results in narrowly assessed tests against very inflexible mark schemes which do not allow markers (who may be inexperienced or non-subject specialists) to credit an unexpected but valuable response.

The result is a pedagogy which seeks to tightly control students' literacy responses so that they have the best chance of fitting the given assessment criteria. This is clearly a problem for researching digital literacy in real school contexts rather than in individual or out-of-school situations. However, in calling for a change in literacy pedagogy it is necessary to be able to envisage how new ideas might be received in current contexts. In the cases reported here the use of ICT encouraged students and teachers to push the boundaries of conventional literacy genres and responses.

A wide range of designs was developed within the English design team, including work on non-fiction, literary study, creative meaning making, media and literacy skills – a range which reflects the breadth of the English curriculum.[7] This chapter focuses on case studies from five design sequences of English work in one primary and two secondary schools in order to reflect on key challenges in taking on the implications of digital literacy.

Multimodal practice: gains and losses

In an interesting discussion of literacy and diversity, Andrew Stables (2003) draws a distinction between literacy which is understood as language, and literacy that is understood as semiotics (the making of meaning through a variety of signs). In the linguistic tradition drawing on the work of the French linguist Saussure (1974) 'language has remained something that happens in words, and literacy is about reading and writing' (p. 69). By contrast, developments of Saussure's thinking about sign systems has led to a focus on semiotics beyond words and an understanding of all signifying systems and practices as a type of 'language'.[8] With this definition, other ways of making meaning beyond language have also gained the status of 'literacies', so we have media literacy, computer literacy and, of course, multimodal literacy. The use of new technology and engagement with new media texts seems to make a material case for the semiotic theory of literacy.[9] When students use technology for writing they tend to draw on the literacy practices with which they are familiar and many of these practices are screen based. Screen-based technologies offer a greater range of resources than that offered by pen and paper. It seems almost unavoidable that students will want to make use of the semiotic resources available, particularly as their models for writing on screen will be colourful, flashing and integrated with sound and image. In current assessment criteria in England the multimodal elements of student productions cannot be formally valued, which may seem unfair and outdated. How far should multimodal literacy be acknowledged within assessment for English?

One of the English case studies which illustrates how a multimodal approach can be used to promote critical thinking and writing involved Year 9 (aged 12–13) students in producing a multimedia presentation about their school for parents and prospective first-year secondary Year 6 students (aged 9–10). Two of the students in the class had very low levels of basic literacy. They were, however, able to produce an effective multimodal presentation designed to appeal to both audiences of parents and young people. Their presentation was framed by a sequence in which a rocket flies from outer space, to Bristol and then to the school.

This sequence of slides was a clever visual pun on the opening caption 'English at John Cabot is out of this world' and the impact

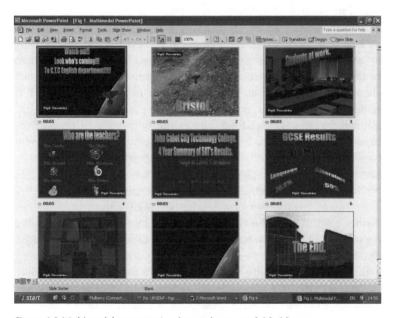

Figure 6.1 Multimodal presentation by students aged 12–13 years

and humour were supported by a rocket launch with sound effects. At the end of the presentation the animated rocket was shown flying off – an appropriate completion.

Students clearly felt motivated by being able to use their design and computer skills to show their understanding of concepts of audience and purpose in a multimodal form. Arguably the most important part of the sequence of work for these students was the 'critical framing', where in both speech and writing they were asked to articulate and evaluate their multimodal production because these were the skills that they needed to develop. Significantly, the official criteria for assessment does not allow credit for the multimodal work. Working with multimedia certainly seemed to enable traditional literacy as it created a sense of mastery and success which students were proud to reflect upon in writing. They each produced a more committed, developed and structured written response than the pieces of work that were collected prior to the project. If the multimodal production had been taken as an end in itself then the written reflection would not have been completed, thus missing out the critical stage of the learning. However, a focus on language as the most important development need for these students does not discount the case for valuing their multimodal products in formal assessment criteria.[10]

This dual need to value multimodal achievement while focusing on the development of language is illustrated in an example drawn from a primary school classroom where students wrote an additional chapter for the classic children's book *Alice in Wonderland* direct to screen. In terms of the process, the teacher had scheduled presentational features to be added only in the final stage of production. However, from the outset, two of the students we observed were working with colour and font and drew on their knowledge of comics and computer game graphics which they both reported enjoying. They produced a highly graphic interpretation of this task.

From the perspective of a teacher of English their text requires further elaboration. The rather abrupt ending of the narrative relies on violent and sensationalist statements: 'destruction' and 'hanged drawn and quartered' to infer a resolution. The statements have a high visual and emotive impact but could be set within a more expanded story or a clearer visual representation. Is 'destruction' a comment from the authors on the plate smashing or does it describe the thought of Alice? Is the sequence of red alerts meant to signify

Destruction

The plate had smashed! Alert! Alert! Alert!
Staff, Goblins, Mr. and Mrs. Bunnybee came fluttering to the rescue.
"How dare you try to escape" Mrs. Bunnybee sneered" This can only mean one thing

Mrs. Bunnybee screamed. That was the story of Alice.

The End

Figure 6.2 Extract from a multimodal response to *Alice in Wonderland*

the sounding of an alarm or an internal reaction from a character? It is as if the pictures are in the students' heads but the uneasy mix of comic book and written story has not quite worked here – and the students themselves acknowledged their frustration with the graphic limitations of Word: 'We could not do what we wanted – the pictures weren't there in Clip Art'.

The issue of how the teacher might best respond is important to consider in relation to students wanting to write 'something a bit different'. Perhaps the students needed support in realising their vision, which differs significantly from the teacher's idea of the task? In order to make their writing meaningful to them they need to write from their cultural experience and their developing literacy practices in relation to the resources they have been given. A critical dialogue is needed with the teacher about how visual design connects with language in their text in the realisation of meaning.[11] Perhaps this would have supported their development of writing and allowed them to make their text more cohesive and developed. However, in this case the teacher viewed their attempts as a distraction from her task of training them for the end of year high stakes written assessment: a reaction which shows the pressure of assessment on classroom practice.[12]

Litter Is A Crime
Make The People Do The Time

♣ Litter seems to attract rats and other animals.
♣ If people cleaned their litter we could reverse this over time.
♣ People don't pick it up because it's not theirs or they think it's dirty to pick up trash from the floor.
♣ So the school's becomes unhealthy and disgusting

People feel that it's the schools job to put it up, but teachers ask pupils to pick litter up if they see it while walking. Although students find it disgusting to put up the garbage, Although they're one of the many people who drop it every day. Which visitors dirty rats and other small creatures, which carries diseases making the school an unsafe place for pupils. Like litter in ponds or rivers around the school becomes polluted.

Teachers and staff have tried many ways to stop litter growing it schools. One of their ideas was no food outside, but it wasn't that smart, pupils hide the food or drink in their pockets and drink or eat it outside.

Figure 6.3 Magazine layout of 'first draft' writing

The next example illustrates how an approach that values the visual might work in practice. This is drawn from a project to create a school magazine in a secondary school classroom. The teacher was successful in working on the language from within the multimodal text that the student had produced. The piece of work was already laid out in the form of a magazine article with an attractive title font, an image downloaded from the Internet and careful layout of the text on the page. Visually this text appeared finished, yet the language of the text was confused and illogical.

The teacher in this case intervened to help the student edit the language from this point in the writing process and from within the 'finished' text. For this student it was language rather than the visual signifiers of the 'magazine article' that needed attention. However, the visual design helped to start the student off in the process of producing a meaningful text.

In many cases we found that the multimodal aspects of text could provide a supportive framework for beginning to write. Using an appropriate font, considering an appropriate image and designing the layout were all ways for students to access voice and genre. Many researchers have noted the way that word processing can change the writing process, making it more fluid.[13] This means that the writing process does not necessarily follow the linear route of 'plan, draft, edit, revise, proofread and present' as laid down in the document for the literacy strategy at secondary level in England.[14] In the case studies reported in this chapter we noticed a repeated pattern that students would strive to begin with presentational features rather than leaving this to the final 'present' stage even when instructed not to do so, as in the *Alice in Wonderland* case study. As this practice is in opposition to the way that teachers and learners are asked to consider the writing process, this sets up a challenge for the teacher to be discerning about when to intervene in the process and to how to decide on the focus for development. The gains in working multimodally were that students had the opportunity to break out of set conventions, which might be the first stage of critical literacy. The danger is that multimodal work can mask problems in coherence and linguistic expression and can reduce the attention given to this by students and teachers. In this case should language remain the focus for development in English?

Writing with language/working with images

Arguably, to produce a piece of written language involves a more complex cognitive process than the manipulation of the presentational features of image and font. It might help to use the distinction made by Gunther Kress between the 'resource' of writing and the use of the resource(s) in a particular communication of meaning, which would be termed literacy. The problem is that when working on the computer the 'resource' of writing and the literacy processes of presenting meaning for particular purposes are often entangled. This makes the teaching (and learning) of writing more complex than that of design and layout. In this section I analyse two case studies of students working with technology to reflect on the different literacy processes involved when working linguistically and when working multimodally: 'Writing Alice' and 'PowerPoint Poetry'.

CASE STUDY 1
Writing *Alice*

Anna and Beth (aged nine), wrote a chapter for *Alice in Wonderland*, working collaboratively on their story and writing direct to screen. Unlike the two boys (discussed above) who produced a graphic text, the multimodal elements were limited to the choice of an old-fashioned font and to final decoration with Clip Art. In the twenty-minute sequence of work captured on video the students were working linguistically. The tool of the word-processing software was, for the most part, unobtrusive in their talk. They were focused on the imaginative world that they were creating through language – both written and spoken.

Both	I ran into . . . I ran into . . . I ran into a . . .
Beth	I ran into the spiral room.
Anna	I ran into a round room with black and white . . . with black and white checked. No, with a black and white floor, with squared black . . .
Beth	No, with squares . . . with a floor that looked like a chess board.
Anna	Yes. OK.
Both	I ran into a round . . .
Beth	*(starts typing)* I ran into a round . . .
Anna	A round room, you want.
Beth	Oh, sorry.
Both	With a floor that looked like a chess board.
Anna	*(Turns from screen)* Is that how you spell 'board'?
Beth	Yes . . . *(types)* a chess board.

They developed a simile of a chessboard for a black and white floor through shared contributions. They also read aloud, voicing the text dramatically, at times reading in unison and in character.

Anna	Then we could have her, then we could have this thing. Then suddenly Alice starts talking. Alice says, Mr Rabbit, Mr Rabbit.

Beth   (*very quietly*) on top of a . . . (*louder and acting*) Mr Rabbit,
          Mr Rabbit . . . um . . . Where am I? No, Mr Rabbit, Mr
          Rabbit, please wait.

They corrected technical errors as they went along, but they were
also able to think about the narrative as a whole, realising that
they needed to revise the structure to clarify the sequence of events
in their story.

Anna   (*Traces finger over the text on screen – reads*) I suddenly
          noticed a glass . . .
Beth   OOH! (*Moves cursor to insert 'table'*) Glass table.
Anna   (*Waits until 'table' is inserted – then reads text through
          aloud from 'in the centre' to 'on top'*)
Beth   Comma (*inserts after 'top'*).
Anna   Then . . .
Beth   (*Starts to type 'Mr Rabbit Mr Rabbit' – stops*) But he's going
          through the door to get to the garden, isn't he?
Anna   Yeah (*turns to Beth*). But before that, remember? Before
          that . . .
Beth   Yeah, and then . . . Oh yeah – he takes the key – opens
          all the doors . . .
Anna   Yeah but remember then Alice comes in . . .
Beth   And drinks the potion.
Anna   No, then Alice comes in and asks (*inaudible*) and the
          rabbit says 'Oh sorry no' (*inaudible*) and then opens all
          the doors.
Beth   I think he picks the key up. (*Pause. Anna nods*) We
          haven't said he picks it up.

The word-processor tool facilitated their shared thinking and
written collaboration without being the focus of the activity. Talk,
creation of story, revision of narrative and performance and editing
were integrated. They did not talk about how to operate the
software although they later used 'help' to find the thesaurus
function.

CASE STUDY 2
PowerPoint poetry

Susan and Carlie (aged fifteen) used PowerPoint to produce a multimodal representation of the poem *Havisham* by Carol Ann Duffy. The students had started working on the opening of the poem:

> Beloved sweetheart bastard. Not a day since then
> I haven't wished him dead.

The students scrolled through the animation options in PowerPoint to animate the phrase 'beloved sweetheart' on a red screen background.

Susan   No, we just want it to go 'bumpff' away *(gestures to reinforce her idea).*
          Preview for the animation of 'beloved sweetheart' is played.
Susan   That's 'disappear' *(an animation option)* Just like that . . . it just goes . . .
Carlie Yes.
Susan   Yes.
Carlie Right, so . . .
          They check the effect on full-screen slide show.
Susan   We'll move it up a bit. Move it up a bit. *(Susan points to the words on the screen)* Up, we want it up.
Carlie . . . then underneath 'bastard' *(seems to be indicating that this would be part of the same slide).*

Figure 6.4 This sequence represents three animations within one slide. 'Beloved sweetheart' appears and is then obscured by 'Bastard'. 'Beloved sweetheart' then disappears, leaving 'Bastard' in place.

> Susan   We're going to have 'bastard' dead centre aren't we?
>   Really big and black (gestures across the black screen).
> Carlie   Yeah, but the trouble with that is that if it just disappears
>   then (inaudible) that means we'll have eleven slides –
>   (querying the need for a new separate slide for this – they
>   have planned for 10). I don't like swearing (an aside).
> Susan   Yeah, but it won't really be eleven slides will it? Because
>   it's all part of the same oxymoron[15] so we'll leave it so
>   it changes right from the next slide. We want 'Bastard!'
>   ('acting out' the text and gesturing across the screen).

Carlie scrolls WordArt and Susan points to a selection. Carlie types 'basterd'.

> Susan   No, 'a, r'.
> Carlie   What? (laughs)
> Susan   Bastard (spells it out).
> Carlie   Bastard.
> Susan   We want it as big as we can get it (gestures). (Carlie is
>   scrolling through different fonts.) Gothic! (decisively)
> Carlie   Gothic. That's it.

The talk was focused on the visual, spatial and practical elements of crafting the PowerPoint presentation, which required fine adjustments to the positioning of text ('We'll move it up a bit. Move it up a bit. Up, we want it up.'). Talk was inexplicit but seemed based on a shared understanding of the poem's meaning, as when both students seemed to decide that 'gothic' was the appropriate font for the word 'bastard', as voiced by the character of Miss Havisham. She would certainly qualify as embodying elements of the gothic, but neither student felt the need to explain or justify this in relation to this particular word within the poem. It is unclear whether Carlie uttered 'that's it' as a reaction to locating the gothic font or as an expression of agreement with the appropriateness of the choice suggested by Susan. Susan seemed to be driving the conceptual aspects of the design while Carlie did the mechanics as directed. Susan showed a confident grasp of the term 'oxymoron' in directing that both words should

continued

be part of the same slide, presumably to show that the feelings of love and hatred are held almost simultaneously, because 'they are both part of the same oxymoron'. The technology appeared to be much more visible in both a literal and metaphorical sense than in the 'Writing Alice' vignette; it announced itself with appearing and disappearing fonts, bright colours and a range of sound effects. The mediation was between the students' response to the poem and the features available within the PowerPoint software. The talk and activity was shared between the manipulation of the ICT tool and the visual representation of the poem, which had become a visual performance, a new artefact and an implicit act of interpretation. 'Gothic' was a one-word answer to the complex play of modern and historical intertextual reference in the poem. Only in language would it be possible to articulate and capture its complexities and alternative interpretations. In this case the value of the activity was as a prelude to the main challenge of a linguistic essay response. If this critical and reflective linguistic element of the process had been omitted then the activity would have lost much of its value for English.

So what reflections on literacy can be drawn from these two case studies? What is the importance of language expressed as speech and writing to a concept of literacy? Both speech and writing have different features and functions related to social purpose. Writing has a tendency towards more permanent realisation (the recording of speech takes place for special purposes) and a greater potential to be revised and shaped so as to develop an argument which can be read and worked on by others. In contrast, speech tends to be revised in the process of conversation and more tightly linked to context, audience and shared reference points. It is certainly true that new forms of communication such as e-mail and text messaging blur the boundaries between the two expressions of language but both remain central to thinking in Western culture.[16] This may not be the case for all cultures and for all times. For instance, the socio-cultural psychologist James Wertsch (1991) cites the example of Aboriginal children outperforming Western children on visual tests. This is part of a critique of Vygotsky, the foundational theorist in socio-cultural psychology, for his ethnocentric assumption that speech is central to thinking. The evidence of Luria suggests that preliterate cultures do not think in abstract categories – so a plate is always a plate rather than a circle.[17]

The argument of educational thinkers led by Kress (1996, 2003, 2007) is that in Western culture we are moving inexorably towards a visual culture, where language and, in particular, writing, will become less central. This is certainly a recognisable trend on the web and in textbooks, but writing is taught, not caught like speech, and we have a choice about how it is valued in the curriculum. Until we have more conclusive evidence that multi-modal design is a better tool for thinking critically and reflecting on abstract concepts, we need to be cautious about recommending less privileged attention to writing. This is particularly the case in that writing is likely to remain the elite mode of communication, as Kress himself points out. Whose children will be encouraged to access the elite expression of writing and the culturally valued but challenging texts? It seems ironic that all the academics who stress so strongly the turn to the visual and argue for teaching multimodal literacy need to do so in densely argued writing, sometimes supported, but not overwhelmed by images.

Green (2001) suggests that we think of writing in the digital age as compos(IT)ion rather than composition. This is a playful attempt to interrupt the way that we think about writing, in that the information technology (IT) becomes central to the process. The metaphor also emphasises the way that written language operates visually as the distinction is only apparent in writing. This seems to fit with the PowerPoint vignette where the ICT resources become central to the work of making meaning. However, it is interesting to observe the amount of routine work involved in actually creating a multimedia presentation. The process involves manual and technical skills in making careful adjustments to sizing, positioning and colour. Often this is slow because of the practical dexterity required to locate, move and create the precise figure desired.

Also, our video data records extended periods of 10–20 minutes where students simply scroll through Google images or Clip Art to find a suitable image. While these may be useful manual and technical skills to acquire they do not seem to require higher order thinking (although students may be conceptualising while composITing in this way, there is not the same pressure to forge their own meaning as there is when writing). For instance, a useful analogy for the process from the non-digital age might be the making of a class display or poster which would involve collating materials, images and writing and arranging them for visual display – this would incorporate cutting with scissors and pasting with glue. It is therefore important to consider the time spent in this type of 'poster making' activity on screen when designing the learning activity.

There is a contrast between this 'compos(IT)ion' process and the fine editing of meaning and form in writing that is required to make a piece publishable. Deciding on how to restructure a sentence or whether to use a different word to get a slightly different shade of meaning involves reflection on the symbolic system of language. Manoeuvring a piece of text to a particular position on the page or selecting an image from scrolling seems to be a more instinctive process (children learn to draw before they are taught to write). Working with design resources is part of literacy using ICT but this may best be seen as playing a supportive role to a focus on language within the English classroom.

Multimodality, the web and literary value

The question of literary value is an important one for English. Both of the previous cases show how digital technology can work within a respect for literary value, as long as language remains the central mode. However, there are dangers in promoting certain uses of technology that privilege the technology at the expense of the literary artefact – this was a consideration in the PowerPoint poetry case study. Carey Jewitt's analysis of a CD-ROM of the novel *Of Mice and Men* offers a more worrying case (Jewitt, 2006). Teachers often use supplementary texts to mediate a novel, most commonly a film version of the text and the differences between the text and the film are commonly highlighted and analysed. The difference between the use of a CD-ROM and 'a film of the book' is that a film version is an artistic text in its own right with its own internal integrity and value, whereas in this example the CD-ROM seems to function as a textbook remediating the text for functional and educational rather than artistic purposes.[18]

The danger is that it may be unclear in the classroom that the CD-ROM is an interpretation of the text – a pedagogical tool – rather than simply the book 'translated' to screen. In the CD-ROM, the novel's problematic representation of 'race' is sanitised. The black character Crooks is presented as well dressed and able bodied and is not referred to as 'nigger', a word that is used repeatedly in the novel. As Jewitt (2006) comments: 'The multimodal transformation of the characters via the resources of the CD-ROM [also] repositioned the novel to account for the imagined concerns of a contemporary audience in an educational context.' (p. 73)

This is a very neutral reaction to censorship and distortion of the novel. The issue of race is crucial to the context of the novel in 1930s America where prejudice was routine. Steinbeck's presentation of Crooks is deliberately unsettling but it is not simplistic – Crooks is well read, clever and vicious. His vindictive treatment of Lennie is both less credible and more reprehensible if Crooks is presented as less victimised and outcast. If such resources are to be used in schools then in terms of literary integrity it is essential that students and teachers are able to critically deconstruct and contest the multimodal representation of the written text. It is not simply a matter of whether or not they are effective in engaging students' interest by introducing 'new resources and practices for navigating, constructing and understanding the entity character' (ibid., p. 74).

Jewitt does not discuss the wider context for the use of the CD-ROM or report whether or not the multimodal representation was deconstructed in this case; the use of the CD-ROM is presented as a point of access to the text (if not a substitute). In many ways this example highlights the need for students and teachers to understand the challenge posed by multimodal representation, particularly as use of a CD-ROM is often an individual or paired activity which takes place without the mediation of the teacher. The critical work needed to deconstruct this multimodal text can only be articulated through written and spoken language. Choosing a poor film version of a text would be counterproductive to teaching a novel; similarly we should also consider the literary value of the CD-ROM as a secondary artefact. Perhaps students would be better off just reading the novel (and watching an excellent film version) if the effect of the CD-ROM representation is to confuse the distinction between the primary and secondary text, substituting a multimodal version for the original.

Another area of concern raised in the PowerPoint poetry case study might be the focus on technological skills rather than literary or linguistic concepts. This is particularly problematic in relation to students making web pages. Year 13 students (aged 17–18) were using the process to research and learn about literature in World War I in one of the English subject designs. In each case students took up different roles in relation to the task. In most cases in the group there was a technical expert, or designer, while others took on the roles of creating the script, searching for images or typing out notes. While this mirrors the production process in real world contexts there are clearly very difficult pedagogical problems to solve here. Some students were involved in the elite literacy practices of reading and writing and others were taking on secretarial and technical roles. Creating a website involves a great deal of very routine and low-level tasks and the students most in need of developing their skills of writing tended towards those tasks in the group situation.

> I found a lot of it was just copying and pasting from the Internet or typing out what you've already got. You don't really read it.
>
> (Emily, interview transcript)

Ironically, in one case this meant typing out the introduction to a play found in a book. A danger raised in Tuman (1992) is the 'cannibalisation' of print where originality is lost in favour of cut and paste. This is the danger in a pedagogy which decentres the idea of self, authorship and creativity in favour of the values of speed, efficiency and information. In interview it was significant that these A-level literature students placed a high value on reading books, seeing the web as a more functional and superficial reading space. Writing about the resilience of old media in the face of new media competition, Freedman analyses US and UK data that suggests the web is used primarily for pragmatic rather than aesthetic or creative practices.[19] The web is not the place to read for pleasure; it is a place to browse and collect information. Far from feeling empowered by reading on the web these students reported a sense of being driven by the pace and scale. Themes raised in interviews with all nine students included: the time taken in searching, dislike of sustained reading on screen and the feeling of a need to scan quickly and move on, printing off relevant sections.

> The fact that there's so many websites you feel the need to sort of look at everything quickly and then like go on to the next one, as opposed to taking a long time just looking at one poem.
>
> (Jane, interview transcript)

These are good skills for research and retrieval and the web can be valuable for collating and presenting a range of views and for organising collective endeavour. Writing a hypertext can also mean leaving the information open to a variety of uses and users rather than marshalling it into a considered argument. In the information age, with the challenge of multiple sources of information, it may be that the skill of interpreting and shaping information in argument becomes more crucial than ever. Certainly, this case study suggests that students still value the materiality of the book, reading for pleasure and the personal and human qualities of English as a subject. This was a surprise in students who were clearly very technologically competent and had been educated in an avowedly pro-technology milieu. Their values were formed in opposition to the values of their City Technology College, which had largely replaced the library with ICT access.

Students as discerners of literacy

We need to think carefully about English as a place that develops the aesthetic and that continues to value cultural artefacts. Green cautions against losing the sense of the literary and places the notion of the imagination as central.[20] As a way forward he makes the case for a broader conception of English as cultural studies. While endorsing the need to rework English in terms of the semiotic shift in communication towards the visual and multimodal he raises the question of the value of a specifically *literary* literacy.

> We run the risk of giving up too much when we shy away from notions of 'imagination' and 'creativity', from an explicit, considered, playfully serious engagement with metaphor and semantic innovation – with the poetic as a distinctive form of knowledge.
> (Green 2004, p. 301)

If we want to prepare young people to engage critically with the myriad and evolving texts and practices of literacy which combine text, sound, image and movement then we need to teach them to be discerning. We need to develop a strong sense of what is and what is not culturally valuable in any future design for literacy pedagogy. Students should be taught how to select texts for their literary merit or rhetorical power and be prepared to give them sustained attention. For literacy to develop it needs to be connected to the cultural and the critical dimensions and these would include situating work on reading and writing in twenty-first-century forms and practices and reflecting on their meanings, potential, limitations and restrictions. Reading and writing with technology involves changes both to the process of reading and writing and the genres of what is produced or read. This has implications for pedagogy and curriculum planning and would indeed seem to indicate a wider range of literacy practices than in the age of print. More than ever students need to be able to articulate arguments in relation to different viewpoints and to produce meaning in a range of forms and contexts. As this chapter has argued, working within multimodal practices should not be incompatible with retaining the focus on language, both spoken and written.

Summary and conclusions

In this chapter the three-part model of literacy – the operational, the cultural and the critical – was used as a holistic way of thinking about literacy. This model encourages teachers to see literacy learning and teaching as centred around cultural values which are shifting in relation to digital technologies. The claims for a multimodal approach to literacy were examined and it was suggested that different modes require different forms of cognition and practice. The key argument in this chapter was that language should remain the keystone of literate practice, the main or 'metamode' of engagement for young people when they create or analyse texts within English lessons. A range of exemplars were analysed, highlighting strategies for teaching and learning which involve multimodal texts. This demonstrated the need for students to be taught discernment when confronted by a range of textual, visual, aural and oral information through ICT.

Notes

1 The concept of 'multiliteracies' (New London Group 1996, Cope and Kalantzis 2000) is widely embraced and diverse practices and skills are named as 'literacies' within a range of educational settings.
2 Here it might be helpful to think of Paul Smith's use of the term 'cerning' (1988) to mean the 'lumping together' of disparate ideas as the opposite of 'discerning' which means to make fine distinctions.
3 See Lankshear and Knobel (2003) p. 11 for a discussion of the development of new literacies.
4 A range of texts which explore the relationship between digital communication and literacy have recently been published; see for instance

New London Group (1996), Kress (2003), Gee (2003), Lankshear and Knobel (2003), Marsh (2005), Jewitt (2006).

5 For further discussion of this see Tuman (1992).

6 For further discussion of this see New London Group (1996), Cope and Kalantzis (2000).

7 For further discussion of work of the English SDT see Matthewman and Triggs (2004) and Matthewman et al. (2004).

8 The key text in translation is Saussure, F. (1974); Course in general linguistics with an introduction by Jonathan Culler; edited by Charles Bally and Albert Sechehaye, translated from the French by Wade Baskin. Revised edition Glasgow: Fontana/Collins.

9 Similarly, Landow (1994) in *hyper-text-theory* discusses the links between literary theory and technological change.

10 For a full account of the literacy issues in this design sequence see Matthewman et al. (2004).

11 See Kress and Van Leeuwen (1996).

12 Standard Assessment Tests (SATs) are taken by students in England at the end of Key Stages 1, 2 and 3.

13 See Balestri (1988), Kaplan and Moulthrop (1990), Snyder (1994).

14 See DfEE (2001) p. 24.

15 Oxymoron: a self-conscious juxtaposition of contradictory expressions, e.g. loving hate.

16 See Halliday (1989).

17 Ong (1982) in Reid (1993).

18 This term is used by Bolter and Grusin (2000) to describe the ways in which a text (or text form) may reappear in a different medium. They show that non-electronic texts have been remediated in the past (novels to films; paintings to poems) and suggest that new media 'refashion older media' in a variety of ways. This theory acknowledges continuities but also raises important questions about the nature and quality of the transformations.

19 Freedman (2005).

20 Green (2004).

Chapter 7*

'Aliens in the classroom 2'

When technology meets classroom life

Using a specific classroom case as a starting point, this chapter explores a number of problematic issues surrounding the deployment of new technologies in conventional classrooms. Using the idea of 'classroom aliens' (in this sense both the students with their technological familiarity, and the technology with its challenge to the customs, culture and norms of subject-based pedagogy) we ask some fundamental questions about how these new capabilities challenge and change the culture and structure (or logic) of contemporary classroom life. These questions are addressed through an exploration of three key concepts: firstly the 'capabilities' of new technologies and, secondly, the 'tipping points' which are reached when these capabilities alter the pace and pattern of interaction, organisation and spatial dynamics of knowledge creation in classrooms. Finally, the idea of 'assemblages' is introduced as a useful metaphor for thinking about the fluid, interconnected nature of classroom life in schools. Capabilities are examined through the possibilities of ICTs, while the tipping points focus on the epistemological diversity that accrues in classrooms and the ways in which new technologies can shift the balance of authority in terms of pedagogy and learning. The final section suggests that new metaphors are needed to open up the 'black boxes' of classrooms and ICTs, making them more readable for teachers as dynamic social formations.

The chapter aims to:

*   highlight the challenges teachers face when new technologies – both embodied in students and emboldened in tools – enter the usual discourses of subject-based classrooms;
*   evaluate the sorts of disruption to conventions that can occur through the use of the creative potential and capabilities of ICT;

* This chapter was authored by Susan Robertson and Roger Dale.

- emphasise the sorts of pedagogical 'tipping points' that can occur when new and sometimes fundamentally different forms of knowledge enter classroom situations.

VIGNETTE
Alien 2

Meet Andy.[1] Andy is a history teacher at an inner-city secondary school with several years of teaching experience behind him. Today he is repeating a lesson to 9C he taught earlier on in the week to 9D. The topic is 'America in the 1920s and 1930s'. Andy has been experimenting with using computers with his history classes, in part because he feels that if he shows an interest in using digital technologies it might encourage more students to take history seriously. However, there is a niggling doubt in Andy's mind about this other 'alien' in the classroom – the computer. Andy smiles to himself at the thought.

Andy has just finished reading a short article by Bill Green and Chris Bigum called Aliens in the Classroom.[2] Peter, one of the university researchers working with him on a technology and learning project, had urged him to read it. 'It's a classic', Peter told him.

Andy has spent some of his lunch break reading this 'classic', but a thought kept occurring to him: that while Green and Bigum argued kids were the aliens because they have grown up in a computer-connected world, half the time for him, as a teacher, it was the technology and more particularly how it intruded into classroom life – or vice versa – that made it feel as if there were two aliens in the classroom and not one. Andy refuses to believe that it was 'him': the term Luddite was too simple. He's been using computers to do all sorts of things at home: book holidays, search for material to teach with, e-mail family and friends; the list goes on. At school he keeps class records on the office computer, uses the school intranet for e-mail, and could search for material for his history classes using the Internet.

He resolves to take some notes after this lesson and use them to talk with Peter.

Andy's lesson with 9C is in the computer room. The room is some distance from *his* classroom. The kids love it – he knows that, even though it means two students sharing a computer, and a lot of noise. However, it also means – and this is the 'rub' – he's spending most of the lesson talking to students' backs as the computers are arranged on benches around the room.

At the end of the lesson, he finds himself noting later, he told the students that the group would be 'going home to Room 24' – his own classroom. Where had this discomfort come from?

As we can see from Andy's situation, not only did he feel events were racing away from him in the computer room, but he also found he was unable to draw upon the repertoire of skills he had mastered since his first unnerving days in the classroom. Why? Because among other things the dynamics changed in ways that meant his repertoire of techniques for managing the pace, content and staging of learning was less than useful. Students were glued to their computer screens and could not see him. There was also another aspect to Andy's discomfort. He was no longer confident about the kind of things young people were learning when they accessed information using the Internet.

Let's go back to Andy's notes and conversation with Peter, for a moment, to look at what actually happened when Andy taught the same history lesson, one located in a dedicated computer room and one in his 'home' classroom.

Andy's notes: 9D – 'We are in our own classroom and I worked with several bits of text on prohibition to help explore "*America in the 1920s and 1930s*". I then asked them to discuss some issues in pairs. The lesson went well; I felt relaxed and I was able to focus on scaffolding the students' learning so they would be able to effectively tackle the source-based questions.'

Andy's notes: 9C – 'I am repeating this lesson in the computer room. I notice that my focus keeps shifting away from the history subject discourse to an ICT technical discourse concerned primarily with procedures required to carry out the activity, such as how to access the relevant files on the computer. This was evident from the start. The board was filled with instructions about the 'C:\' drive and accessing files. I also found myself constantly checking the students, making sure that they were using the computers for this lesson and not something else. I kept thinking: what's happened to my history lesson?'

In Andy's later discussion with Peter they compare the two lessons. They muse together over how, in Andy's lesson with 9C, an ICT technical discourse had supplanted a subject discourse. It felt like a different logic was at work. In Andy's lesson with 9D in the history classroom, he sat behind his desk and launched the lesson by spending eight minutes reading through two sources, discussing their content, and framing possible ways of answering the first question. In doing this he was modelling the 'history discipline processes' by demonstrating this to the students. This provided a collective focus of attention for the group.

By way of contrast, in the computer room, only three minutes were spent giving a general summary of the prohibition era and the nature of the task before the students were sent off to independently access sources using search engines, to read the results of the search and to decide for themselves how best to approach the first question. Andy prowled around the classroom, checking the screens and the tabs at the bottom, reassuring himself that the students were doing the tasks he had assigned, like 'searching' for material related to the lesson rather than skiving off in cyberspace. Peter and Andy agreed that a neutral observer watching might easily conclude that the students were being introduced to two completely different learning activities.

Introduction

In this chapter we use Andy's experience with what he called this second 'alien' in the classroom as a starting point, to ask where his discomfort comes from and to argue that something quite profound is taking place in the social domain of learning and the social relations of classroom life.[3] We will be suggesting that the introduction of information and communication technologies into the various institutions and spaces of modern and modernising societies – including schools and homes – is reconstituting these domains and relations socially, politically and culturally. In part it has to do with the 'newness'[4] of the technology itself and, as we will argue, the *capabilities*[5] of the new information and communication technologies.

These capabilities, we will suggest, are not simply in the form of hardware and software but in the range of experiences and understandings they enable. The students and the teacher bring with them ICT-mediated experiences that, in combination, reconstitute the classroom as a very different kind of learning space. We might imagine each classroom as an 'assemblage'[6] made up of combinations of elements (such as students, teachers, curriculum, texts, pedagogical practices, community) that are 'fixed' together by cultural norms, roles, official policies and so on – their specific form making up the grammar of schooling in any particular social formation. Each assemblage both constitutes and is constituted by a specific 'ecology of knowledge production'. ICT-mediated classrooms draw upon knowledge and skills from across the assemblage (home, peer group, schools and so on) which add new elements to the ecology of knowledge production in the classroom, in turn transforming the learning assemblage.

In order to take these ideas forward, we will build on the ideas of instrument and instrumentation introduced in Chapter 3 by linking it to the idea of capability (developed below). In our view, if teachers like Andy have a way of understanding the 'why', 'how' and 'with what consequences for learning' of an ICT-mediated classroom, they will be in a better position to mediate, manage and capitalise on ICT in ways that are productive for learning. We begin this process by opening the technology 'black box' to understand better the changing form of the technology-society relation. We explore the way in which ICTs are changing knowledge practices using the idea of an attention economy. Finally, we explore the way in which the capabilities of the new ICTs act like tipping points, transforming the logics shaping classroom learning and the overall grammar of schooling through dynamics such as organisation, interaction and space. This new logic places very different demands on teachers and requires different regulative and pedagogical practices. Finally, we conclude by suggesting that we need a more open way of conceptualising the fluid and dynamic and connected nature of classroom life to wider social process, if we are to improve learning.

Opening the technology 'black box'

What is it about ICTs that make them sufficiently powerful to interrupt and disrupt Andy's classroom-based lessons? Writers like Manuel Castells (1996) argue that the power of digital technologies lies in the fact that these tools enable us to make endless connections between different domains, as well as between the elements and agents of such activities. Take, for instance, a routine task – such as creating an activity sheet for student work – that teachers like Andy might have undertaken in preparation for this lesson. Andy has used the Internet (www.icteachers.co.uk/teachers/links/thistory.htm), with its links to the BBC history and British Museum websites, to check for ideas for his lesson. He has also used 'Google.image' to search for images that might enhance the activity sheets before sending the final 'document' to the office for printing. Andy has not left his office. Instead he has used the school's recent installation of wi-fi technology to rove the world from his laptop before finally sending on the completed worksheet for printing. In Castells' view, ICTs have the capacity to enable workers, like Andy, to labour more efficiently and productively. Castells also argues that ICTs have now changed the way organisations and institutions work, as well as the kinds of societies we inhabit.

It is this latter point about the transformations of societies that we are particularly interested in exploring, for a number of reasons. First, the official policy discourse that linked technology to learning was characterised by a high degree of technological determinism.[7] This is all too evident in the UK government's 1997 *National Grid for Learning* policy costing £1 billion to create a 'connected society'.[8] Through supplying hardware, connecting more than 30,000 schools to the Internet, creating online resources for teachers and offering large-scale programmes for teacher professional development, the policy aimed to meet the technological revolution head on. The formula was relatively simple. Simply add ICTs to schools and there will be a transformation in learning. The problem with this simple-minded technological determinism is that the theory of how this was supposed to work – the programme ontology – was one of $\boxed{\text{T (technology)} + \text{L (learner)} = \text{L}_t \text{ (transformed learner)}}$. What makes it determinist is that T, when added to L, is regarded as sufficient to bring about $\boxed{\text{L}_t}$.

There are a number of problems with this formulation. First, technology is homogenised, yet ICTs are not simply a single resource. They take different forms because different softwares have different potentials and thus offer possibilities for a range of practices. Second, the formula homogenises the learner. As a result there is no way of accounting for the different experiences the learner might have had with ICTs, nor the levels of expertise these learners might have acquired in other out-of-school settings that might mediate their engagement with classroom-based learning with ICTs.

Third, there is no theory of what it is about ICTs, as a resource, that might enable – or require – teachers like Andy to think about the capabilities they offer and then to use this knowledge to build up lessons rather differently. In other words, ICTs tend to be black-boxed and thus closed off from close analysis. Fourth, the learner is extracted from the classroom and other learners. Yet classrooms are profoundly social spaces and particular kinds of social formations – an insight that Andy must take into every lesson he gives. 9C and 9D are very different groups, not only in terms of social class, gender and race, but also in terms of the different career trajectories of the students.

Fifth, the teacher is absent from the formulation above and yet the teacher's own views and experiences with ICTs, their concerns about how to incorporate their subject matter into ICT-based learning, their experiences as a teacher, along with experiences with different kinds of digital resources, all matter and will act to mediate the dynamics. Sixth (and consequent on points four and five), neither the student nor the teacher are given sufficient agency in this crude causal formulation, with the result that there is neither a recognition of contingency (not being able to predict exactly what it is that the student will learn) nor the possibility of complexity (not being able to predict the range of outcomes or effects). Here we need to ask: what range of meaning-making activities is taking place? How and for what purpose are these resources mobilised? What kinds of performances/knowledges are being produced? And so on.

Finally, this simple policy formula, to bring UK learners into the twenty-first century, failed to take into account the policy and management environment that placed real limits on Andy's opportunities for experimentation in his classroom. For instance, Andy's promotion in the profession was dependent upon the 'value-added' his teaching was recorded as contributing to each learner. Andy was unsure, if not sceptical, of the kind of value-added ICT-based history teaching offered. There was little research evidence he could find that might inform him. Yet, in a climate of school audits and league tables that now characterised the English education system, Andy felt pressured to be sure about which innovations he incorporated into his classroom and what value they could add to student learning. This kind of policy and practice regime left little space for experimentation and threatened possible chaos. It also limited the learning he, Andy, might acquire from failure. In other words, the wider social and political contexts that shaped the everyday realities for teachers and their work in English classrooms were erased, and thus absent in such formulations.

Toward a local ecology of knowledge production with ICTs

In our research on the InterActive project we began by inserting these absences into our representations of what we called *a local ecology of knowledge production*. We started by placing the student and the teacher in the classroom with ICTs and called this a social formation. We then nested this social formation within the school, the wider community to include homes, peer groups and agencies like local education authorities, and finally the national and global domains that are influential in shaping agendas as well as offering the potential for new kinds of connectivity.[9] In its totality, we viewed this complex of interconnections as an 'assemblage' – an idea we return to in the final section of the chapter.

In the project we were aware that this was a natural experiment and also that teachers would be concerned about their performance and student learning. However, our intention was to work with the teachers in our study in such ways where they could begin to ask different questions that might enable them to 'see' and 'mediate' learning with ICT. Only then, we argued, might teachers be in a position to generate a rather different programme ontology[10] – in other words a theory of how ICTs worked in the classroom. This theory would come from their own experiments and insights following using ICT in real learning settings; this was to be an alternative to the crude and pedagogically stifling technological determinism which we believed was embraced in official policies. This meant teachers would have to become researchers of their own practice in a process that was facilitated by university-based researchers. The learning that took place would inform and benefit both the teacher researcher and the university researcher, and, we hoped, the overall opportunities for student learning.

In order to help Andy open the black box on technology, Peter suggested that he look at some of the writings by Manuel Castells, but then use his own experience and discussions with, and observations of, the students to make a list of what it was about ICTs that might make them powerful 'new' tools. 'After all', said Peter, '. . . some writers argue that we can trace complex IT-based technologies back to the early nineteenth century'.[11] Andy jotted down a list of notes in his diary for discussion with Peter:

- lessons and students' work can be taught/presented using a complex mix of text, images, sound, interaction;
- instant feedback, e.g. from spelling a word wrong to game playing;
- search engines to access all kinds of information out there in the wider world so that the students are not dependent on what is in the library at school or at home;
- communication . . . using e-mail, chat rooms . . . enabling students to get in touch with people and places instantly around the world;
- knowledge can now be produced by the students through making their own web pages, blogs, wikis, small film segments, and so on . . . the old experts are no longer needed;
- classroom is now more linked into the outside world;
- . . . students can have their own addresses separate from 'home' – e.g. gmail.com;
- . . . *it does not mean they happen!*

Andy cast his eye down his notes. Several ideas in his notes stood out. *ICTs enable a multiplicity of links with lots of activities taking place around the globe . . . it is a communication resource . . . it opens up many very different ways of producing and sharing knowledge.* He then cast his eyes to the final line he had underlined: *it does not mean they happen!.* The way he saw things, there was nothing predetermined about how any of his students would use ICTs and that was part of the problem, as he needed to be in more control than this. Andy also saw a range of attitudes and practices in his classrooms. Some of the students were highly skilled with the computer; they had their own web pages, could do programming, and used software like AdobePhotoshop to create and manipulate images.[12] Other students were more ambivalent.

Earlier in the chapter we introduced the idea of capabilities as a heuristic or way of thinking about ICTs. According to Sasken (2006) 'capabilities' are '. . . collective productions whose development entails time, making, competition, and conflicts, and whose utilities are, in principle, multivalent because they are conditioned in the character of the relational systems within which they function' (pp. 7–8). This way of thinking about ICTs enables us also to see them as evolving, as socially produced. One way in which this becomes evident is where there is competition over which is the better tool (for instance, over which search engine is the best – Google or Yahoo!); another is exposing conflicting ways of understanding the world, such as through blogs, wikis, and so on. ICTs are also appropriated and reappropriated for different uses. In other words, actors have 'interpretive flexibility', meaning that different groups of people involved with particular 'socially frozen' moments of a technology can have different understandings of that technology, including understandings of its technical characteristics. Peter reminds Andy of the history of the microwave oven as an example of this; it was a direct descendent of military radar technology used to heat up food in Navy submarines. Initially microwaves were marketed as a 'brown good' to sit alongside hi-fis and televisions, and were aimed at young males' leisure activities. However, this way of representing the microwave was unsuccessful and was eventually reconstituted as a 'white good' for housewives.[13]

ICTs are thus part of the social and cultural worlds of meaning making. As a result, their production, distribution and uses are contingent, diverse and dynamic. However, there is also sufficient convergence in students' knowledge and skills in technology and the wider social and cultural dynamics which shape young people's lives, for Andy to understand something of the profound changes that are taking place in students' lives. As Peter pointed out, some young people have never known the text-bound world that their elders have come from – or at least not in the same way.[14] For Andy to appreciate this more fully in his teaching, Peter has suggested Andy think about the wider social settings in which young people live and learn,[15] and to draw on the students' capabilities developed through using ICT outside school to restructure learning activities in the classroom.

For Andy, this means thinking about teaching and technology more broadly, to take account of the 'mutually constitutive' relationship between technology and society. The point of doing this is to enable Andy to make more explicit the links between classroom life and wider social, political and economic processes. It is helpful, Peter suggests, in order to see better the relationship between technology and society as a fluid, dynamic co-constitutive process – it shapes us and we shape it.

New economies of knowledge production

So what is it about the ways in which new ICTs are reshaping the social domains and social relations that is particularly important for how teachers use ICTs in their classroom? We have argued so far that ICTs are powerful because of their scale and speed capabilities: capabilities that make them stand apart from other technologies. In this section we focus on how these elements, in combination, alter knowledge production, its distribution and use in a number of profound ways.

A number of writers have begun to argue that ICTs are involved in new economics of 'attention'.[16] Given that gaining 'attention' is a key means for teachers engaging students in learning, and given the importance of viewing classroom life as one element in the assemblage that constitutes opportunities for student learning, it is important to examine the claims about new economics of attention in order to shed light on how this might also have an impact on social practices and students' identities. Cognitive scientist Herbert Simon (1971) argued that information is dependent upon consumers' attention and that in a virtual sea of information there is a 'poverty of attention'. This kind of insight has been used in the media and ICT-based worlds to help developers and advertisers think through how they might structure interfaces, such as web pages, in order to grab the viewer's attention. That said, there are several different 'takes' or views on the economics of attention that are worth outlining.

In the first approach it is argued that in some kinds of information, such as model answers to school exams, there has been a great deal of attention given to the shaping of the information, while other information, such as a teacher's quick e-mail to her colleagues in the school, might be viewed as almost raw data.[17] In the first case there has been considerable time put into the shaping of the model answer, the kinds of students who might read the model answer, the overall purpose of the exam, and so on. In the second example, the attention given has been both more limited and more specific to the receiver as person rather than the receiver as group. The focus in this approach is how much attention is given to the *production* of an item.

The second approach to the attention economy focuses on the *subjects* themselves, and on how and why they pursue attention.[18] That is, when people live in economically advanced societies they are socialised in ways that orient them towards the pursuit of attention, and this pursuit is pleasurable. Andy, for instance, became acutely aware of the fact that the students were easily drawn away from the intended learning about a specific event in history when using the Internet. This presents all kinds of management and teaching problems. He was also aware of the considerable effort spent, and pleasure gained, by students in 'making' websites, blogs and school presentations in ways that attract attention. This new economy of attention-getting sits in sharp contrast to the comparatively dowdy, static and authoritative attention economy of conventional learning settings.

The third approach comes from the advertising field; that is, how best to capture the attention of potential *consumers* of knowledge.[19] These techniques have been translated into a whole range of practices and activities on the Internet, from having websites and pages picked up in the search process to how games capture the long-term attention of the player. These ideas have direct relevance to teachers' use of the Internet for learning activities.

If we return to Andy's classroom, there are two fundamental elements comprising the 'alien-ness' of ICT. They tend to overlap and even disguise each other, but it is important to recognise that they are distinct. One is that when we talk about students knowing more than teachers, having access to the Internet and different forms and sources of knowledge, what we are talking about is a new form of *epistemological* diversity introduced into education, the curriculum and the classroom. This is superficially similar to the kinds of linguistic and cultural diversity to which we have become accustomed, but the challenges it produces are quite different. They constitute not just different ways of accessing knowledge but different forms of knowledge and different ways of representing knowledge. They generate issues of 'author-ity', for instance, which are fundamental to curriculum, so that when Andy is wondering about what has happened to his history lesson, it is not solely because of technical issues but because of potential problems of comparability and commensurability of the information students may retrieve, which are of a quite different order from that of the responses they may generate discussing shared texts in pairs.

As an example of what this might involve, we put the terms *'America 1920s 1930s prohibition'* into Google (see excerpt below – captured 13 May 2007). Google came up with around 740,000 possible responses. In the image capture we show only the first four results, but even here we find very interesting examples of the kinds of changes we are talking about. The first entry seems to be quite tangential, and thus raises questions of what we might call the 'meta-authority' of Google – how Google determines the priority of matches becomes an important issue. Our normal assumption (learned by us and communicated to our students) might be that the order is determined by 'closeness of fit', perhaps as demonstrated in the coincidence of titles of books or papers with the same search terms. At the same time it raises the issues of epistemology and 'author-ity' we have just mentioned, the 'legitimacy' of literacies other than print – jazz tracks and fashion drawings, for instance.[20]

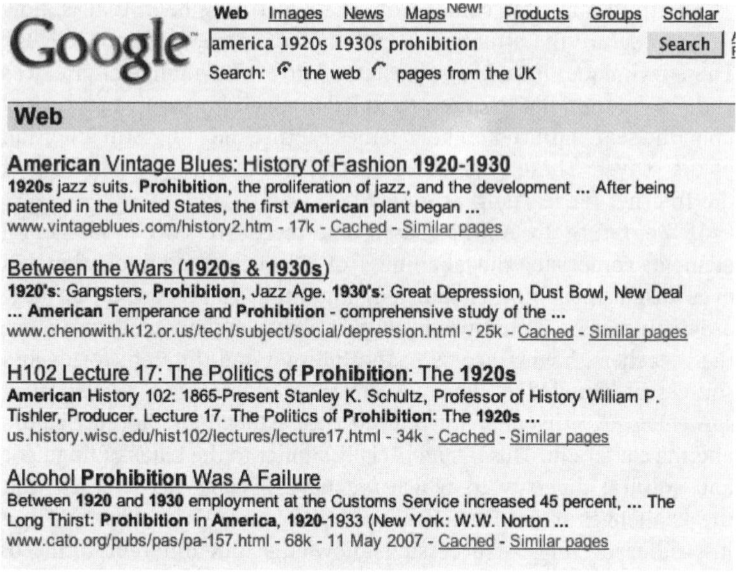

Figure 7.1 Excerpt from Google search 'America 1920s 1930s prohibition' 13 May
2007

The second entry is especially relevant. It comes from a school in
Oregon, and displays what might be considered an example of the
'orthodox' means of utilising ICT to *enhance* the curriculum, with a
range of links to other useful sites, presented under subheadings that
might be used to structure a course on the topic. However, it could
also present different kinds of challenges and opportunities to a
classroom teacher like Andy. Will the class be comparing the resources
he has brought to the class with those made available by the 'alien'?
Will they generate discussions of how American history is seen in the
US and UK?

The third entry is a lecture on the politics of prohibition that had
been posted on a university website: the sort of information that Andy
might have preferred his students to consult and use. It had the kind
of information authority that Andy understood and had learned to
respect from his own studies in history and in his teacher training
days.

The fourth entry raises a most interesting issue, of a quite different
order. It comes from the Cato Institute, which is a right-wing liber-
tarian American think tank, whose view is that any kind of prohibition

may be seen as an infringement of individual freedom by state authorities. This clearly raises a set of issues that transcend that of the topic being taught. For instance, it is quite conceivable that many history teachers would consider this a very useful resource through which they could introduce a range of such issues. However, in that case, rather than appearing as one among thousands of apparently equivalent a-historical, un-contexted, de-politicising entries, demarcated only by their relevance (to Google), the provenance of the report would be built into the discussion, and possibly balanced by other views, such as by the health profession and so on.

The use of Internet resources also raises issues of originality, plagiarism and indeed what is being rewarded. This is especially significant in an era when accountability of teachers, as judged by the results their students receive, dominates the management of contemporary education systems. This is, of course, perhaps the central point of tension in the introduction of ICT into education, because new technologies afford greater power and rights to young people to decide for themselves what they can see, think and do.[21]

This leads to a second basic issue raised by the introduction of ICT to schools. That is, that it challenges deeply embedded orthodox assumptions of pedagogy at a level, and in ways, that make it very difficult to rely on those assumptions as a guide to what ICT will mean and how it can be best used by teachers. In a nutshell, it is qualitatively different from existing approaches to pedagogy. It cannot easily be incorporated into any of them. Introducing ICT in the classroom is not like introducing a new history curriculum or work package, or even like modifying existing work packages to make them more accessible to students from different cultural or linguistic backgrounds.

Empirically, what we see in classrooms like Andy's is an attempt to incorporate the new epistemological challenges into the existing curriculum, and the pedagogic capabilities of ICT into existing pedagogic assumptions. We can see what is involved in the first of these in the example we gave above. The example from the Oregon school shows the possibility of enhancing the curriculum through quantitatively increasing the range of materials available to students, and we can see the potential for this quantitative enhancement to bring about qualitative change – that is, to transform our conceptions of history and how it might be taught, rather than add to the range of ways it is taught now.

The obstacle to that development lies, however, in the second of the problems outlined above: that our existing pedagogic assumptions do not stand alone, as easily detachable and replaceable elements of teaching, like plugging in a new software application. Rather, they are deeply embedded in a wider grammar of schooling:[22] that is, the set of organisational assumptions and practices that have grown up around the development of mass schooling and have come to be seen as defining it, to become, in effect, education as practised. It frames what is possible in schooling, and acts as a major barrier to significant change in schools. For Tyack and Tobin, that grammar of schooling comprises a number of interrelated features, such as a structure of subjects; a schedule of classes; a system of age grouping; a given duration of a 'class'; a grading system; and curricular materials.

Within that grammar of schooling the place of, and assumptions about, pedagogy are especially important. To put it over simply, within the grammar of schooling the place and role and importance of pedagogy are framed by the other assumptions (such as the content of schooling and how it is assessed, the role and management of teachers, and the fact that education is compulsory), so that 'teaching' becomes how we were taught, with any variation being seen as an aberration or deviation (witness the outcry whenever 'progressive' modes of teaching are bruited abroad).

One consequence of the traditional grammar of schooling, then, is that pedagogy has come to be widely regarded as a neutral means of transmitting the knowledge designated as of most importance, and as having little, if any, independent contribution to make. New forms of pedagogy may be introduced, but they tend to be variations on the existing themes, different ways of doing the same thing, rather than doing different things. It is here that we see the main obstacles to the development of the potential of ICT in schools, for the implementation of ICT has tended very much to follow the former route, doing the same things differently rather than doing different things. There are two reasons at least for this: one relatively theoretical; the other relatively practical. The theoretical reason is that the place of pedagogy in the grammar of schooling has led to the potential of ICTs being deeply underestimated.

The practical reason is the serious underestimation of what would be involved in preparing teachers to carry out and introduce deeper and further-reaching changes in pedagogy through the use of ICT. The InterActive project was particularly sensitive to this issue; for this reason we developed very close research/teacher/practice/ research relations around designed experiments intended to also reshape teacher practices. This stood in sharp contrast to the forms of professional development currently found, such as technical acquaintance courses, or short courses in the use of particular softwares, that appear to assume, and reinforce, precisely the use of ICT as an 'add-on' to existing teaching that we have just been discussing. If the capabilities of ICT are to be realised, something far more extensive will be needed. A further aspect of this point is that ICT is constantly changing – which in itself creates major financial obstacles for schools – but this also means constant obsolescence, especially in comparison to what is available to students on the Internet.

Classrooms as particular kinds of digitally mediated social formations

In this final section we explore, briefly, the way the capabilities of ICT in the classroom – that is the combination of: (i) ICT as an instrument; (ii) young people's ICT-mediated knowledge and experiences within and outside school; (iii) the teacher's ICT/subject and pedagogical-mediated knowledges and experiences; and (iv) official policies on learning, and learning with ICT – change the logic or grammar of the classroom as a particular kind of digital formation. Not only do ICTs interrupt the existing grammar of schooling but this combination of capabilities transforms the organisation, interaction and spatialisation of social relations in the classroom, thus tipping the logic in a new direction.[23] By *organisation* we mean the ordering of practices (for example, via rules and roles), content (data and images) and relations among actors (individual, collective and machine); by *interaction* we mean the flow of exchange and transmission among actors; and by *spatialisation* we refer to the electronic 'staging' of the content and social relations at play in a classroom-based digital formation. Here the idea of staging implies the coordination of views, visualisations and narrations that unfold in time – such as the possibility of multiple screens of one form or another on the desktop, or the organisation of actions and practices within digital formations with implications for who has access, to what kind of information, on what basis and so on. In combination, spatialisation practices shape the possibilities for interaction and *inter alia* social relations.

In Andy's classrooms, both when using ICTs as part of the lesson, or when students use ICTs to complete their work, there is an array of new roles that are now possible and new rules to be followed in the creation of knowledge. For instance, there is an expansion of the literacy horizon well beyond the text-based literacy that underpins non-ICT-based knowledge creation. New kinds of expertise and competence are also possible, as we see with areas like music, mathematical problem-solving, and so on, so that the previous balance of power between expert-non-expert, which was almost always tipped in the direction of the teacher, is now recalibrated to include, if not favour, the student. Furthermore, students are able to access many more resources from the available knowledge pools. However, this also requires rather different competencies in assessing truth claims, the inter-textual nature of knowledge, its genealogy and so on.

The spatialisation of classroom life is profoundly disrupted by the fact that ICTs offer more open and multiple stagings. However, in ICT-based lessons, the teacher is less able to control these performances, not only because of how computer-based work stations tend to be organised in contemporary learning settings, but also because there is the real possibility for the student to connect to sites globally. Here in ICT-mediated classrooms we see a new logic at work; the teacher-directed classroom is replaced by a set of multivalent performances that are, in turn, enabled through this now leaky space. The challenge for Andy as a teacher is how best to understand this very different grammar in ways he can manage and incorporate into his pedagogy to enhance student learning. Finally, students' ICT-mediated experiences are shaped by the spatialised politics of access, experience, quality and support – where new learning divides emerge and old ones are reinforced. As a result, not all students in Andy's class will participate in these various stagings. Andy is increasingly aware of this, and the need to take these diverse experiences into account.

'Assemblages': a metaphor for seeing classrooms as dynamic social formations

What has become evident to us in working on this project is the tendency to view schools as islands, loosely connected to society. This kind of metaphor represents the school as an institution for teaching and learning, sitting outside of, rather than constituting, society. Several things follow from this metaphor. First, schools are viewed as being unique holders of a particular mandate: to develop the abilities of the learner.[24] As a result, what young people learn in other places and spaces has little currency in the classroom, unless of course it is officially sanctioned as 'homework': that is, essentially school-assigned learning in the home. When that knowledge is taken into account, as with students' ICT-mediated learning as a result of connectivity, they are likely to be constructed as 'aliens' in the classroom, rather than differently knowledgeable. Second, schools are also represented as enduring features of the landscape, immune to change. The typical example used to make this point is the architecture of schools – where, aside from some re-engineering from decade to decade, it is argued schools 'look' the same. Changes in school infrastructures, like the addition of ICT hardware, are just as likely to be constituted as additions – as aliens too. Maybe schools look the same, but this is to miss the point about their location in societies, and this is the nub of our argument.

Schools and classrooms are particular moments in wider social relations. They are also particular configurations of social relations. As we have argued, students come to school and learn a wide range of things. However, as we discuss more fully in Chapter 8, they bring with them learning from different locations – the playground, the home, their online communities, and so on. Schools, as official sites for learning, are also connected to a wide range of other activities – some of which shape what it is that schools, teachers and students do in direct ways; others more indirectly. This ensemble of linkages and social relations is given coherence through particular logics, what it is that these various actors should do, how they are governed in pursuit of this, and so on. We might call this an assemblage – a particular set of linkages that form, like a constellation around a classroom, but which extend outward to a range of locations and with a range of effects on the learner, the teacher, the classroom, the school and so on. Viewing classrooms as an assemblage, on the one hand, keeps the system more open and, on the other hand, also opens to the possibility of seeing it as far more dynamic and open to changes, both small and big. ICTs have the potential to generate *big* rather than 'small' change, and they have, in our view, the potential to profoundly alter the social relations of classroom life. We see signs of this already, and as certain chapters in this book reveal, some teachers are well advanced in managing the implementation and consequences of the learning that is made possible.

Summary and conclusions

In this chapter we have used a specific classroom case based upon Andy, a secondary history teacher, to explore a number of issues surrounding the use of new technologies in conventional classrooms. We showed how ICTs, both in the ways that students bring their ICT-mediated knowledge and experience into the classroom and in the incorporation of ICTs into the history curriculum, alter the dynamics of classroom life. Knowledge creation, the distribution of expertise, forms of interaction, organisation and the re-spatialisation of classroom life, tip the logic of the old assemblage into a new one. There are now new actors, practices and linkages which make up this new assemblage and ecology of knowledge production. Rather than seeing aliens in the classroom, by connecting classroom life more closely to wider social relations, Andy might now be able to ask questions that reveal to him different kinds of possibilities for working with and improving learning.

Notes

1 Andy's story is a composite of several teachers that we worked with on the InterActive project. We want to acknowledge the contribution of Tim Shortis who worked on the InterActive project as a Research Fellow to thinking about these issues more generally, and to his insights about Andy's case specifically.
2 See Green and Bigum (1994).
3 We take this argument in different directions in Robertson, *et al.* (2004).
4 See Latham and Sassen (2005). Latham and Sassen talk about the 'newness' of information and communication technologies, suggesting that there are novel formations that we have not seen before: for instance cyberspace, multimedia connected communities, and so on.
5 See Sasken (2006) for further discussion of capabilities.
6 'Assemblage' is a term taken from Deleuze and Guattari (1987).
7 Technological determinism is a concept used to describe the assumption that it is the technology itself that brings about change rather than the agents who mobilise technologies. The technological determinism of early UK policy on technology was softened following accruing evidence that it was by no means inevitable that such high levels of investment were followed by equal transformations in learning outcomes.
8 See Selwyn (1999).
9 See Pawson (2002).
10 See Dale, Robertson and Shortis (2004).
11 See Beniger (1986).
12 See also Facer, Furlong, Furlong and Sutherland (2003).
13 See Wajcman (2002).
14 See Castells and Jensen (2004).
15 See Chapter 8 for further discussion.

16 See Lankshear and Knobel (2003).
17 See Lantham (1994).
18 See Goldhaber (1997).
19 See Adler (1995).
20 See Lankshear and Knobel (2005).
21 See Castell and Jensen (2004).
22 See Tyack and Tobin (1994).
23 See Latham and Sassen (ibid., p. 10).
24 Though we would point out that this is not the only thing that schools do. Schools also socialise students into the workplace, produce compliant citizens, and so on.

Chapter 8*

Connecting cultures
Home and school uses of ICT

This chapter occupies an ambiguous position in relation to many of the chapters in this book. While it is concerned with exploring learning with digital technologies, it comes at this question not from a focus on the school but via an investigation of children and young people's use of computers and the Internet in the home. As such, it occupies something of the same position in relation to the rest of the book as 'informal learning' often does to the school – its relevance needs to be made visible and articulated clearly for fear of simply being overlooked. We began this process by arguing in Chapter 7 that the idea of 'assemblage' enables us to view learning as located in multiple sites and made up of multiple elements, not simply schools. This chapter pursues this idea through a more systematic exploration of the articulation of these elements and sites.

As such, the chapter has two areas of focus: first, it documents our observations of children's out-of-school use of computers and the Internet gathered through the InterActive project; second, it focuses on one example of ICT use in the classroom and uses this to explore how 'schooled' and 'leisured' cultures of ICT use are mobilised and collide. The chapter then asks whether the relationship between school and leisure uses of technology is leading to new relationships between formal and informal knowledge. To summarise, the main aims of the chapter are:

- to provide insights into young people's use of computers and Internet in the home;
- to explore how classroom-based interactions with ICT are connected with and influenced by young people's out-of-school digital cultures;
- to consider what new relationships might be developed between formal school knowledges and informal out-of-school knowledges.

* This chapter was authored by Keri Facer and Rosamund Sutherland.

Using computers and the Internet in the home

Any attempt to understand learning outside the school makes visible the ways in which schools actively select and manage the multiple knowledges and expertise that enter its doors each day.[1] Understanding the relationship between learning in the home and learning in the school always, therefore, requires an engagement with questions of power and knowledge and an exploration of the ways in which different practices and knowledges are permitted, negotiated and transformed as they move between different sites. As we increasingly witness educational software companies designing technologies intended to draw on leisure practices such as gaming, as we see teachers using technologies in order to enhance 'engagement' and enjoyment of learning, we will increasingly be confronted with the question 'what happens when we appropriate young people's out-of-school cultures for the goals of formal education?' 'When these different cultures collide – which wins? And why?'

Before exploring these more theoretical questions, however, we begin the chapter with a description of the sorts of activities we understand children and young people to be engaged with in using digital technologies in the home, based on data collected within the InterActive project.[2]

Constructing the computer and Internet in the home

Within the survey carried out in 2003 88 per cent of young people reported owning a computer and 73 per cent reported having access to the Internet. For many of these young people the computer was a shared resource for several members of the family (only 6 per cent of the young people with home computers reported that no one else used the computer that they used most of the time at home, with 57 per cent reporting that at least three other people also used it). The survey also revealed that the majority of computers most regularly used by the young people in the study were located in 'family' spaces within the home, with 24 per cent in living rooms, 27 per cent in attic/computer room/kids room/study, 7 per cent in kitchens/halls and landings, 12 per cent in someone else's bedroom. The minority (24 per cent) were located in the young person's bedroom.

Our questionnaire asked about participation in 20 activities – from using the computer to write, to using the Internet for shopping or downloading software. Figure 8.1 shows the percentage of all young people surveyed who reported that they were involved in these activities at least once a week.

By 2003, outside school the computer is popularly used as an information resource to be explored for pleasure, a machine for textual production and a resource for entertainment, mainly in the form of games-based activities. It is also, for many young people, a means of communication and connection with others: levels of participation in e-mail, chat rooms, or online games suggest a connected conception of the computer rather than a stand-alone conception. Multimodality similarly is part of the picture of 'computing' in the home – games play draws on simulation, visual imagery, sound and text – and many young people are playing with images/photos and pictures. The digital world is also, by 2003, beginning to be seen as a site of consumption – not necessarily commercial consumption (as the low levels of Internet shoppers would suggest) but for consumption of media, software and information.

While there are differences between individuals, these principles of play, of easy access to information and people, of ever-interconnected images, words and sounds, are the taken-for-granted and everyday assumptions that inform the ideas that young people have about the

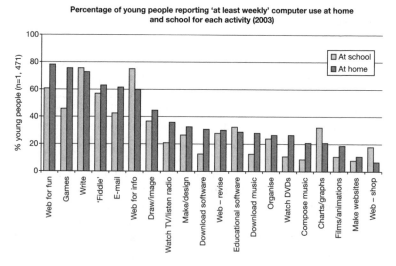

Figure 8.1 Young people's experience of computer activity at home and school (2003)

purpose and 'point' of computers and the Internet outside school. These are beginning to form the basis for the new literacies of digital cultures, literacies which, as we discuss in Chapter 5, constitute not simply interactions with texts but specific cultural and social practices. It is these ideas and practices that young people potentially reference when engaging with digital technologies in the classroom.

Looking at these figures now and, indeed, at the questions we asked to generate them, however, raises interesting questions about the processes of researching young people's use of computers outside school. Let's consider what is missing from this list of activities: Instant Messenger/Myspace/Bebo/YouTube, to name just a few. Let's also consider the wording of some of the questions – we asked about 'talking in chat rooms', and 'playing computer games against other people on the web'. The lists and languages used to generate this data betray their point of origin and their time. They ignore some of the features that became apparent through interviews as crucial to young people's use of ICT outside school between 2001 and 2003 – such as the use of the Internet not to 'talk in chat rooms', but to maintain friendships and talk with those people they already know. They also fail to respond to the changes in digital cultures over time – notably, the emergence of social software or Web 2.0 practices that have developed since 2003.[3]

What is the value of these figures then? We would argue that it is primarily in explaining the cultural practices young people were engaged in when they entered the classrooms described in the remainder of the chapters in this book. They also have a value, when we look at the next level of granularity, in highlighting the potential factors through which home use of computers and the Internet are filtered. For, as Steve Woolgar has argued in relation to the lessons that might be learned from the study of apparently 'obsolete' technologies:

> Although claims about the obsolescence of technologies under academic focus are exaggerated, it is undeniable that the longevity of a careful social scientific research project will probably exceed the period when the technology under study is deemed cutting edge. Against this, it should be remembered that technology is only ever cutting edge for certain specific groups – for example, the supply side of the electronics industry and some (self styled) sophisticated users. Thus, for example, the telephone is still out of reach to large proportions of the population of the world as a whole. But this does not invalidate the study of its adoption and effects. There may be

important lessons to be learned about the situations and circumstances that enabled and/or constrained take up.

(Woolgar 2002, p. 20)

Contours of participation in digital cultures outside school

The surveys revealed the persistence of socio-economic factors in determining access to computers and the Internet in the home. In 2003 reported computer ownership among those young people from the highest socio-economic areas[4] was 96 per cent compared to 81 per cent for those in the lowest. Similarly, reported Internet access stood at 87 per cent for the highest groups against 65 per cent for those in the lowest.[5] Although those young people from lower socio-economic areas were more likely to have access to digital TV, games consoles and mobile phones with Internet connections, this did not translate into a consistent pattern of greater use of these alternative devices to access the Internet. They were more likely to use mobile phones to access the Internet, but not games consoles or digital TV.

Gender differences were visible primarily in the area of use of the computer for entertainment purposes. Boys were more likely than girls to report at least weekly use of the computer 'for fun' (92 per cent compared with 85 per cent). More significant gender differences are apparent if we look at daily use of the home computer: 46 per cent of boys compared with 35 per cent of girls reported using the computer for fun every day. By far the greatest difference is in the area of games playing, with 32 per cent of boys playing games daily compared with 17 per cent of girls in 2003. This is consistent with other research that identifies the area of games playing as the most significant gender difference in use of computers.[6]

There is a general pattern of increasing use of the computer (and particularly the Internet) by age with a significant jump in Internet use between primary and secondary age ranges. As age increases there is an overall trend in declining use of the computer for entertainment (particularly games) purposes, compared with increases in use for school-related activities.

Family practices

So far we have talked about the overall patterns of use of computers and the Internet in the home as reported in our surveys. Our interviews, however, revealed a more nuanced set of practices in the home. The following vignettes illustrate the ways in which young people's choices about what and how they use the computer and the Internet are always situated within the social and cultural context of their extended family and friends.

VIGNETTE 1
Alan the family information gatherer

Alan, a 12-year-old student, lived in a small terrace house with his father and mother and older brother. His older sister, who worked from home for a leading European computer company, had recently moved into her own flat in which she had organised an office in the attic. Alan had recently moved into the largest bedroom of the house (with his parents now sleeping in a smaller bedroom) so that his bedroom could become the 'space' for the use of the computer in the home ('I persuaded them that I have this room simply because I have the most technology'). Alan's dad, who usually worked on a night shift, would use the computer in Alan's bedroom when he was at school. When Alan was not at school, keeping in touch with his school friends, through MSN Messenger, was clearly important to him, and as well as generally chatting, the friends used this medium for arranging out-of-school activities such as going swimming together. Alan also used the computer for playing games, e-mail, designing websites and doing homework.

Interestingly Alan seemed to have become the family information gatherer, who was always willing to use the Internet to search for information for his family. He helped his father find the best places in England for carp fishing and his grandmother to find a holiday and also to 'research on things which she wants to find out, like crystals . . . that's what she collects . . . like quartz'. For his grandfather he searched for Internet sites on 'old coins and woodwork'. Alan was teaching himself to create his own website, and this was clearly a challenge for him. In order to do this he was cutting and pasting script from an already developed website into his own, and from this process was beginning to make sense of the website scripting language.

VIGNETTE 2
A teacher in the corner of the home

Sian's family had first bought a computer when her elder sister was in primary school, to help her with school work. Her mother explained that it was 'mainly used for research rather than for writing up'. By the time Sian was at secondary school they had a computer with Internet access at home. Mum was using it to keep in touch with friends in Canada and booking holidays, and occasionally she used spreadsheets at home for work-related activity. Dad was less confident about using the computer, occasionally using it to play solitaire, but he said that, 'what I can't understand is why it won't do what you are telling it to do'. The computer was in the main living room of the house so that the parents could keep an eye on what their children were using it for. Sian's older sister was using it for 'Internet research' for college. Although both sisters used the computer for playing games, their father said that, 'it's an educational tool, not a games machine'. Both parents said that they were learning about how to use the Internet from their daughters and the father had gone to 'night school' to do a basic computer course. 'They were doing things I didn't know, and I kept on asking to be told, so I thought, well, the best way to do it was to go to night school and find out what they were doing'. Both parents were positive about the educational benefits of their daughters' use of the computer at home, with Dad saying that it is like 'having a teacher in the corner'. However, Sian's mother said that she was now less involved in her daughter's homework when she was using the Internet 'for research' than when she had previously used books: 'like without the computer she would come to us and say where can I go and can I go to the library. Whereas it's now all at her fingertips so we don't have to give the time so much as we probably would to take her to the library ... she does all the researching herself, whereas we used to do it with her'. However, Sian pointed out that now she discussed her 'research' homework with her school friends using MSN.

VIGNETTE 3
Being a rock musician

John's mother categorises people as a 'people person' and a 'machine person', saying that she is a 'people person' and that John is a 'machine person'. The family computer was on a desk in the dining room, and the father also brought a laptop computer home from work, and used the software Word and Excel (and less frequently PowerPoint) when working at home. Mum, a school librarian, used a computer at work and was not interested in using it at home. John (aged 16) used the home computer for playing collaborative games on the Internet, for communicating with his friends on MSN Messenger and for downloading tabs for his band ('if I need vocals for like anything I'm doing in my band then I'll get them off the Internet') and for school work (for 'scientific research').

These interviews were carried out in 2003, and in 1999 we had carried out an earlier study of young people's use of the computer at home as part of the Screen Play Project. What had changed since the 1999 study was the type of computer-based technology that was available in the home. In comparison with 2003, in 1999 the vast majority of young people in our study did not have access to the Internet, or to MSN Messenger or to music software. As we discussed above, by the time of writing this book the specific software and resources available to young people in the home had changed again, with a wide range of social software becoming available. So the type of technology entering the home is continuously changing and in relatively rapid ways.

However, analysis of the 2003 interviews suggests that despite this, what stays the same is the way in which young people's use of ICT in the home is embedded within the social and cultural practices of the home and friendship groups. What young people choose to use the computer for outside school very much relates to their personal interests and identities (for example, being a rock musician). Within some families (for example, Alan's family) the young person is constructed as the 'expert' computer user and home use centres around this expertise. Interestingly, in Alan's family it seems that his appropriation of a large bedroom for his computer and associated technology is (possibly unknown to him) modelling his older sister's home office. Within other families there is more of a distributed approach to the development of expertise, and the home is a space for shared knowledge creation, with everyone bringing into the home what they know and have learned from outside.

By 2003, when the Internet was widely available in the home, schoolwork seemed to be being constructed as doing 'research', and in some families the computer was being constructed as 'a teacher in the corner'. As we discuss in Chapter 10, at the heart of high-quality teaching is the ability to make skilful judgements about the knowledge students need to learn, in what order it is made available and how it is engaged with. Whereas family and friends can also play a role in supporting learning in the home we might want to question the impact on learning if parents delegate this responsibility to the 'computer in the corner'.

Comparing patterns of computer and Internet use at home and school

So far we have provided an indication of the types of activities young people are involved with in the home setting. How different is this, then, from their experiences in school? Analysis of the survey data suggests, surprisingly, that there is often broad congruency between the categories of use of computers and the Internet at home and at school, with schools reflecting home use and vice versa. For example, the patterns of high reported use of computers and the Internet for writing and for 'fiddling' (a term we coined to reflect the often non-purposive but exploratory use of the computer across a range of software packages) that we saw in the home, were equally frequently reported in the school. Similarly, those activities often seen as exotic in the home – creating web pages, making films and animations etc., were also rarely reported in the school.

The differences between home and school in terms of activity, then, are not black and white. It is not a case of completely 'different worlds'. Rather, activities in different sites tend to be 'inflected' with particular practices. For example, the home tends to be a site in which young people engage in computer activities often associated with 'leisure', such as games play or media activities, which are less common (or sanctioned) in school. In contrast, schools seem to offer opportunities for young people to engage with the use of computers for modelling and mathematics (using charts, graphs, tables) activities which are only infrequently reported in the home environment. At the same time, while the school seems to act as an important site for young people to experience a diversity of computer activities, the home offers the opportunity for more frequent and lengthy engagement with a narrower set of practices. This is unsurprising given the different systems of access to technologies in home and school and the ways in which the home offers, as discussed earlier, the opportunity for children to 'specialise' in particular uses of ICT relating to their family, peer and personal interests.

What remains to be understood, however, is how these different practices come into contact and whether and how they transform each other. This question – how to understand the dynamism of the boundary between 'schooled' and 'leisured' digital cultures – will form the focus for the remainder of the chapter.

When games go to school

We argue in Chapter 7 that schools and classrooms are particular moments in wider social relations which might be conceptualised as a dynamic 'assemblage' which connects a diverse range of locations, resources and practices. In Chapter 3 we argue that: 'from the "artefact" VirtualFishtank students construct the "instrument" gaming software'. Both of these chapters suggest that we need to pay detailed attention to the moments in which out-of-school and in-school cultures, practices and expectations come into contact.

In Chapter 3, we suggest that the lesson with the VirtualFishtank 'failed' because at the heart of the lesson were two different ideas of the activity: where the children saw the software as a 'game', the teacher saw it as a 'science learning tool'. This difference provides a powerful and interesting example of what happens when children's informal digital cultures come into contact with formal education. In order to probe more deeply into this type of interaction and into this example in particular, we want to draw on the conception of the classroom as an element in a wider assemblage which makes up young people's learning and is connected with wider sets of resources, discourses and practices (discussed in depth in Chapter 7). As such, we will attempt to explore how the 'process of instrumentation' (see

Chapter 3) mobilises connections to different contexts, cultures and networks of activity outside the classroom walls.[7] (It will help readers to refer back to the more detailed transcript of the Virtual Fishtank lesson in Chapter 3 on pages 50 to 55).

Let's return to the point where the teacher introduces the software in the VirtualFishtank lesson.

Teacher It's not real, it's *like a simulation*. So it's a bit of a . . .
James   It's *a bit like a game*
Teacher It *is a bit like a game*

At the heart of this exchange, and the activities and events which followed, is the question of what 'a bit like a game' *means* to the children and teacher in that setting.

For the teacher, constructing the activity as a game is a means of engaging the students' interest in the activity and relies also on an understanding of games as, themselves, similar to simulations, tools which are sanctioned and familiar in science classrooms. For the students, however, the naming of the activity as 'like a game' mobilises a set of expectations and cultural practices intimately associated with their home and leisure experiences. What is important here is that teachers and students bring with them very different sets of experiences of gaming to the classroom. A recent study, for example, highlighted the difference in teacher and student participation in games practices – with over 80 per cent of young people reporting at least fortnightly games play compared with less than 25 per cent of teachers ever having played games.[8] As such, for teacher and students, the 'game' is connected with very different cultural practices; it implies association with *different* assemblages (in the terms defined in Chapter 7).

For the teacher, the naming of the software as 'a bit like a game' associates it with principles of simulation and practices of prediction, recording, hypothesising and reflection. Simulation is an important element of scientific practice as a means of testing conjecture and building theory (the practice which the teacher expected the students to participate in in this lesson).

In contrast, for the students, the naming of the software as 'game' is associated primarily with informal play practices outside school using mainstream commercial computer games. As such, it is associated with immersion, rapid feedback, complex interactive environments, imaginative identification with the avatar and playful 'roaming' behaviour.[9] The exchange above, and the ambiguity of what 'a bit like a game' means, brings into play two radically different networks of meaning, resources and practices.

If we examine the conversations in the classroom around the software we can see how teacher and children articulate the practice they are engaged with in the classroom with these two different cultural activities.

The children, for example, immediately mobilise a language of leisured play, starting their observation with 'Ready steady go!' They begin to test the limits of the game; one girl, for example, wants to try to kill the fish quickly by not feeding it. They mobilise a language of competition with each other and 'against' the software: 'Don't die! We gotta beat people!' Another child begins to click around on different elements of the interface, searching for interactivity not immediately associated with 'the mission' (a key element of many mainstream games being the ability to interact with characters/ elements not immediately tied to the overarching game's narrative). We see the children identifying themselves with 'my fish' on screen. The children are impressed with the fish's 'skills' in avoiding the shark. They play with being in control and losing control of the avatar (one of the pleasures of games play being the ambiguous nature of identification with the avatar on the screen). One of the boys plays with the mechanics of control – challenging the mouse control by another girl and looking to use the keyboard.

In contrast, we can observe the teacher interacting with the children in ways which attempt to reconstruct the 'game' as simulation. She ties the game to the cultural practices of the scientific domain:

Teacher What conditions are you making sure your fish has got? [. . .] cos if you need to then recreate it then you know exactly what you've done [. . .] [. . .] you're not recording, first of all, what was your prediction – what did you think was going to make a good fish [. . .] I want you to jot down some of your learning that was happening.

While the students, following the logic of domestic games play, are moving immediately into immersion – expecting to learn through rapid feedback and trial and error from the 'game' – the teacher is asking the students to step back, to reflect upon their decisions prior to starting activity, to carefully observe and document the implications of their choices – to learn from practices of scientific method.

In order to understand what is happening in this classroom, then, it is not enough to consider the world of the school. Instead, we need to understand the sorts of multiple communities and cultures that are mobilised and referenced in this situation. This example makes explicit the idea discussed in Chapter 7, namely that moments in school are situated within wider social relations, and are also particular configurations of social relations. Viewing the classroom as an assemblage opens up the possibilities for seeing it as dynamic and open to changes, both small and large.

This lesson, however, needs also to be seen in a much wider context than a discussion of the relative models of learning that science simulation and gaming bring into play.[10] What is of particular interest, for example, is the relationship between teachers, children and software in the lesson and the way in which an ambiguity is introduced into the classroom through the construction of the software as both 'educational' and 'entertaining' (see also Chapter 2). This ambiguity, we would suggest, goes to the heart of current ambiguities in the relationship between adults and young people, between formal schooling and informal knowledge, in the context of digital technologies today.

Since the emergence of the home computer we have witnessed a battle in homes over whether this new technology should be understood as a leisure or an educational/work device – whether it should be seen as being for 'games' or for 'learning'. The last 15 years have seen local skirmishes over these competing interpretations in the home between parents and children[11] and increasing anxieties at policy level over children's use of computers for games rather than educational purposes: 'the divide which sees some playing games while others are developing the skills that will equip them for the twenty-first century'.[12]

By 1992, however, researchers were already suggesting that the home computer had, for the large majority of households, been irrevocably identified with games play.[13] By 1998, researchers were suggesting that it was through games play that young people came to be competent actors in the digital world.[14] By 2001, we witnessed the emergence of ideas of children as 'digital natives', able to act fluently and ably in the 'information age', a fluency developed through their early and confident engagement with computer games.[15] Computer games play, it was suggested, was equipping children as more competent navigators of the information society than the adults who attempted to teach them. At the same time, we also witnessed the construction of a new conflict between home and school digital cultures. Tom Bentley, influential director of the think tank Demos, for example, argued in 1998 that:

> Young people have a far wider range of distractions and alternative pursuits on offer than ever before. The growth of multi and mass media, including computer games, pop music and the Internet, as well as the proliferation of retail and consumer goods, and leisure activities and facilities, means that young people choose between an increasingly wide range of alternatives. [. . .] Information is accessible in ways which older people are still struggling to get to grips with, while the young, more often than not, take to them like ducks to water. Educational institutions must compete with a dazzling array of alternative information, distractions and sources of motivation and example. [. . .] Whether we think that teachers ought, in principle, to have to compete with such influences on their students' attention, they already do.[16]

The home and the school, in this context, are seen as in competition for students' attention and engagement and, at the heart of this competition, lies students' engagement with the 'dazzling array' of digital technologies, including computer games. This sort of opposition – familiar not only from policy discourse but from newspaper articles and family conversation – in turn produces a new role for children in relation to education: it begins to imply that children should be understood as consumers and, reciprocally, that teachers and educators have to play a role in 'selling' education to children. This idea of childhood is, in more recent years, appropriated as justification for a shift towards a new model of education in which the child's 'choice' is central to new educational agendas. Consider, for example, the association made by Will Hutton between games play and personalisation of education:

> On my son's Xbox we choose each member of the football teams we pit against each other. I inevitably lose. 'You can have Beckham, Lampard and Gerrard' goes his challenge. 'And I'll be Northern Ireland with 10 men'. This is personalisation à la mode, even if the result never changes. The Xbox generation is growing up in a world which it expects to shape to meet its particular needs. From the iPod playlist to the blogging sites, it's all about

choice. [. . .] These phenomena – personalisation and plural, diversified production – are the unavoidable realities of modern business life [. . .].[17]

What we have seen in recent years, then, is an articulation of ideas of children and young people as games players, children and young people as consumers and the demand on schools to transform in response to technological and societal change. This is a process which not only transforms ideas of children's relationship with formal education but which also transforms the identity of the teacher. As Bauman argues, we may see the emergence of:

> . . . a gradual yet relentless replacement of the orthodox teacher-student relationship with the supplier-client, or shopping-mall-shopper patter. This is the social setting in which today's educators find themselves bound to operate. Their responses and the effectiveness of the strategies deployed to promote them, are likely to remain a paramount concern of pedagogical science for a long time to come.[18]

In this context, then, teacher identity is constructed in relation to student identity as one of salesman to consumer; and in the school setting, digital technologies are increasingly harnessed to support this identity. Computers, the Internet and mobile devices are mobilised in support of the call to 'sell' education to the child-consumer; software packages are appropriated because they are seen to be sufficiently ambiguous to be able to meet both the teachers' educational objectives and because they are potentially 'sellable' to the child as engaging and attractive.

This model is, to some extent, visible in the interactions in the 'VirtualFishtank Classroom' in which the teacher attempts to engage the students with apparently 'undesirable' formal education through a 'desirable' language of play. The teacher is, in Bauman's terms, attempting to 'sell' the science by mobilising the potential link between the VirtualFishtank software and children's digital leisure cultures. Indeed, this to some extent echoes the teachers' own analysis of the 'failure' of the lesson.[19]

One response to this 'failure' is to see the attempt to engage with children's interests and enjoyment as a mistake, to recoil from this first step toward dialogue between in- and out-of-school experiences and to reinforce the boundaries between 'schooled' and 'informal' practices. Indeed, the earlier analysis by teachers and researchers suggests this interpretation of the events in the classroom is dominant:

Teacher Also I allowed the fun and gaming element of the lesson to become the main factor and lost the learning objectives. The science element became secondary.

This analysis reproduces the opposition between school cultures and informal cultures. It suggests that they are in competition with each other, and that one can only be acknowledged when mobilised in order to entice children to engage with the other. Where the out-of-school culture is not valued in its own right, where it is understood in subordinate relation to the official, valued knowledge of the classroom, the implications of this lesson are clear: we should move away from attempting to engage with children's out-of-school cultures. A return to understanding scientific cultures and practices and enculturing children into these discourses should remain central.

However, this lesson could be interpreted in a different way. We could argue, instead, that the failure of the lesson resulted from a failure to fully understand children's expectations of gaming cultures, and the higher demands that children would consequently have for interactivity, rapid feedback and responsive environments as soon as this association was mobilised in the classroom. The problem was *not* that the classroom 'dumbed down' to meet children's informal cultures; was *not* that engaging with children's enjoyment and pleasure was a mistake, but that the sorts of interactions on offer simply did not match the challenging interactions that children were familiar with from their out-of-school settings.

This is not, in any way, a criticism of the teacher in the classroom. It is an indication of the extent to which even such micro-interactions as these are evidence of the uncertainties over 'what to do about children's digital cultures' in the wider context of relationships between formal schooling and informal learning. These micro-interactions are the sites where not only teaching approaches are negotiated and transformed, but in which the multiple cultures connected to each classroom are negotiated, debated and changed. Specifically, in this instance, we saw the opening-up of school and scientific discourses to discourses of play, experimentation and fun, a process which is bound to lead to change of some sort. As Fairclough argues:

Recontextualising the new discourse is both opening an organisation (and its individual members) up to a process of colonisation (and its individual effects) and, insofar as the new discourse is transformed, in locally specific ways by being worked into a distinctive relation with other (existing) discourses – a process of appropriation.

(Fairclough 2004, p. 232)

Colliding or concurring cultures

What remains to be seen, however, is where we go next in classroom practice on the basis of these observations. Our suggestion would be that the next step is not to reinforce the boundaries between home and school, and to exclude all attempts to engage with young people's digital cultures. Instead, we would suggest that the change needs to be around the relationship between teacher and child. After all, the appeal to the child as consumer – evidenced in the demand to 'engage' children through using 'their' technology – can serve as a shortcut to effectively ignoring the complexity, richness and value of children's out-of-school cultures. The diversity of these cultures and the range of experiences they may offer to children are evidenced in the three vignettes we talked about earlier. This diversity, however, is routinely ignored and homogenised in the construction of children's digital cultures as purely 'fun and games'. The more successful approach to drawing on children's out-of-school experiences, therefore, might not be the assumption that 'all children like games', but in the development of an attentiveness to the diverse and surprising resources and knowledge that children might bring into the classroom.

There are examples from the InterActive project in which the out-of-school and in-school cultures were articulated in a productive way. For example, in the case study discussed in Chapter 2, students in Dan Sutch's primary school were working in school on an investigation of the spelling of 'hard words' in English. For homework they were asked to investigate the possible spellings associated with words that end in the phoneme /e/. In class Joe had made the conjecture, 'The spelling strand ey only makes the sound /e/ when at the end of a word'. For homework Joe used the search engine Ask Jeeves[20] to find words with the 'ey' letter strand at the end of the word, in the middle of the word and at the beginning of the word. He had not learned to use Ask Jeeves in school, he had learned how to do this at home through interacting with family or friends. What is interesting and important about this example is that when Joe brought his knowledge into the school the next day the teacher, Dan, valued Joe's expertise and supported him to share these techniques and what he knew with the whole class, using it as a basis for a very productive discussion (in the end Joe accepted that his conjecture was incorrect). This enabled both the teacher and the students to also learn from Joe about how to use Ask Jeeves.

Similarly, when Simon Mills was working with 8–9-year-old students on the interpretation of graphs and charts, using the spreadsheet Excel, Simon became aware that some students were bringing their previous knowledge of Word to their learning of spreadsheets in order to generate pie charts and bar charts. Interviews with students also revealed that at least one of them had previous experience of using spreadsheets at home, as the following interchange shows.

Int.   Do either of you use Excel at home?
       (*Alan shakes head*)
Ray   Sometimes. My dad uses it for his paper work.
Int.   And when you use it, what do you use it for?
Ray   Umm, he uses it, 'cos when he's got paper calculations and some are hard like for him, he puts it in Excel and then he circles it and then presses the equal button and it tells him what the sums are.
Int.   What do you use it for?
Ray   Maths homework.
Alan   Cheat!

Although Simon did not know that one of the students in his class had previously used spreadsheets at home, he approaches his teaching in such a way that he is always attentive and open to whatever students bring to the lesson and this adds benefit to the whole process of knowledge production in the classroom. The view expressed by the student, Alan, that it is 'cheating' to use a spreadsheet for homework seems to reflect a view that homework must be carried out by an individual alone (that is, person-solo). This view contrasts with our argument throughout the book that young people should become resourceful learners, that is learners who draw on people and technologies, learners who know how to become a person-plus.

Summary and conclusions

What does this evidence about out-of-school uses of ICT suggest for productive use of ICT in school? It tells us something different from the suggestion that we either turn away from engaging with students out-of-school cultures or reduce the pedagogic relationship to one of salesman and consumer. Instead, it suggests the potential for a hybrid approach: the mobilisation of all elements in the assemblage to support learning. It suggests that if we can find ways of noticing, valuing and drawing on both 'official' and 'unofficial' knowledges, and building lines of communication between them, we might create valuable learning experiences. This is not about the abnegation of responsibility by the adult: the reduction of teaching to 'selling' and enticing children. It is about a more evolved stage of engagement with children's and young people's experiences in which we view them as able to bring resources and knowledge into the classroom. The Virtual Fishtank example, after all, shows what happens when we do not fully acknowledge the strength of expectations and practices that are associated with different forms of learning outside school.

A key question for the future might therefore be not 'how do we use young people's out-of-school learning to support our existing goals', but 'how do we draw on the resources children and young people bring into the school setting to enable them to add to and extend the aspirations we have for them'.

At a time when we are seeking to understand how to encourage young people to develop responsibility for their own learning, at a time when there are increasing concerns about a predetermined curriculum incapable of responding to local concerns or the changing nature of knowledge, at a time when we are keen to understand how to support young people to act as active participants in society, maybe it is time to consider young people's out-of-school knowledges and cultures not as 'distractions' from the main business of schooling, nor as consisting of one general mass of commercialised pleasure, but as rich, complex, diverse and powerful sources for young people's learning and an important place to start in designing education for the twenty-first century.

Notes

1 See Bernstein (1990); Barton and Hamilton (1998); Heath (1983 and 1986).
2 This section is based on a mix of survey and interview data. For further information on this data see the Methodological Appendix.

3 For more information about Web 2.0 practice see Owen *et al.* (2006), Social Software and Learning, Bristol: Futurelab.

4 The analysis refers to children coming from areas with the highest/middle-high/middle-low/or lowest socio-economic profiles. This is not to say that the individual child is necessarily from the highest/lowest socio-economic background, but that the area in which they live (to a detail of 14 houses) can be characterised along those lines.

5 These patterns of ownership of technologies among families with school-age children are replicated in the UK population as a whole still today. ONS data suggests that income and education level are significant in predicting ownership of home computer and levels of Internet access. This data also suggests that there may be important geographical differences to consider as well – with lower levels of access in rural areas, and with access declining in the north, Scotland and Wales compared with the South of England. See Selwyn and Facer (2007).

6 See, for example, Colley and Comber (2003).

7 This discussion is informed by sensitising concepts from Norman Fairclough's discourse analysis, which theorises social change as emerging through social practices acting as dynamic sites of negotiation, appropriation and colonisation. This approach is particularly pertinent when considering how the different cultures and practices of home and school use of ICT encounter and are transformed by each other. See Fairclough, N (2004).

8 See Sandford, Ulicsak, Facer and Rudd (2006).

9 See, for example, Gee (2003) and Sandford (2005).

10 Angela McFarlane, for example, has written widely on the challenges and tensions involved in the introduction of simulation and/or gaming software into the science classroom, for example McFarlane, Sparrowhawk and Heald (2002) Report on the educational use of games, for TEEM/DfES.

11 See, for example, Facer *et al.* (2003); Holloway and Valentine (2003).

12 David Blunkett, quoted in McGavin, H. (1997).

13 Haddon (1992).

14 Downes (1998).

15 Prensky (2001).

16 Bentley (1998).

17 Hutton (2006).

18 Bauman (2005).

19 For an insightful account of the lesson by the teacher, see Armstrong and Curran (2006).

20 www.ask.co.uk.

Part 3

What are the overall implications?

The final part of the book raises theoretical issues of relevance to policy makers and practitioners and summarises the overall implications of the research from the InterActive Education project.

We start by recounting the history of computers and schooling, discussing how this has always challenged the subject-based curriculum being used to imagine educational futures.

We then move to highlighting the key theoretical ideas that have been introduced throughout the book and explain why these theories are valuable to help us see things differently, to understand what is happening when ICTs are improving learning and also when they are not improving learning.

In the final chapter we discuss the importance of finding a new language to talk about teaching and learning with ICT and reintroduce some of the terms that we have used throughout the book. We argue that transformations in learning will only come about when teachers, researchers, policy makers and students are all given a prominent role in contributing to what we know about technology-mediated learning.

Chapter 9

Breaking into the curriculum

The impact of information technology on schooling

This chapter highlights the complex relationships between ICT and 'subject cultures'. The school system in England and Wales has been characterised as dominated by a strongly classified curriculum based around school subjects. Since the mid-1960s an increased number of commentators have argued for alternative forms of 'integrated' curriculum. ICT has played an important part in this challenge to the subject-based curriculum, because it is seen as signalling a different view of knowledge. At the same time, one of the main routes into schools of ICT has been through its adoption and integration within existing school subjects (the other route has been the ICT component of the National Curriculum). When considering the role of ICT in the curriculum there is a tendency to talk as if it has an agency and power of its own – it is as if the technology is simply there waiting to be picked up. But of course ICT is used as a resource by specific groups who have an interest in promoting its use. This chapter aims to:

- consider the ways in which ICT is located in schools in a wider social and cultural context;
- consider how it has played its part in the 'subject culture' of school geography;
- discuss more recent arguments about the way ICT offers challenges to the curriculum.

ICT and society

When I started teaching geography in 1988, the 'information revolution' that was taking place in schools had not reached me. Though the first affordable PC hit the UK market in 1976, I don't recall seeing a single computer during my time at a comprehensive school on

* This chapter was authored by John Morgan.

the outskirts of Bristol. During my undergraduate years' studies we did some work with a statistical package using the 'Computer Science Lab', but I wrote my final year dissertation by hand and had it 'typed up' by a person who advertised her skills to students in the local paper. My PGCE[1] course was little different, and though reference was made to the potential of computers for geography teaching, we received no explicit training, and I don't recall the schools I trained in having any computers.

Things changed when, in 1988, I moved to London to take up my first teaching post. Immediately I was sent on a variety of training courses (many of them run by the local authority) designed to develop my information-handling skills (word processing, spreadsheets) as well as introducing me to specific humanities packages such as the HiT (Humanities into Technology) and 'Domesday' projects.[2] At this time there was a great push to get industry and schools working together. No doubt most teachers who have worked in schools over the past twenty or so years have their own recollections of these times, and no doubt things have changed. By the time I joined the University of Bristol to teach on the PGCE course in 2000, Information and Communications Technology (ICT) as it was now designated, was a central part of my working life. As and when required, I had learned to use Microsoft Office, routinely used e-mail to maintain professional networks, and was beginning to use Internet as a research tool. At Bristol, the increasing availability of electronic journals and online databases has transformed my research practices. In addition, teacher training courses now require significant elements of ICT training and, though the picture is varied, most of the school geography departments I visited during the mid-2000s incorporated elements of geography-specific ICT in their schemes of work.

It would be possible to interpret this account of ICT in terms of gradual progress and development. If we remember that the first affordable PC only became available in 1976, there has indeed been considerable progress in the 'technologisation' of the school curriculum. The adoption of ICT within schools may not be as fast as some people wanted or imagined; there remain problems of access and training, and a small number of teachers are resistant, but these are temporary 'barriers' to adoption that will eventually be overcome.

However, I want to suggest a different reading of this account, one that seeks to put my 'personal account' of ICT in a broader historical and cultural context. The decision to write in a personal voice is deliberate; I was not directly involved in the InterActive project (though the involvement of colleagues allowed me to follow its progress). I also do not claim to be telling *the* history of ICT and curriculum – this is one particular narrative, and, as I'll try to illustrate, the geographical and social location of this story matters a good deal.

As I noted above, the introduction and spread of ICT in schools in the UK has taken place in the past thirty years, and an important part of that process has been a discussion of what happens to the school curriculum as a result of the introduction of ICT. Of course, to mention the word curriculum immediately entangles us with questions of culture, since, as Raymond Williams (1961) argued in his chapter on education in *The Long Revolution*, curriculum is a selection from the culture, and, since the industrial revolution and the development of state education, different educational ideologies were struggling to gain ascendancy. One of the dominant themes in the forty-odd years since *The Long Revolution* was published has been the rise to prominence of the idea that schooling should be the place where young people are prepared for the 'world of work'. To some extent this has ousted the 'liberal humanist' view of education, but it is more complicated than that. However, there can be little doubt of the pre-eminence of the view that schools should provide students with the skills and attitudes to take their place in a competitive employment market. These were played out in different ways at different times and places, as the following 'personal histories' suggest.

I started secondary school in September 1977, at a mixed comprehensive school about thirteen miles north of Bristol. The town – Yate – was relatively new, having expanded from the early 1960s as housing developers built family homes for young couples seeking to live away from Bristol. The fathers of most of the children I went to school with made the daily commute to Bristol, while the mothers either stayed at home to look after the children or worked locally in the local shops or in the factories that assembled household goods. The development of Yate was based on the relative stability of the post-war economy. Employment was steady and this allowed for the expansion of credit (which enabled people like my parents to have a mortgage) and the development of a consumer culture. I think as children we took on an optimistic world-view. We assumed we'd all get work of some kind, and for the boys an 'apprenticeship' at Rolls Royce or British Aerospace was the glittering prize. The large majority of students in my year left school at 16.

By the end of the 1970s the picture wasn't looking so rosy. Throughout the 1970s there was a loss of manufacturing jobs and unemployment was increasing. There was a sense in school of some dark times ahead. As teenagers we were dimly aware of the troubles ahead which only became clearer to me in my later studies when I realised the extent of the economic recession between 1979–81.[3] In school, this was brought home by the shock of the riots that took place in St Pauls in April 1981.[4] I recall sitting listening to an English teacher telling us that she lived in the area and informing us of some of the context for these events. It is worth remembering some of the basic educational 'facts' of this period. The passage from primary school to secondary school to university in England was followed by less than 10 per cent of the population, and approximately 50 per cent of young people in 1980 left school without at least one O level.[5] Strikingly, 67 per cent of students left secondary school at the minimum leaving age of 16 and over 50 per cent had become almost permanent truants in their final year. This system may have worked well enough in the 1950s and 1960s when there was an abundance of jobs in a booming economy, but in the context of a declining manufacturing sector the spectre of high levels of youth unemployment led to calls for radical change in the education system.

Looking back now, I understand that my experience of schooling took place in the context of a dramatic shift in the economic and political structure of the UK. In October 1976 the prime minister James Callaghan[6] made a speech at Ruskin College that launched the so-called 'Great Debate' in education. Callaghan focused on the extent to which schools were producing students with the skills needed in the economy. 'I am concerned,' he said, 'to find complaints from industry that new recruits from schools sometimes do not have the basic tools to do the job that is required'. He went on to stress his concern about the lack of school-industry cooperation, the anti-technological bias in the school curriculum, and the standards of numeracy and literacy among school leavers.

I didn't think too much about schools again until I started training to be a geography teacher in 1987. Once more, the place is important. I was working in Swansea, a town adjacent to the South Wales coalfield, that was suffering from the impact of economic recession and in particular closures in the mining and steel industries. There was much talk of the potential effects of the new hi-tech industries (Sony had opened a factory at Briton Ferry), but for the most part this was not yet realised and there were concerns that the jobs created would be low-paid and relatively unskilled. The focus of all this work was about employment. The teachers I met were committed and pragmatic. There was a sense that people were talking about a new economy and recognised that the old industries and skills were no longer enough, but the tools and technologies that would enable this transformation had not yet arrived. There was also a sense that an older gender division of labour was being broken down, represented symbolically in the headteacher's introduction of a mixed staffroom, although male teachers and female teachers still largely chose to sit apart.

This sense of change was brought home to me when I took up my first post as a teacher in a school in the London Borough of Sutton. This was a selective single-sex school, located in an affluent part of the Home Counties, which drew many students from what was sardonically called the 'Deep South' of Croydon. These were the children of the professional middle classes. Looking back, I realise that when I joined the school it was in the middle of a struggle over the nature of the curriculum: a struggle in which IT was enlisted. There was a group of teachers (loosely represented by one of the deputy heads) who sought to modernise what they saw as an outdated and traditional curriculum. In order to do this, they looked to models of the vocational curriculum and drew heavily on the TVEI[7] model which allowed access to funds within the local authority. An important part of this was IT, and the computers that came into the school were largely used to support this curriculum. At the same time, there were those who argued for the continued salience of the traditional curriculum, and although IT was increasingly used in these classrooms there was a paucity of resources. There was an additional factor at work in this curriculum debate – that of gender. This was a girls' school that had a tradition of high achievement, with many students going on to study traditional subjects at 'good' universities. The issue about the curriculum was about the extent to which the traditional subjects provided the skills that young women would need to take their place in the new economy where there were real opportunities for women. IT was essential to this new economy and the school needed to modernise (ie. vocationalise) its curriculum to meet these needs.

So, in the late-1980s, I worked in two schools where IT was at the heart of discussions about the nature of the curriculum. Information technology (IT) seemed to have tremendous power to mobilise people and resources. It seemed to symbolise the division between modernisation and tradition at a time when questions about the future were being discussed. In her essay 'The old and new worlds of information technology in Britain', Maureen McNeill discusses how, in the 1980s, IT played a central part in attempts to construct 'a new social consensus'.[8] In the context of public concern about unprecedented levels of unemployment (particularly acute among young people) and regional imbalance, IT played the role of offering a bright new vision for the economy. Whereas in the 1970s, technology had become associated with industrial decline and job losses, by the early 1980s, a new term – information technology – came into circulation, which put a different spin on things. Information Technology sounded 'cleaner, more optimistic, more attractive'. McNeill argues that this shift was solidified in the recession of 1979–83 where, increasingly, unemployment was associated with lack of competitiveness and the new IT could be embraced as a way out of the recession. The positive associations of IT were signified by terms such as the 'sunrise' industries and the 'sunbelt' (the area of the country in which the high-skill end of IT industries was concentrated). Particular places became associated with these industries – high-tech places such as Cambridge and the south-east:

> ... the shift from microelectronics to information technology opened the way for a linguistic repertoire which highlighted a benign image of this technological revolution – 'sunrise industries' and 'sunbelts', 'cottage industries' and 'teleworkers' ... The benevolent imagery encouraged the belief that this would be a technological revolution without victims or losers or social costs.
>
> (McNeil 1991, p. 123)

McNeill's argument makes it clear that information technology is never a matter of pure hardware. It is linked in complex ways to ideas about the national interest (we need IT to develop skills needed to compete), of visions of the future (e.g. cleaner, ecologically sustainable industries) and of specific social relations (e.g. a fairer balance between men and women). In the two schools I have described in this section, all of these meanings were variously attached to IT. The important thing to take from this discussion is that an understanding of (what are now called) ICT's role in the curriculum requires us to think about the wider social and cultural context of schooling. In the remainder of this chapter, I will suggest how this insight applies to more recent debates about subjects and curriculum change in which the InterActive project was involved.

ICT and school geography

The previous section suggested how debates about ICT in education are never merely debates about technology but are wrapped up in complex issues related to class, gender and social change. Arguments about the role of ICT in the school curriculum are ultimately arguments about the type of society we imagine we are living in and would like to live in, in the future. Although it may sometimes feel static, the school curriculum does change; subjects come and go, and even those subjects that endure are subject to change. There are important arguments about the nature of change within school subjects, but the position taken here follows Goodson (1991, p. 236) who stresses that: 'Subjects are not monolithic entities but shifting amalgamations of sub-groups and traditions. These groups within the subject influence and change boundaries and priorities.'

Geography's history as a subject is one of aspiration. It has been characterised by anxiety about the definition of the subject and its relationship to others such as social studies, environmental studies and, more recently, citizenship. One of the problems geography faced as a school subject was its 'expansiveness': its tendency to take on ever-new subject matter with the result that the boundaries of the discipline were ill-defined. From the late-1960s onwards, one solution to this was to hand over power to geographers in universities, who were embarked on the task of transforming a descriptive and particularistic discipline into a predictive and generalisable 'science' based on mathematics and models from the physical sciences. Through its newly acquired methodological rigour, geography's position as a real science could be assured. The new geography stressed the scientific and theoretical side of the subject. Goodson argued that this was a case of school geography teachers seeking to improve the status of the subject in schools, command greater resources and secure better career prospects for teachers.[9]

The attempts by some in the subject to make geography more 'scientific' were quite successful in the 1970s and early 1980s. The subject moved away from a descriptive and regional approach towards the production of generalisations and systematic studies. Academic geography had gained status by applying itself to the 'technics and mechanics of urban, regional and environmental management'[10] and geographers used opportunities for curriculum reform to tighten the connections between school geography and university geography. New technologies played an important part in this process of legitimation and geography educators have been at the forefront of moves to 'modernise' the curriculum. This is in line with Goodson's argument that by promoting the subject as a science, geography teachers could promote themselves. This project was more convincing if geography could lay claim to the new technologies finding their way into schools.[11] The introduction of ICT in geography teaching has been wrapped up with a particular form of geographical knowledge, which is the geographer as problem-solver. The following statement is indicative of the types of claims made for ICT within school geography:

> Throughout a huge range of human activity, including commerce and the public sector, ICT is playing an increasing role in decision-making, ranging from locating a road or superstore to the identification of flood or weather hazards. ICT can better enable decision-making as it is possible to take into consideration a wider range of variables, as well as supporting the monitoring of natural hazards and systems to provide greater warning and providing the opportunity to take action to reduce impact. As a result, ICT can provide better and faster tools for decision-making. These changes have an impact in two ways; first, they change the geography we teach, but second, they change the decision-making skills and processes that we should be developing in children. The key issue in this area is how can the subject community ensure that the geography of formal curricula that is taught and examined keep up with these changes?[12]

This passage suggests how ICT has been incorporated in school geography in ways that confirm the status of geography as an empirical and 'problem-solving' science. The examples used to illustrate ICT opportunities to support geography are revealing. They include: 'use a presentation package to combine various types of information to argue the case to the class on the new superstore location'; 'investigate the changing traffic pressure on a locality using a mapping package to present flow rates over time from a series of observations of major roads'. Although these activities are perfectly valid, they reflect a particular view or interpretation of what constitutes geographical knowledge – one which 'accepts the basic structure of society, and seeks to manipulate certain aspects of its superstructure only . . . It is involved in patching-up the future, rather than creating it'.[13]

   This section has shown that ICT is firmly ingrained in the subject culture of school geography. It is important to realise that its use is not necessarily linked to any learning benefits for students – indeed, it is possible to argue that the use of ICT in school geography has prevented the development of alternative forms of geographical education based on philosophies derived from humanism and critical theory.[14] As Gregory (1981) pointed out at the height of school geography's 'dash for ICT':

> . . . the appearance of geographers capable of calling on computer-assisted techniques to solve particular problems in the subject may have dealt most satisfying body-blows to the sneerers who can be found in most common rooms, but it certainly did not guarantee that the questions which they were asking were any more meaningful or that the answers to them were any more incisive.
>
> (p. 124)

Future subjects/geographies

In the previous section, I described how, within school geography, ICT was used to support and legitimise a dominant strand within the subject culture. Reading the work of those who argue most strongly for ICT in schools, one senses their frustration that things are not moving fast enough and at the obstacles to the incorporation of ICT. However, there is also a body of writing that makes grand claims for the significance of ICT. These include:

- ICT has the potential to challenge the basis of a fragmented, subject-based curriculum;
- ICT allows students to take greater responsibility for the content and direction of learning;
- ICT suggests that the teacher's role is less as the transmitter of skills and knowledge and more as the co-constructor of knowledge;
- ICT allows for a focus on learning (learning skills and orientations) as opposed to knowledge acquisition.[15]

There are a number of recent examples of this type of argument, which come from both academic and policy sources. Typical of this type of analysis is a recently published paper by Futurelab[16] which explores the potential of recent developments in ICT such as blogs, wikis and bookmarking to support the 'new' types of education that are emerging. The background to this is that 'there is a shift in emphasis at policy level from a focus on the content of what children should be taught, to a concern with how best to enable children to learn'. This shift is based on the 'recognition that we live in a fast-changing world in which the young people leaving school today cannot expect to remain in the same career or even the same sphere of work for the whole of their lives' (p. 8). These new approaches are 'premised on the notion that we are moving into a new form of information society which is characterised by changes in the use of technologies and the forms of knowledge and learning that are valued in society' (p. 30). It is worth quoting at length how these changes are imagined:

> Firstly, there is a shift in the nature of knowledge and how know-ledge is created and organised, and secondly there is a cultural shift growing from the use of information and communications technologies, the so-called cyberculture. These two strands mirror the twin concerns of those arguing for a shift in educational processes to align with the perceived demands of a knowledge economy: namely the concern with developing young people able to act as innovators and creators of knowledge; and the concern with developing young people able to operate effectively within digital and information-rich environments.
>
> (p. 30)

This statement is indicative of a type of approach to technology and education that celebrates the potential of ICT to transform existing social relations in schools and classrooms. The authors argue that these developments have radical implications for the school curriculum. They state that for most of the twentieth century there was a 'remarkable' consensus about what it meant to be educated, a consensus eventually enshrined in law in the National Curriculum.[17] This resulted in a 'strongly defined' curriculum where the boundaries between subjects are clearly maintained and patrolled:

> Today, however, as we witness the demand for new ways of working, living and learning outside school, and as we see the emergence of new forms of interaction mediated by digital technologies, we need to ask whether what we teach and the way we teach in schools is still a sound basis for our current common culture, or has the world moved on?
>
> (Schostak 1988, p. 86)

The place of school subjects within this vision of education is downplayed in these accounts. If we assume for a moment that the current generation of school students are not busy writing blogs with a geographical content, contributing their views about burning issues to wikis, and using Web 2.0 to create collaborative maps, it is interesting to think about what a geographical experience based on these ideas might look like. An example of this new type of 'literacy practice' is the Urban Tapestries project[18] run by Probiscus, a group of artists, technologists and educators based in London. The Urban Tapestries project allows users to walk through the city and, using a PDA-application,[19] record their impressions of specific places in text, sound and digital photos. As they move around they can also access the words, sounds and pictures created by others at that location. The idea is that users can create their own experiences of places. This might take the form of a treasure hunt or a trail, creating a thread of local resources (specialist shops) as places to learn new things. The test area was Bloomsbury, an area of central London, and testers used PDAs with a base map with no directions, points of interest or street names; it was up to the participants to go outside and 'write their city' by marking the places they visited and sharing their stories and impressions through the network.

This seems to be the type of collaborative knowledge creation and sharing that is envisaged by those who extol the potential of Web 2.0. Indeed, it is the type of application that is becoming increasingly feasible. Those involved in the Urban Tapestries trials were engaged in a form of public authoring. They produced their own personal or idiosyncratic geographies with titles such as 'Arguments I had with my ex-husband', 'A day in the life of an urban knitter', and 'Chocolate with that', a fictional journey. The participants in the project reported that they were not concerned with whether the postings of public authors were factually accurate, but were concerned with how to deal with the issue of large amounts of content.

Probiscus argues that:

> As we move into a new century, new paradigms of communications are beginning to take hold. The range of sources of information have multiplied exponentially with the arrival of satellite communications and the Internet. No longer are we reliant on a single or limited number of sources that define our understanding and opinions, but we may gather information from a heterogeneous collection of places. Although much of it is the same,

we now have at our disposal an unprecedented ability to see from other perspectives, through different eyes.

(p. 4)

Here we have an example of ICT in which the experience of the individual is prioritised over any formal curriculum. There is no *formal* geography of the city to be taught here. However, I hesitate to use the term 'learning' here; where is the opportunity for distanced and disciplined reflection on the meanings made public? There is no doubt that the type of activity involved in urban tapestries represents a 'new literacy practice' (albeit a marginal one). However, its value as an educational experience is not clear, especially if it is claimed that it is this type of experience that renders the formal curriculum an 'irrelevance'.

The Probiscus example illustrates the importance of inquiring into the 'politics of knowledge' that surround the role of ICT in schools. Indeed, in all the examples used in this chapter, the question of the 'social imaginary' that underpins its use inevitably surfaces.

Summary and conclusions

By way of concluding this chapter I want to return to its title, 'Breaking into the curriculum: the impact of information technology on schooling'. This was the title of a collection of essays edited by John Schostak (1988). Schostak's work is motivated by the desire for people (including school students) to be freed from the shackles of control. He argues that school children are capable of serious critique and yet are prevented from contributing to any debate upon their schooling and are in the main denied access to the resources they need to fulfil their abilities.

Schostak wrote about the possible ways in which ICT could overcome this situation. He pointed out that technology is an open book; it has possibilities for enslavement or transformation. He was gravely concerned that it will be used to reinforce patterns of schooling which limit the imagination. For Schostak, schooling as a way of canalising thoughts, feelings and actions through prescribed courses and historically determined structures sets limits to the exercise of imagination and self-expression and directs attention and energy less towards the possible than the given. Schooling has historically been associated with social control and socialisation and, through this, reproducing the social order. On the other hand, education becomes a way of 'breaking into the social order'. This idea has its parallel in computing – the idea of 'hacking' into a system. Hacking reveals the hidden rules and structures that shape experience. Schostak is interested in the extent to which ICT could allow those whose experience of school is negative to break into the curriculum. He suggests that ICT can foster networks or 'intelligence communities' which put people in touch with each other and which can foster critically reflective relationships.

> The end of education is to produce intelligence. Intelligence is not a finished product, nor a given quotient of ability. It is a process which depends upon community and communication. To form a community whose members are capable of critical reflection, expressing experience in a range of forms, imagining new ranges of possibility and forming courses of creative, constructive action is the end of education.
>
> (Schostak 1988, p. 256)

The examples provided in this chapter suggest that ICT is intimately bound up with questions of what Fred Inglis (2004) recently called 'the good society', and highlight the need for an understanding of school subjects and curriculum in their wider social and cultural setting. The aim of this chapter has been to prompt reflection on the social relations of education in which ICT is inserted. As stated at the start of this chapter, it is important to remember that moves to develop ICT in schools have occurred in the past thirty years, a period of major economic, social and cultural upheaval. This should remind us that ICT is being used to imagine new educational futures. What all the examples presented in this chapter have in common is that they use ICT as part of the argument about why schooling and the curriculum should change. Hopefully the type of analysis developed in this chapter can serve as a method for teachers and educators to reflect on the relationship of ICT to wider questions of education and social change.

Notes

1 PGCE stands for 'Post-Graduate Certificate of Education'. It is a one-year course that leads towards Qualified Teacher Status.
2 These were widely publicised 'flagship' projects for computer assisted learning in the 1980s.

3 This was a period in which many manufacturing jobs were lost and unemployment rose dramatically, reaching 3 million in 1982.

4 St Pauls is an area of Bristol characterised by a multi-ethnic population. The 'riots', which were the first of a series of disturbances in large English cities, were widely regarded as the expression of economic and social problems.

5 The Ordinary level (O level) examination for 15–16-year-olds in England was replaced in 1986 by the General Certificate of Secondary Education (GCSE).

6 See 'Towards a national debate', the Education speech given by Prime Minister James Callaghan at Ruskin College, Oxford in 1976. See http://education.guardian.co.uk/thegreatdebate/story/0,9860,574645,00.html.

7 Technical and Vocational Education Initiative.

8 McNeill (1991).

9 Here we are discussing how geography as a school subject has developed in Britain.

10 See Huckle (1985).

11 This argument is developed in more depth in Morgan and Tidmarsh (2004).

12 See Hassell and Smith (2002), p. 155.

13 See Johnston (1986), p. 11.

14 The diversity of philosophical approaches to geographical education and their relevance to teaching the subject are discussed in Morgan and Lambert (2005), Teaching School Subjects: Geography 11–19 (Routledge).

15 Moore (2006).

16 Futurelab (2006) Social software and learning, Bristol (available at www.futurelab.org.uk). Futurelab is a not-for-profit organisation that specialises in promoting and understanding educational innovation.

17 Schostak (1988).

18 See http://urbantapestries.net/.

19 Personal Digital Assistant. See Wikipedia entry http://en.wikipedia.org/wiki/Personal_digital_assistant.

Chapter 10*

Designs and theories for learning

> Humans are irrepressible theorizers. We can't help but note similarities among diverse experiences, to see relationships among events and to develop theories that explain these relationships (and that predict others).
>
> (Davis *et al.* 2000, p. 52)

Introduction

At the heart of the InterActive project was the idea of designing for learning with ICT, where design involves both out-of-the-classroom thinking, reflecting and planning and in-the-classroom teaching and learning. Video data captured the processes of teaching and learning and were central to the analysis, interpretation and reflection phases of the design process. The process of design was iterative, with the emphasis being on learning from the in-the-classroom teaching and learning with ICT in order to inform a new cycle of design and research.

One of the distinctive features of the project was the way in which teachers, teacher educators and researchers worked together to create a multi-layered professional learning and research community. At the centre were the meso-communities of the subject design teams who worked together to critically examine ways in which ICT could be incorporated into teaching and learning in the classroom. Within these meso-communities each teacher worked closely with a university colleague (the micro-community) to design and realise a subject design initiative (SDI). In this respect the micro-level and meso-level communities were intimately involved in the process of designing for learning, drawing on appropriate research literature and expertise. Whereas using and developing theory was a part of this process it was at the level of the macro-community that we were able to step

* This chapter was authored by Rosamund Sutherland and Susan Robertson.

back and work in a more explicit way on theorising the processes of teaching and learning with ICT.[1]

As the quote above highlights, humans are irrepressible theorisers; we all construct theories as we interact with the world. Much of this theorising is intuitive and implicit; we are often not aware of our theories and beliefs. However, the language we use to communicate with others often reflects these theories and beliefs. For example, if we talk about whether a person 'has' or 'does not have' a particular ability, the use of the word 'has' relates to a metaphor of possession. The use of this word implicitly links to a belief that people 'do have' certain abilities (for example intelligence) and that these are somehow an invariant property of the individual. Wertsch (1991) argues that such a metaphor of possession is often used by people involved in education. A metaphor of possession, he suggests, gets in the way of thinking about how tool-use shapes mental action. Wertsch puts forward the alternative perspective that differences between people can be better understood as how they 'recognise and create contexts by using various items from a tool kit' (p. 96).

An important aspect of research is making the theories we are using explicit and also developing new theories which emerge from engaging in empirical work. This book is a 'whole book', a coming together of the work of a large team. However, as we said in the preface, there are many voices speaking within the book and although these voices have converged throughout the work of the project (which includes the writing of this book), we have not attempted to resolve tensions inherent in some of the different perspectives of the various authors. At the core of the InterActive project were socio-cultural theories, but we recognised from the beginning that these might not be adequate to theorise learning with ICT in schools and in particular the political and sociological structures and constraints which impinge on learning institutions. For example, in Chapter 7 we take a more sociological perspective, looking from the outside towards the individual in order to explain the way in which society and schooling structure the possibilities for an individual. In contrast, in Chapter 3 we take a more cognitive perspective, looking from the individual outwards in order to explain the ways in which people appropriate the same ICT tool differently.

Within this chapter we revisit some of the theoretical ideas that have been introduced throughout the book in order to weave them together in a way that throws fresh light on improving learning with ICT.

Learning, tools and culture

At the core of the InterActive project was the idea that all human action is mediated by cultural, social and cognitive 'tools': that is, all human action involves interaction and dialogue with multiple 'knowledgeable others' and with multiple tools and technologies. The idea of interacting with 'knowledgeable others' incorporates both the more intentional teaching and learning situations which have been crafted by teachers and the more informal interactions that occur outside the classroom in schools and out-of-school. The idea of interacting with 'tools' is interpreted broadly to include interaction with material things, which can be both digital (calculator, music composition package, wikipedia) and non-digital (book, violin, ruler), interaction with semiotic systems and language (map, graph, language) and interaction with social and political structures (curriculum, assessment system).

Learning, then, is a dynamic process which involves interaction between a person and their social and physical environment (always located within a particular socio-cultural setting) and through which a person emerges changed in some way. In this sense learning is inextricably linked to a process of 'change', which can appear as capabilities to use 'tools' in order to think and produce things differently and capabilities to engage in discourses which relate to different knowledge worlds.

Culture is both present within the here and now when a person interacts with the world and is also embedded within the tools that a person chooses to use. In this respect all tools (and language) have been developed within a particular socio-cultural setting and carry with them the provenance of this culture. PowerPoint, for instance, was developed primarily for use within a business context and the preset templates can influence users towards business genres of presentation. However, we cannot predict in advance how a person will make sense of and use a particular ICT tool. In Chapter 3 we introduced the concept of 'instrument' as a way of paying attention to the idea that people creatively adapt tools for their own purpose, which may be very different from what the teacher or the designer of the tool intended. In this respect a tool can be transformed into several instruments according to the interpretation a student brings to the situation. So software that has been designed for educational purposes can be transformed into a computer 'game' (for example when simulation software for learning science is transformed into a computer game) and software that has been designed for the business world can be transformed into a tool for learning (for example the use of spreadsheets for learning algebra).[2] This is perhaps one of the most important and difficult messages of the book and one which it seems that policy makers find hard to learn. For example, merely making interactive whiteboards available in the classroom does not lead to more interactive and productive teaching and learning. Teachers have to learn how to use the interactive whiteboard as an instrument for effective teaching and learning. This involves taking risks and experimenting with new pedagogic practices.

Teaching and learning in schools is nested within multiple and overlapping cultures, which include subject knowledge, the school culture, national and international policy and young people's out-of-school cultures. In Chapter 7 we introduced the idea of 'assemblage' to enable us to think about the fluid, interconnected nature of classroom life in schools and to help us to view schools as being connected to and not separated from society. We also discussed the ways in which introducing ICTs into the classroom brings about a new form of epistemological diversity, which relates to different ways of accessing knowledge, different forms of knowledge and different ways of representing knowledge.

CASE STUDY 1
Learning data handling in the primary school

In order to illustrate the concepts discussed above we return again to the work of Simon Mills, who presented a personal account of his involvement in the InterActive project in Chapter 1. Working with his University 'research' partner (the micro-community) Simon developed an SDI for 8–9-year-old students to learn about handling data. Simon's class can be viewed as an assemblage, a particular set of linkages that form, like a constellation around the classroom, but which extend outward to a range of locations and with a range of effects on the learner, the teacher, the classroom and the school.

Simon's SDI was situated within the influence of the policy initiative of the Numeracy and Literacy Strategies in England and

Wales.[3] In this respect he was working within a framework that consists broadly of objective-led teaching with a starter activity, individual/group work, extension and final plenary. This structured episodic approach contrasts with the dominant espoused ethos of individualised and more child-centred approaches that were prevalent in primary mathematics classrooms prior to the introduction of the National Strategies. Whereas some teachers might feel constrained by top-down policy initiatives such as the Numeracy Strategy, Simon worked creatively within the constraints of the system to develop his design initiative. He adapted the Numeracy Strategy so as to follow a rhythm of whole-class and individual work which fitted his understandings of student learning; this process enabled him to integrate ICT into his pedagogical practice so that it supported learning. He was prepared to take risks, sometimes working outside the strategy framework and other times creatively adapting the strategy framework for his own purposes. We suggest that Simon was able to use this particular policy structure as a 'liberating constraint' that enabled him to make creative decisions related to teaching and learning with ICT.

Simon's SDI centred around the activity of investigating the distribution of the colours of sweets in a Smartie tube. The design work involved thinking through the ways in which students would use both digital and non-digital tools to support their learning, and he took into account relevant research throughout this design phase.[4] He started the 'Smartie' investigation with the questions:

> Does every tube of Smarties contain the same number of each colour?
>
> How many tubes of Smarties would I have to buy to get a fair share of my favourite orange ones?

Students worked in pairs at the computer and used the spreadsheet Excel as a mathematical tool, together with paper-based charts and graphs, to carry out their investigation. Simon also used an interactive whiteboard as a basis for creating a community of inquiry in the classroom.

As we discussed more fully in Chapter 7 when students come to school they bring with them new learning from different

continued

locations – the playground, the home, their online communities. This was very apparent in Simon's classroom.

> Some children began exploring the software environment unprompted. The children had used several other Microsoft applications in the past, and were familiar with the use of 'Wizards' as tools and templates. They were also aware that usually they needed to highlight by 'drag and drop' in order to use features within these applications. I noticed that one pair of students had begun using the chart wizard feature to explore independently the different types of chart they could present using Excel. I decided to draw on this opportunity, and the following day encouraged one child to present what he had learned to the rest of the class.
>
> (Mills 2004, p. 19)

Analysis of students' use of language as they interacted with the spreadsheet shows that initially they were not appropriating the spreadsheet as an instrument for doing mathematics. The data reveals the ways in which Simon supported the students to shift their language from the language of word processing ('I high-lighted') to the language of data handling ('I selected the data'). In this respect Simon was supporting students to begin to appropriate the spreadsheet as a mathematical instrument for creating and representing charts. Students initially used colours to visually match the charts they were constructing with the colour of the Smarties, and they were not necessarily aware of the mathematical meaning of what they were doing. Simon encouraged students to begin to see the 'coloured' charts as mathematical representations of the distribution of Smarties, again supporting the transformation of the spreadsheet tool into a mathematical instrument.

In summary the theoretical idea of all human action being mediated by social and technological tools enables us to begin to examine the potential interactions with people and tools that were central to Simon's SDI. The idea of assemblage enables us to expand the concept outwards to examine the ways in which Simon's class was situated within a network of linkages, all influencing what was possible at the level of teaching and learning in the classroom. The idea of instrumentation enables us to expand the concept inwards to interrogate the possible instruments that students might develop when using the spreadsheet tool in a mathematics lesson.

Improving learning with ICT – developing a toolkit

If we incorporate the notion of a tool kit into Vygotsky's approach, action continues to be shaped by mediational means but several new questions arise: what is the nature of the diversity of mediational means and why is one, as opposed to another, mediational means employed in carrying out a particular form of action.

(Wertsch 1991, p. 94)

Returning again to the core idea of the InterActive project, namely that all human action is mediated by social and technological tools it becomes important to find a way of discriminating between different tool use. This involves considering the relative potential of a tool for a particular learning purpose. Wertsch introduced the word 'privileging' to refer to the fact that a particular tool can be viewed as being more appropriate or efficacious in a particular setting. For example we argue in Chapter 6 that mono-modal language is the most effective tool for critically reflecting on multimodal texts. In Chapter 5 we suggest that Cubase might be a more appropriate tool for composing in music than Dance eJay, if the intention is that students have the freedom to input a range of musical sounds into the composition process. In Chapter 3 we suggest that the Virtual Fishtank might not be an appropriate tool for learning science. The process of deciding which ICT tools to use in the classroom can be examined as part of a 'thought experiment' which constitutes the first phase of designing for learning with ICT. Such a 'thought experiment' will also involve playing and experimenting with potential tools, imagining and critically examining their potential for learning. From this perspective we do not consider that all tools are 'equal'. Which tool to choose will depend on the aims and intentions of the particular learning situation. This involves learning to discern the potential of a tool for a particular purpose.

Nowadays most ICT tools are both sophisticated and extensive and so having made a decision about which tool to use there are still many decisions to be made about how to use the tool for teaching and learning, which relates to the instrumentation process. Wiki software, for example, could potentially support knowledge-building networks in the classroom. However, in a recent study Lindsey Grant found that 'the social and cultural practices of collaborative working that needs to accompany the use of such software in order to take advantage of the functional affordances of the software were not in the students' repertoire of shared practices. Instead they imported practices of individualized written assessment that they saw as important from the broader economy of education and the practices of the school economy'.[5] We suggest that one reason why the students did not use the wiki as the teacher had intended, was that he had not paid attention to the need to orchestrate the use of the wiki as an instrument for collaboratively building knowledge, believing instead that it was sufficient to introduce the tool into the classroom to produce the intended effects. But in most schools students have learned that knowledge relates to individual competition for grades in the high-stakes assessment system, and so the idea of collaboratively building knowledge is alien to their normal classroom practices. Pausing to carry out a thought-experiment before introducing the wiki software into the classroom might have enabled the teacher to think about the 'normal' cultural practices around knowledge-building in schools. Reflecting on this situation might have led the teacher to realise that he had a role in orchestrating different types of collaborative knowledge-building practices among this group of students.

When considering how to use particular digital tools in the classroom it is also important to decide when to use non-digital tools (for example whether or not to use digital software or an acoustic instrument such as a piano, when composing a piece of music). As we have argued throughout the book digital tools do not necessarily replace non-digital tools and teachers and students should learn to discriminate between the potential of different tools for particular purposes. We suggest that there can be no inherent ranking of tools in terms of their history of development and a tool that emerges later is not inherently better than a tool that was developed earlier. So for example a digital interactive whiteboard is not inherently better than a non-digital whiteboard, they can both be used in different ways and for different purposes. Similarly as discussed in Chapter 5 multimodal literacy is not inherently more richly meaningful than mono-modal written language.

Finally in developing a toolkit for a particular purpose it is important to consider both the effects-with and the effects-of technology, where the effects-of can be considered to be the residue which is left behind when a technology is no longer present.[6] The idea of residue which relates to a process of 'internalising' a tool, is often an explicit aim within education, where tools are sometimes introduced for the particular pedagogic purpose of 'scaffolding' learning, with the ultimate aim being to remove the tool. This process of 'scaffolding' is highlighted in the Modern Foreign Languages case study in Chapter 4, where we see the idea of a digital writing frame being adapted and customised so that the linguistic structure of German might be better understood. The intention from the beginning was that there would be a 'residue' left behind, with students being better able to write in German when the writing frame was removed (which is what happened in this case). In other cases we are concerned with the effects-with technology: there is no expectation that the tool will be removed. This is the case when the use of an ICT tool makes the production of something possible, that would have been impossible without the use of such a tool: for example, the creation of multimedia hypertexts or the production of a digital video, which can only be produced using a digital tool.

Within this section of the chapter we have emphasised the idea of experimenting with and critically reflecting on the potential of digital tools in order to make decisions about which tools to introduce into the classroom. But such a 'thought experiment' or out-of-the-classroom design for learning will not be adequate to anticipate the different ways in which students will develop their own instruments from the chosen tools. This is why it is important to examine what happens when ICT tools begin to be used in the classroom for particular learning purposes, and reflecting on these processes can be greatly enhanced by viewing and analysing digital video of the teaching and learning processes.

Ways into knowledge worlds – the role of language

From the beginning of the InterActive project we acknowledged that 'language is the master tool' which permeates all our interactions in the world. However in foregrounding the role of ICTs in learning we did not always pay enough attention to spoken and written language when designing learning initiatives. It was only when we began to analyse the video data in depth that we realised that in most of the cases when ICT was not being used effectively the language being used by the teacher and the students was not appropriate language in terms of the intended learning and the particular knowledge domain. This is starkly illustrated by the VirtualFishtank case study discussed in Chapters 3 and 8, where students (and the teacher) used the language of gaming, instead of the language of science, when interacting with the 'science simulation'.

So what are the mechanisms for developing the language practices that are associated with learning about new knowledge domains? A person's language use is constrained by the types of social languages that are available to them. How, then, can different languages become available? Drawing on the work of Bahktin, Wertsch uses the word 'ventriloquation' to describe the process by which we learn to speak with a new language. We learn new words by 'copying' and appropriating the words used by other people. In order to speak we do not learn words from a dictionary, rather we learn them from 'other people's mouths'. This is not to say that we completely 'parrot' someone else's language; we creatively adapt the words and language of others.[7] In order to appropriate the language of a new knowledge world we need to hear this language spoken, and this is why teachers play particularly crucial roles in inducting young people into different language practices. They do this by being aware of their role as gatekeepers of new knowledge practices, by using the language of the knowledge practices themselves and by supporting students to shift their attention to the appropriate use of language, for example the language of science, the language of mathematics, the language of history or the language of music.

The classroom as a knowledge-building community

In emphasising the key role of teachers we do not wish to suggest that students themselves do not also have an important role. Within the pool of knowledge that is part of the classroom, there are likely to be students who are more knowledgeable than the teacher in particular ways. The example of music-sequencing software is a case in point, and as we have argued throughout this book teachers should always be attentive and open to whatever students bring to the classroom. In many respects there is an irreducible tension between teacher as gatekeeper and students as knowledgeable beings. Whereas the teacher does have a role in deciding what is appropriate and what is not appropriate related to the particular intended learning, it is also important to find mechanisms for students to present their work for critical feedback from others as a way of shifting emphasis from individual to more collective and shared knowledge. Some subjects, music and English for example, have more of a tradition of such a practice. In the music design initiatives students were often offered opportunities to share their music compositions with the whole class. Many of the English teachers within the InterActive project also incorporated an element of critical feedback from students into their learning designs. Some of the mathematics teachers also worked in this way. For example when Marnie Weeden worked with 13–14-year-old students on learning about proof and geometry she explicitly built in a process of students presenting their mathematical proofs to the class for critical feedback. This, we argue, supported students to enter the difficult world of mathematical proof.[8] In summary we suggest that collective and critical discussion can support students to enter the 'inner world' of a school subject.

Our emphasis on collective knowledge-building could be seen to be at-odds with the current push for 'personalised learning'. We argue that personalisation should not view learning as an isolated endeavour, preferring to emphasise the collaborative and mutual aspects of learning. Of central importance is the negotiation process where students, in conjunction with teachers, decide upon a learning cycle which relates to a collective (and negotiated) desire to learn about particular knowledge areas. This makes it important to discuss explicitly what these knowledge areas are, so that students can become aware if they are being detracted by particular capabilities of ICT into focusing on 'other' knowledge. This is rather more subtle and difficult than becoming aware that students are, for example, 'wasting time' by using the Internet to shop instead of for a history inquiry. We are arguing that students (and teachers) have to learn to discern the differences between, for example, what written language offers and what multimedia offers, what mathematical proof offers and what measurement offers, and to learn to discern between what different software packages offer when composing music.

The push for personalised learning seems to relate to a view that the ideal situation is a personal tutor for every student. We are arguing

strongly that this does not take into account the importance of collective knowledge-building. We are also arguing that classrooms can
become productive knowledge-building communities. This involves
reinventing the classroom as a space where students work together
in a collaborative community to build new knowledge, a collaborative
community that is linked to the outside world through ICT. It also
involves acknowledging that a classroom is part of an assemblage of
knowledge production, and taking account of and working with the
epistemological diversity that is inherent in any classroom community.

Summary and conclusions

What characterises this book from other books on teaching and
learning is our focus on the role of ICTs for learning. We have argued
throughout the book that ICTs have the potential to profoundly alter
the social relations in the classroom, to impact on ways of interacting
with knowledge, and to impact on teaching and learning approaches.
We have argued that there are qualitative shifts when ICTs are
introduced into the classroom and that these shifts can tip over into
enhancing learning. However, we have also argued that without a
teacher carefully crafting and orchestrating learning, the incorporation
of ICT into the classroom is much more likely to tip over in the other
direction, into learning that is at-odds with what the school and the
teacher intends students to learn.

Our emphasis on both theory and design relates to our view that
it is important for teachers and policy makers to understand the
complex interactions between students, teachers and ICTs. Theory
offers a way of seeing things differently, a way of understanding what
is happening when ICTs are improving learning and understanding
what is happening when ICTs are not improving learning (from the
point of view of the intended learning). Design offers a way of rethinking the process of embedding ICTs into classroom learning, and
an approach to teacher learning that involves an iterative cycle of
design and reflection.

We see teachers as being key to the whole process of designing
for learning with ICT, and we are optimistic about the potential of
ICTs to improve learning if teachers are supported to become enabled
practitioners, supported to become members of communities of
professional learning, and supported to work in partnership with
researchers to develop new knowledge about teaching and learning
with ICT.

Within the final chapter of this book we highlight the importance of opening up the space for a range of new kinds of collaborations – between teachers themselves, between teachers and learners, between learners and learners, and between university researchers and teachers. We argue that such collaborations should be built upon a strong commitment to enquiry and practice. From these collaborations we suggest that it will be possible to build a relevant evidential base on improving learning with ICT that is iterative, dynamic, context sensitive and deep, and which teachers believe is authentic.

Notes

1 For further details on this approach see the Methodological appendix.
2 For discussion of how a spreadsheet can be used to introduce students to algebra see Sutherland (2007).
3 For information on the National Numeracy Strategy see www.standards. dfes.gov.uk/numeracy/; for information on the National Literacy Strategy see www.standards.dfes.gov.uk/literacy/.
4 This work is discussed more fully in Mills (2004) and Sutherland (2007).
5 See Using Wikis in Schools: a Case Study, at www.futurelab.org.uk/ resources/publications_reports_articles/discussion_papers/Discussion_ Paper258.
6 For further discussion of effects-of and effects-with see Salomon (1993).
7 For further discussion of 'ventriloquation' see Wertsch (1991) p. 127.
8 For more discussion of these issues related to learning mathematics and mathematical proof see Chapter 2 and Sutherland (2007).

Chapter 11*

From 'should be' and 'can be' to 'will be'

Reflections and new directions on improving learning with ICT

The findings from our research speak to all of the key players involved in delivering learning. Beginning with teachers, we asked: how can they, as researchers, take these insights and evidence and continue to add to them through reflexive iterations and innovations in their own understandings and practices? What are the conditions that make this possible? Can these conditions be sustained? Second, how can policymakers and managers learn from our research that will, in turn, enable them to better support teachers and learning inside and out of classrooms? Third, how can university researchers develop productive and mutually supportive researching/learning partnerships with teachers that are aimed at building a community of learners/ researchers and an ecology of knowledge production?

We began this book by stating that one starting point for our research into the use of information and communication technologies (ICT) to improve learning in classrooms was on the 'can be' nature of this relationship, so aptly framed by John Bransford and his colleagues in 2000. That is, new information and communication technologies *can be* powerful pedagogical tools. However, the challenge for us in this research was to understand how *can be* (which we might view as a working hypothesis or problematic) might be shifted along the continuum to *is* or *will be* (a statement of fact or confident prediction based on evidence) and, most importantly, to specify the processes involved, the conditions under which change occurred, the learning outcomes for students and teachers, and so on. Yet we also detected that there was a very powerful *should be* discourse which accompanied ICTs which has, on the one hand, resulted in a major investment in infrastructures but, on the other hand, also impeded our understanding of the very complex nature of technology itself and how it might be embedded in classroom practices. While the title of this chapter – *from*

* This chapter is authored by Susan Robertson and Rosamund Sutherland.

'*should be*' and '*can be*', to '*will be*' – looks something like a rollercoaster ride, we think this is an accurate reflection of the state of affairs. Hype and promises are one thing, but teaching and learning in classrooms have to be based on more than that.

We began this project knowing that there was a very large gap in our knowledge about teaching and learning with powerful digital technologies in classrooms. That meant that there was a great deal to learn about how the 'should be' and 'can be' discourses around technologies might be transformed into a more confident claim of 'is a powerful tool' contributing to learning improvement. There are several reasons why this gap has been so undeniably and under-standably huge. The most important, of course, is that the new digital technologies are, as they declare themselves to be, 'new'.

A consequence of this newness is that, as educators and researchers, we have had very little time to assess how best to bring ICTs into classrooms; how these technologies interact with existing pedagogical knowledges, classroom norms and regulatory practices; how they might change the possibilities for knowledge-building; how they are used out of school by young learners; how young learners bring their knowledge and skills back into the classroom; and how teachers draw upon learning from outside the classroom.

This gaping chasm in our knowledge about these processes has, in turn, created an enormous 'evidence vacuum' with consequences. Part of the problem, of course, is that our view of student learning has tended to be centred on what is taking place in classrooms. Yet, all of the experiences around us tell us that young people are learning a great deal with technologies – outside of classrooms and outside of the researcher's gaze.

Also contributing to the 'evidence vacuum' is the fact that, until recently, the content of education and ICT policy is that it has tended to be filled with powerful ICT 'futures' rhetoric. In anyone's reckoning, this kind of discursive content has more in common with the wizardry of slick advertisers and sales merchants than the prescriptions of an evidence-informed innovation policy. Here, new digital technologies are viewed as the path to the new future; a way out of the malaise of the crisis of industrialisation; a means for securing the shiny, new, service economy. This is a rhetoric high on promise and low on the mechanisms of process.

However, as teachers well know, viewing new technologies as the magical solution to the future closes down, rather than opens up, lines of questioning and investigation which might, in turn, become the basis for reconceptualising new and effective teaching and learning strategies and practices. Furthermore, 'technology as magic' is likely to lead most teachers to seeing themselves as failing in their ability to master this conjuring act. In fact, turned around the other way, we might say that the early introduction of new digital technologies largely failed teachers and learners, as something considerably more is required to realise improvements in learning other than magic and metaphors of the future.

So how might we take this research forward? The first move is to do what John Morgan calls for in Chapter 9 of this book. That is, we must 'break open' in order to 'break into' those tropes about technology that play with our imaginations, fears, hopes and desires. This means seeing ICTs not as some kind of modernisation magic, but as a very sophisticated set of tools that are both socially shaped and socially shaping. The second move is to critically engage with the possibilities and limitations of ICT as a tool to extend student learning inside and out of classrooms. Many of the chapters in this book explore how to do this by helping teachers become researchers of their own practice in classrooms. While this in itself is not a new insight, what is new is that the teachers in our study were encouraged to think about their teaching, learning and assessment practices *in relation to technology* so that they, and other practitioners, might learn more about this innovation. The third is to reflect upon the bigger insights we have gained in our research about the relationships between the triad of policy and management, teaching and learning, and new technologies.

'Breaking open' to 'break into' ICT discourse to insert curriculum and pedagogical substance and meaning

New digital technologies, of the kind that our teachers have been working with, emerged at a time when questions of national economic interest, competitiveness, the modernisation of public sectors, new forms of work, globalisation, and the possibilities of a new kind of society (network) were being discussed. Technology promised a way out of recession, unemployment and economic decline. They were the means to build a new economy, a new society, and a nation. In short, ICTs were a 'metaphor for the future'.

Now the problem with ICT as 'metaphor for the future' is that this has left a great deal of work to be done before we can understand both when, how and with what outcomes ICTs might be used to support learning across the curriculum areas. In other words, ICT as metaphor for the future is rather like a black box; it sheds no light on the politics, processes and practices that necessarily shaped both its history, nor on the assumptions that are necessarily embedded in ICT policy and programmes. To make matters worse, we have lacked a language, or set of mutually understood concepts, to talk about the technology, learning and pedagogy. What kinds of tools are these new technologies? How did these tools reshape the social worlds in which young learners operate? What makes them different from other learning tools that teachers have at their disposal? What is it about these tools in particular that can so quickly result in lessons being disrupted in the way they are? How is the learner conceptualised in this ICT discourse, and what is the role of the school in relation to other sites and spaces of knowledge production? These are big and important questions, and ones of which we are only beginning to grasp the full importance. There is much work to be done.

One challenge the project team faced was how to build a set of concepts that captured important dimensions of the relationship between ICTs and learning, and for describing the research relationship between the teachers and the university researchers. For example, in answer to the question: *how might we think about the relationship between the learner and the tool?* we settled on the idea of 'instrumentation' to capture the idea that a learner can construct different instruments starting from the same ICT tool. Similarly, we drew on Wertsch's ideas, based on socio-cultural theory, to represent the learner/technology relationship as one of 'person-acting-with-mediational-means' to emphasise that a person's capabilities are potentially enhanced by working with a technology. We also introduced the idea of 'privileging' to draw attention to the idea that it matters what kind of technology a learner might be using, in that different technologies will privilege the enhancement of different kinds of capabilities.

We also found it useful to draw on Goldhaber's ideas (1997) – that ICTs are involved in a new 'attention economy' – and to reflect upon what this means for young learners in all of the settings that they find themselves. If, indeed, attention is scarce, and the competing claims on attention are able to mobilise multimodal resources to capture the imaginations of young learners, then teachers need to be able to take account of these developments when structuring curricular experiences and pedagogical practices. Like all of us, young learners are also potential consumers of an exponential increase in the information that is out there. How can we turn attention into knowing;

how can we ensure that knowing is more than accumulating the bits of incidental knowledge acquired in the course of attending? For surely education is about ensuring that attention is turned on the construction of intended knowledge that is more than the sum of the incidental parts. This is an important challenge to educators, and one that will increase in veracity, rather than diminish, as ICTs become more and more powerful.

Similarly, we developed the idea of 'epistemological diversity' to grasp hold of the idea that new technologies seem to have injected into the curriculum new ways of accessing knowledge, new ways of knowing, and different ways of representing knowledge. However, as we also argued in the book, this generates new issues of 'authority' because of the incomparability and incommensurability of the knowledges that students might access. This not only places teachers in a central role in helping interpret and mediate such 'epistemological diversity', but, as we argue in Chapter 7, the new economy of knowledge production generates very different challenges for teachers and students in terms of how they might develop critical literacy practices that enable them to 'read' the new politics of knowledge production.

We also spoke about our teacher partners as teacher researchers rather than as 'teachers' to signal the nature of the work that they were involved in, and also as a way of overcoming the divide that results from claims about research being the province of university academics and not teachers. Our view was, and is, that to build a community of practice, we need a language that both reflects our shared commitment to co-producing knowledge and that also communicates that this partnership is a valued way of working.

What also became evident to us, as our work with teachers and students progressed, was the need, on the one hand, to revisit old metaphors about schooling and learning and, on the other hand, to construct new metaphors that opened up the possibility of different, indeed more productive, ways of thinking about the relationships between learners, classrooms and schools, and the wider society. For instance, the metaphors that guided how we talked about education tended to essentialise the classroom as the 'only' place where learning occurs. As a result, learning taking place outside of the classrooms tended to be trivialised and devalued. Yet, it is hard to ignore the fact that many young learners have acquired high levels of ICT competence and can expertly deploy this knowledge in schools.

We found introducing new metaphors, like 'assemblages', into our conceptual vocabulary enabled us to bring into view the way in which schools are particular moments of wider social relations and social practices. Learners do go to school, but they also learn important knowledges and skills in other settings. We need a language that can grasp this complex, open and dynamic way in which learning takes place, and draw this back into our repertoires of teaching in schools.

Generating a new language to talk about learning and teaching with new technologies, as well as how to research these processes in ways in which teachers are able to design, experiment, reflect and transform their pedagogical, curriculum and assessment practices, is still in its early days. However, we argue that if we are to move beyond black boxes, essentialising assumptions and naturalising tendencies, this is a critically important move. More importantly, all stakeholders should be involved in this process, for they have important things to say, and we all have much to gain as a result.

Designing the conditions for learning with technology

In the previous section, we reflected on the challenges ICTs pose for educators, policymakers, learners and researchers for thinking about how to give substance to contemporary pedagogy and the curriculum. We now turn attention to the practical pedagogical/knowing/ economy of knowledge production – questions that have been a constant theme in our research. What did we learn about how best to work with teacher researchers, with schools, and young people that might be added to an evidential base about teaching and learning in the twenty-first century? Mostly research tends to focus on the 'findings'; the 'what we know now' that we did not know before, leaving aside important epistemological and methodological – or how we know – concerns.

How we know, and how we produce knowledge, is not a technical act; it is a profoundly political one that is shaped as a result of the prioritisation of some agents or actors over others, some knowledges over others, some ways of looking at the world over others.

Our view is that teachers need to be brought into the circle of knowledge production about their own practice rather than be bystanders in a process that treats them as objects. This is important if we are not only to help teachers develop the skills of researchers that justifies the teacher researcher linkage, but for it to become a basis upon which teacher researchers can model a learning-to-learn approach to knowledge production for young learners.

In this project we worked closely with teachers to design learning experiments that ranged from the more immediate 'thought experiment' to a more systematically enacted '*thoughtful* experiment' as in a subject design initiative (SDI). These ways of supporting teachers to make choices about what they do, of taking an interest in designing and interpreting the effects of what they do, and using this knowledge to feed back into ongoing, refined and reflective practices, is what Schon (1983) had in mind when he talked about the reflective practitioner. By helping teachers design learning experiments, collect data, systematise analysis, and so on, 'action' is brought into conversation with reflection. As a result it is situated and dynamic, relevant and responsive, to the learner.

'Thoughtful experiments', however, require 'space' for experimentation and risk. As all researchers know, not only are some of our hypotheses wrong, and our hunches or diagnoses incorrect, but we must also be open to surprise. We learn through our successes *and* our failures. Indeed, failure might encourage us to think outside of the box. We might learn to invent new methods, new strategies, draw on new metaphors, encourage new learning relationships, and so on. However, current policy and management practices in schools and colleges in the UK, driven by concerns about accountability and control over professional labour have, in our view, closed down the space for experiment and risk. This has had a damaging effect on the creation of a more experimental and experiential pedagogical space.

We suggest that critical to the development of the evidential base around learning with new ICTs, is that we review out policies and management practices so that they do open up space for experimentation and risk. In our research with teacher researchers in schools, where we were effective in opening up that space we saw that it was filled with all kinds of exciting new learning, even if some of that learning was to realise the limits of technology.

Opening up the space for a range of new kinds of collaborations – between teachers themselves, between teachers and students, students and students, university researchers and teachers, and so on, built upon a strong commitment to enquiry and practice – is crucial. It is only then that we will rapidly be able to build a relevant evidential base that is iterative, dynamic, context sensitive and deep, and which teachers feel is authentic. Such an evidence base will help guide their decisions about 'is' and enable them to contribute to 'will be' knowledge about ICT and learning. How, otherwise, might we keep pace with the very fast-changing nature of ICT innovations and how they mediate learning? How, otherwise, might teachers come to believe in, experiment with, reflect upon, and alter their teaching practices in relation to ICT? How, otherwise, might young people come to see themselves as creative knowledge producers and not simply ciphers or consumers of the latest software, the latest gadget, the latest thing to circulate in the attention economy. To build an ecology of knowledge production, we must take the idea of 'ecology' seriously. Central to the notion of ecology is the understanding that all elements in the learning environment matter – from the teacher researcher to the students to the tools to the range of settings for acquiring knowledge, including the home.

Concluding remarks

Education has, and will continue to be, a trade-off between regulating the conditions for teaching and learning, and exploiting the possibilities that learners of all shapes, sizes and colours bring with them to new experiences. Learning is not just for students. Rather, we are all learners. With this in mind, we might then say: transformations in learning will only come about when we can square the circle between the following elements: the policymakers' knowledge about the parameters for innovation with technology; the need for teachers' ICT-mediated teaching practices to develop in an environment where time and space is given, and value assigned to, taking risks and experimenting with what works, under what conditions, for whom, with what outcome; when university researchers see the value of negotiating research/learning partnerships with teachers to enhance learning; and young people themselves are given a prominent role in contributing to what we know about technology-mediated learning.

Methodological appendix

Objective and aims

The overall objective of the InterActive project was to examine the ways in which ICT could be used in educational settings to enhance teaching and learning. Specific aims were:

i)   to describe and theorise the links between teaching and learning in ICT-rich settings;
ii) to characterise young people's and teachers' out-of-school learning with technology in order to draw on this potential within school-based learning situations;
iii) to characterise productive professional development practices;
iv) to identify the conditions which give rise to effective management practices enabling the creation of innovative ICT learning environments;
v)   to highlight the similarities and differences between subject cultures with respect to both pedagogic practices and students' approaches to learning which incorporate ICT;
vi) to identify the ways in which research evidence can be transformed and developed to be of value to educational practitioners.

Organisation and partnership

The InterActive project centred around developing research partnerships between teachers and researchers in order to design researchable learning environments which were supported by research on teaching and learning. From the outset partnerships were established with ten institutions: one further education college, five secondary schools and four primary schools, and overall fifty-nine teachers from these institutions became teacher researchers. The secondary schools were chosen so that a) their students represented a spread of socio-economic and ethnic backgrounds and b) their history of ICT use represented a spread from extensive to minimal, with all schools having adequate ICT provision. Three of the primary schools were chosen because they 'fed into' the secondary schools; the fourth approached the project team with a request to join the project.

A principle of management of the project was that our belief about the characteristics of 'good' learning environments should permeate all aspects of the project. From the outset we considered the following to be important: devolving responsibility for creating and solving problems to 'learners'/members of a team; creating communities of inquiry which harness the potential of distributed intelligence; and creating environments in which students focus their energy on the object of learning.

Subject design teams and initiatives

As discussed in Chapter 4, the project focused upon a multi-level set of overlapping communities of practice. At the meso-level, the project was organised around subject design teams (SDTs). Within these teams teachers, teacher educators, researchers and research students worked together to develop learning initiatives, designated as subject design initiatives (SDIs). Whereas the meso-level was the starting point for the SDI, much of the working through of the initiative took place at a micro-level where a teacher and researcher worked intensively together on the design, realisation and evaluation of the SDI.

At the macro-level the core team of university researchers, teacher educators and research students worked together to develop the theoretical and methodological coherence of the project. A steering group (consisting of project school heads and LEA advisers) was set up to ensure communication between the university and school teams, and review the development of research instruments. Additionally, an advisory group consisting of academics and non-academics met annually to give critical feedback on project output.

The project was predicated on the view that teachers would need support to begin the process of integrating ICT into teaching and learning and the majority of partner-teachers had not previously embedded ICT into teaching and learning. Support for doing this was organised around SDTs within the following subject areas: English, history, geography, modern foreign languages, science, music and mathematics. The SDT consisted of teachers from the project partner schools, researchers, teacher educators and research students (see Table A.1). Each SDT (coordinated by a member of the university research team) constituted the core of the professional development which was central to the project. These teams developed SDIs: these were sequences of work and research involving the use of ICT, which were designed, implemented and researched in individual teachers' classes. SDIs were planned to address key learning areas within a particular subject domain and to incorporate both digital and non-digital technologies as appropriate. Design was informed by theory, research-based evidence on the use of ICT for learning, teachers' craft knowledge, curriculum knowledge, policy and management constraints and possibilities and the research team's expertise. The focus was on iterative design and evaluation of SDIs, and initiatives were piloted before substantive evaluation. These classroom-specific, collaboratively designed and progressively adapted initiatives gave the project theoretical and methodological versatility. The aim was to develop understanding and change practice through a long-term shift in conceptions. Over the two years of the school/college-focused phase of the project, each teacher was funded to work out of the classroom for the equivalent of fifteen days.

In focusing on 'designs for learning' we took as a starting point the idea that all activity is a creative application and combination of 'available designs' (New London Group 1996). Through accessing

Table A.1 Number of researchers, teacher educators, research students and teachers in each subject design team

Subject area	No. of researchers	No. of teacher educators	No. of research students	No. of teachers			Total
				Prim.	Secon.	FE Colleges	
English	2	1	1	7	8	1	20
Geography		1			2		3
History		1			2		3
Mathematics	2	1	1	2	10	2	18
MFL		1			8		9
Music		1	1	4	5		11
Science	1	2			8		11
Total	6	8	3	13	43	3	75

'available designs' a person can begin a design process, which involves re-presentation and re-contextualisation. The outcome of this process is called the 'redesigned', where:

> the redesigned may be variously creative or reproductive in relation to the resources for meaning-making available in available designs. But it is neither a simple reproduction (as the myth of standards and transmission pedagogy would have us believe) nor is it simply creative (as the myths of individual originality and personal voice would have us believe).
>
> (ibid., p. 75)

Research themes

The project was framed by the following research themes which related to the project objectives.

Research Theme 1: Educational Policy and Management of ICT in Schools
Research Theme 2: Teaching and Learning
Research Theme 3: The Role of Subject Cultures in Mediating ICT Use
Research Theme 4: Teachers and Professional Development
Research Theme 5: Learners' Out-of-School Uses of Computers

Each research theme was organised around specific questions, which were refined throughout the life of the project. Research in Theme 2 (teaching and learning) focused on the work of the SDIs and the teacher partners. Research in Theme 4 (professional development) focused on the work of the SDTs, and also drew on the work of the SDIs. In contrast, research in Theme 1 (policy and management of ICT) focused on the work of all teachers (ie. not only the fifty-nine partner teachers) and senior managers in the partner schools. Research in Theme 3 (subject cultures) drew on the data which was collected for Themes 1 and 2. Research in Theme 5 (out-of-school uses of computers) centred on a study of samples of young people from the project schools.

Research methods

The research was structured around a range of methods and the team had collective responsibility for collecting data used within the different strands of the project (see Table A.2). The SDI was the unit of analysis for researching learning at the level of the classroom and the use of digital video was crucial to this process. We also developed digital video as: a) a tool for transforming teachers' practice and associated enhancing of learning; and b) as a tool for communicating research to the academic and practitioner communities.

The following provides an overview of how the research instruments were piloted and the data was collected.

Questionnaires to students on out-of-school uses of ICT

The questionnaire was designed drawing on an instrument previously used in the ScreenPlay Project (Facer *et al.* 2003) in 1998 which was altered to reflect categories of computer use that had emerged during the qualitative stages of that project. In total the questionnaire comprises over 200 questions concerning young people's computer ownership, access and use in home and school. It also carries questions on Internet access (via multiple devices), mobile phone use, and location of and access to ICTs in the home. The questionnaire was initially tested with colleagues and then the instrument and analysis were piloted in a local Bristol primary school in May 2001. The first survey was conducted in the summer and autumn of 2001. All students from Years 5, 7, 10 and 12 in four primary schools, five secondary schools and one FE college in the Bristol area were sampled in order to cover young people in different stages of their schooling, covering Key Stages 2, 3 and 4 (ages 9 to 18). This survey was then repeated with the same year groups in the same institutions in the summer term of 2003.

A letter explaining the research was sent to all young people and their parents providing them with the opportunity to opt out of the survey. In the primary schools children completed the questionnaire in prearranged lesson time with their class teacher and project researchers were present to answer any queries arising. In the secondary schools, detailed written instructions were provided to form teachers who administered the completion of the questionnaires in form time, PSE lessons or equivalent. In 2001 an overall response rate of 71 per cent (N = 1,818) fully completed questionnaires was achieved and 78 per cent (N = 1,471) was achieved in the 2003 survey. The sample profiles for both surveys are detailed in Table A.3.

Table A.2 Overview of data collected within the project

Data collected	Used within research theme				
	RT1: Policy and manage-ment	RT2: Teaching and learning	RT3: Subject cultures	RT4: Profes-sional develop-ment	RT5: Out of school
Questionnaires to students on out-of-school uses of ICT (2001 and 2003)		✓			✓
Focus group interviews with students about their out-of-school ICT use (2002)					✓
Case studies of young people's out-of-school ICT use (carried out in 2003, to include video data)					✓
Questionnaire to teachers on use of ICT in and out of school (2001 and 2003)	✓	✓	✓	✓	
Interviews with senior management and ICT coordinators (2001 and 2003)	✓		✓	✓	
Interviews with partner-teachers carried out in 2001 and 2004	✓	✓	✓	✓	
Key policy documents	✓		✓	✓	
Participant observers' notes and occasional video recordings of SDT meetings		✓	✓	✓	
For each SDI		✓			
Interviews with selected students		✓	✓	✓	✓
Diagnostic assessment		✓			
Video recordings of lessons		✓			
Notes of lessons		✓			
Student projects/output		✓			
Observers' notes		✓			

Table A.3 Sample profile for 2001 and 2003 surveys (%)

Total number of respondents	2001 survey 1,818	2003 survey 1,471
Ethnicity		
White	77	71
Mixed	5	6
Asian	4	4
African	3	4
'Other'	1	2
Missing data	9	13
Gender		
Male	50	50
Female	50	50
School year		
Year 5	11	12
Year 7	41	47
Year 10	35	32
Year 12	13	8
*Socio-economic background**		
Highest quartile	24	18
Middle-high quartile	18	25
Middle-low quartile	29	25
Lowest quartile	9	9
Data not available	21	23

* Derived using postcode data, see Facer *et al.* 2003

Focus group interviews with students about their out-of-school ICT use

Young people from Years 5, 7, 10 and 12 from each of the participating schools were selected, drawing on the 2001 questionnaire as a sampling frame. The survey data was used to allocate young people into two groups: 'high home computer user' (defined as reporting home computer and Internet use on a daily or 2–3 times weekly basis) and 'low home computer user' (defined as reporting home computer and Internet use less than weekly). In total 192 young people were interviewed in school, in groups of between four and eight students, all of the same year group and level of home computer use as described above. The semi-structured peer group interviews lasted approximately an hour and comprised questions concerning participants' access and use of computers both at home and school. Interviews were recorded and transcribed.

Case studies of young people's out-of-school ICT use

Young people and their families were selected for home interviews using the 2003 questionnaire data as a sampling frame. They were purposively sampled to ensure the inclusion of young people with a range of backgrounds in terms of age, school, gender, socio-economic area and also differing types of home computer usage. Of twenty-eight families approached, eleven agreed to participate. The first interview included a family discussion covering the history of ICT within the household and current use of ICT, family learning resources/support networks and also an individual interview with the young person about their current ICT usage and practices and the social context of their computer use. The second visit to the family involved an observation of the young person's computer use, using a diary completed in the previous week as a prompt, an interview with the young person about home and school uses of ICT and also a follow-up interview with parents about their perceptions of their child's computer use.

Questionnaires to teachers on use of ICT in and out of school

Teachers questionnaires were developed, piloted and administered (October 2001 and October 2003) to survey the views of all the teachers in our research sites on ICT, teaching and learning, with specific questions on policy and the management of ICT in their school (TQ1 = 263 and TQ2 = 226). The return rate was 30 per cent. While lower than we would have wanted, it was evident that teachers in the schools saw additional activities such as filling in questionnaires as adding to their workloads. This return nonetheless was adequate for enabling us to provide an overview. The questionnaire was developed from a teacher questionnaire which had been used within a Becta-funded survey of teachers so that we could identify changes over time, and was designed to give us a better sense of teachers' experience of ICT in and out of school. In TQ2 we were also able to establish whether and in what ways the teachers who participated in the InterActive project were similar or different to the broader population of teachers within the school. The aim was to help us understand better how teachers were using ICT for administration, planning, and working with students. All responses were anonymous and confidential. The questionnaire had eight sections.

Interviews with teacher researchers

We interviewed the participating teacher researchers twice throughout the life of the project (in 2001 and 2003). These were semi-structured and focused on a range of themes as summarised below.

1   Historical and contextual influences on pedagogical attitudes and practice.
2   Views about subject (e.g. English, mathematics) teaching.
3   Views about teaching and learning.
4   Strengths and areas for development.
5   Attitudes to change in subject (e.g. English, mathematics) teaching.
6   Attitudes to ICT and subject (e.g. English, mathematics).
7   Views about the impact of the InterActive project on practice.

Interviews were tape recorded and transcribed.

Interviews with senior management and ICT coordinators

Two extended interviews were conducted with each headteacher and ICT coordinator at two points over the project (2001 and 2003). These were piloted and transcribed.

Key policy documents

A significant collection of policy and related documents was assembled, from the school, local education authority, national agencies such as DfES, Becta and TTA, and global institutions (OECD, EC) and agents (Microsoft, Cisco Systems).

Participant observers' notes of SDT meetings

The observations of substantive meetings were summarised in detailed field notes as well as some being video and audio recorded and then transcribed. The planning sessions were typically summarised in terms of decisions reached and issues arising that were shared among the team. The regular debrief sessions also allowed participants to reflect on the activities they had been involved in and to discuss the research evidence that was being introduced at regular intervals. For instance, written research reports and papers were used as a basis for discussion around a video sequence or as supporting evidence for the introduction of a new idea into the planning process. Whenever research evidence was introduced and shared with participants their comments and critique were noted. The documentation of this process provided valuable insight on the nature of collaboration and the relationship between the research and practitioner communities.

SDI – video data

In order to capture the interaction between teacher and students a video camera was placed in the corner of the classroom and left to record without interference. This technique records classroom processes of interaction, including teachers' and students' talk. In order to capture the interaction between students and the computer two forms of data capture were used: (a) dynamic electronic recording of the computer using software; (b) video recording of social interactions and interactions with the computer. In the case of music it was also important to record the process as shown on the computer screen, while also capturing the ways in which the student(s) used the musical keyboard – and to ensure that these were synchronised (capturing the sound from the computer as well as the sound of the students talking). This involved using two cameras for each pair of students; one focused on the screen, the other on the music/computer keyboard. A mixer was used to capture the sound from the students' individual microphones as well as the sound from the computer or keyboard, since the students often wore headphones. Video footage was viewed along with the musical products that were saved in files. We also used a screen-save program or discretely named multiple-saves to capture the process of the work.

SDI – diagnostic assessment

Where appropriate we developed diagnostic instruments to measure learning within each SDI. These diagnostic instruments were used both to evaluate learning and to support teachers in reflective practice.

The diagnostic instruments were aimed at assessing learning outcomes as they related to the aims of the subject-based design initiatives.

Analytical techniques

Analysis of questionnaire data

The questionnaires were mostly pre-coded and this information was entered into SPSS version 11.0 for analysis. Where questions were not pre-coded a coding scheme was designed and responses coded accordingly. Data verification checks were carried out. Initial frequency distributions were requested based on the total number of respondents. Two-way frequency distributions were then produced between questions and specific subgroups of respondents (e.g. gender, age, school, primary or secondary, Interactive Education teacher or not).

Analysis of teacher interviews

Analysing interviews involved a careful step-by-step iterative process where the transcripts were read and re-read in order to create 'sentence units'. These were then given labels or category descriptions using single word labels or short implying phrases. The initial coding of the data using these categories was then checked for reliability using two independent experts to adjudicate using 10 per cent of the transcripts. Inter-coder reliability co-efficients were then applied using standard formulae. The 'sentence units' then formed the basis of a more fine-grained qualitative exemplar-based analysis thus allowing more detailed descriptive data to be deployed to support specific findings.

Discourse analysis

(i) corpus linguistics analysis
Corpus linguistics techniques were used to analyse policy documents. Corpus analysis, as a method, is the computer-assisted study of patterns of vocabulary use in texts. The software package Wordsmith Tools was used to examine how words are used in individual texts and large corpora of texts, such as reports produced by DfES, Becta and Ofsted. The tools perform a number of functions: analysis of frequency of word use (Wordlist); unexpected frequency of word use (Keyword); word use in context (Concordance); words used together (Collocation). In our case we were able to examine the ways in which

words like technology and ICT are linked to words like knowledge economy, economy, knowledge society, and so on.

(ii) critical research

Critical research draws from the work of Jupp (1996) who proposes a method for discourse analysis which consists of asking particular questions of documents produced by institutions: in our case the range of institutions in our study including the schools, LEAs, government agencies, firms and so on. Our questions set out to reveal the assumptions which underline official documents and to identify what has been concealed or left out. This consideration of content is supported by an analysis of the institutions that have produced the texts and which interests they represent. Fundamentally, this approach sees that the texts can be interrogated in terms of content, author (who says it), authority (on what grounds), audience (to whom) and objective (in order to achieve what) (Jupp 1996, p. 300).

(iii) critical discourse analysis

Our third approach to analysing texts was critical discourse analysis (CDA). It resists the conventional distinctions between theory and method. Instead it offers a way to 'operationalise' the investigation of texts through identifying different domains of textual analysis: text, interaction and context. In terms of methodology, CDA involves a continual movement between text and theoretical perspectives so that theory and method are part of a dynamic process of textual exploration rather than being separate analytical moments. Having said that, CDA is textually oriented discourse analysis and linguistic features should always ground the developing understanding of power and ideology. Significantly, the importance of interpretation is constantly emphasised in CDA. Texts can be understood in different ways and the validity of any explanation is open to argument and empirical challenge based on the linguistic features of the text. For Chouliaraki and Fairclough, 'a text does not have a uniquely determined meaning, though there is a limit to what a text can mean: different understandings of the text result from different combinations of the properties of the text and the properties (social positioning, knowledges, values, etc.) of the interpreter' (Chouliaraki and Fairclough 1999, p. 67). In producing explanatory accounts of texts therefore, CDA does offer particular explanations and particular readings, and their validity is determined by the placement of properties of the texts within theoretical frameworks.

Video cases of teaching and learning

Our theoretical perspective implies that learning is closely related to activity and the cognitive and cultural tools that are harnessed within this activity. Thus our focus of analysis of learning was on the nature of activity and the interactions between students and their use of digital and non-digital tools. Each SDI was analysed from a holistic perspective, using all the data sources that had been collected (see Table A.2). Analysis was often carried out in collaboration with a teacher partner and written up in an academic journal or teacher journal. Those teacher partners who decided to study for a higher degree (Masters (4), doctorate (2)) have (or are in the process of) analysed their own SDIs. The process of analysis involves developing analytical categories that relate to both socio-cultural theory and the particular knowledge domain (see for example Taylor and Lazarus, 2005; Sutherland *et al.* 2004; Sutch, 2005). The analytical process focused on teaching and learning processes (through an analysis of video data) and learning outcomes (through an analysis of students' work, diagnostic assessment and interview data).

The video data was viewed in real time and passages identified for more detailed analysis using the constructed analytical categories. In order to explore the learning dimension of what students had been doing we developed conjectures from our analysis and played back critical episodes of video data. The video- and computer-based textual record was therefore both a source of data and a stimulus for reflective discussion with teachers. We edited excerpts of the video data (subject to ethical considerations) in order to produce teacher development videos. Selected excerpts of the video recording were transcribed in detail (to include capturing of images, etc.).

Bibliography

Adams, J. (2000) *French Writing Frames 11–14, Creative and Imaginative Writing*, Dunstable: Folens.

Adler, R. (1995) *The Future of Advertising: New Approaches to the Attention Economy*, Washington, DC: Aspen Institute.

Ainley, J. (2000) Constructing purposeful mathematical activity in primary classrooms, in C. Tikly and A. Wolf (eds), *The Maths We Need Now*, London: Bedford Way Papers, pp. 138–53.

——, Nardi, E. and Pratt, D. (2000). The construction of meanings for trend in Active Graphing, *International Journal of Computers for Mathematical Learning*, 5(2): 85–114. (pdf 305kb).

Airy, S. and Parr, J.M. (2001) MIDI, music and me: students' perspectives on composing with MIDI, *Music Education Research*, 3(1): 41–9.

Alexander, R. (2000) *Culture and Pedagogy*, Oxford: Blackwell.

Armstrong, V. and Curran, S. (2006) Developing a collaborative model of research using digital video, *Computers & Education*, 46(3): 336–47.

——, Barnes, S., Sutherland, R., Curran, S., Mills, S. and Thompson, I. (2005) Collaborative research methodology for investigating teaching and learning: the use of interactive whiteboard technology, *Educational Review*, 57(4): 457–69.

Artigue, M. (2002) Learning mathematics in a CAS environment: the genesis of a reflection about instrumentation and the dialectics between technical and conceptual work, *International Journal of Computers for Mathematical Learning*, 7(3): 245–74.

Ashby, J. (2007) General Teaching Council for England Survey of Teachers 2004–6 Report on Trend Data, GTCE www.gtce.org.uk/shared/contentlibs/126795/93128/126346/207305/trend_rpt.pdf.

Baggott La Velle, L., Brawn, R., McFarlane., A. and John, P. (2004) According to the promises: the sub-culture of school science, teachers' pedagogical identity and the challenge of ICT, *Education, Communication & Information (ECi)*, 4(1): 109–29.

Bahktin M.M. (1981) Discourses in the novel, in M.M. Bahktin, *The Dialogic Imagination: Four Essays by M.M. Bahktin*, Austin, TX: University of Texas Press.

Balacheff, N. (1988) Aspects of proof in pupils' practice of school mathematics, in D. Pimm (ed.), *Mathematics, Teachers and Children*, London: Hodder & Stoughton.

Balestri, D. (1988) Softcopy and hard wordprocessing and writing process, *Academic Computing*, February: 14–17, 41–5.

Barton, D. and Hamilton, M. (1998) *Local Literacies*, London: Routledge.

Battersby, J. (1995) *Teaching Geography at Key Stage 3*, Cambridge: Chris Kington.

Bauman, Z. (2005) Education in liquid modernity, *Review of Education, Pedagogy and Cultural Studies*, 27: 303–17.

Becta (2007a) Harnessing Technology Review 2007: progress and impact of technology in education, *Summary Report*, Coventry: Becta.

—— (2007b) Harnessing Technology Review 2007: progress and impact of technology in education, *Evidence Review*, Coventry: Becta http://publications.becta.org.uk/display.cfm?resID=33979.

Bell, M. (2004) *Understanding English Spelling*, London: Pegasus.

Beniger, J. (1986) *The Control Revolution, Technological and Economic Origins of the Information Society*, Cambridge, MA: Harvard University Press.

Bentley, T. (1998) *The Classroom Without Walls*, London: Demos, Routledge, pp. 80–1.

Bernstein, B. (1990) *The Structuring of Pedagogic Discourse*, Vol. IV, *Class Codes and Control*, London, New York: Routledge.

Blunkett, David, quoted in H. McGavin (1997) 'Blunkett fears two tier cyber-space', *Times Educational Supplement*, 10 January 1997.

Bolter, D. and Grusin, R. (2000) *Remediation: Understanding New Media*, Cambridge, MA: MIT Press.

Bourdieu, P. (1980) *The Logic of Practice*, Cambridge: Polity Press.

Bransford, J.D., Brown, A.L. and Cocking, R.R. (2000) *How People Learn: Brain, Mind, Experience, and School*, Washington, DC: National Academy Press, pp. 206–30.

Breeze, N. (2008) The mediating effects of ICT upon music composition in the classroom, unpublished doctoral thesis, Bristol: University of Bristol.

Butt, G. (2002) *Reflective Teaching of Geography 11–18*, London, New York: Continuum.

Butt, S. and Cebulla, A. (2006) *E-Maturity and School Performance – A Secondary Analysis of VOL Evaluation Data*, London: National Centre for Social Research.

Cain, T. (2004) Theory, technology and the music curriculum, *British Journal of Music Education*, 21(2): 215–21.

Carney, E. (1994) *A Survey of English Spelling*, London, Routledge.

Castell, S. and Jensen, J. (2004) Paying attention to attention: new economies for learning, *Educational Theory*, 54(4): 381–97.

Castells, M. (1996) *The Network Society*, Oxford: Blackwell.

Chouliaraki, L. and Fairclough, N. (1999) *Discourse in Late Modernity*, Edinburgh: Edinburgh University Press.

Colley, A. and Comber, C. (2003) Age and gender differences in computer use and attitudes among secondary school students: what has changed?, *Educational Research*, 45: 155–65.

Cope, B. and Kalantzis, C. (editors for the New London Group) (2000) *Multiliteracies: Literacy Learning and the Design of Social Futures*, London: Routledge.

Dale, R., Robertson, S. and Shortis, T. (2004) 'You can't not go with the technological flow. Can you?': Constructing 'ICT'and 'teaching and learning', *Journal of Computer Assisted Learning*, 20(6): 456–70.

Davis, B., Sumara, D. and Luce-Kapler, R. (2000) *Engaging Minds: Learning and Teaching in a Complex World*, Mahwah, NJ: Lawrence Erlbaum Associates.

Day, C. (1999) *Developing Teachers: The Challenges of Lifelong Learning*, London: Routledge.

Deleuze, G. and Guattari, F. (1987) *A Thousand Plateaus: Capitalism and Schizophrenia*, Minneapolis, MI: Minnesota University Press.

DfEE (1997) *Information Technology in Schools: Statistical Bulletin 3/97*, London: Stationery Office.

—— (2000) *Framework for Teaching English: Years 7, 8 and 9*, London: Stationery Office.

DfES (2004) A National Conversation about Personalised Learning: www.standards.dfes.gov.uk/innovation-unit/personalisation.

—— (2007) Computer:pupil ratios from Pupil Level Annual School Census 2005 and 2006, available online: www.teachernet.gov.uk/wholeschool/ictis/facts.

Dillon, T. (2005) Future music: investigating the role of technology in enhancing public appreciation of and participation in music. An insight paper, available online: www.futurelab.org.uk/research/innovations/music_insight_paper_01.htm (accessed 23 October 2006).

Downes, T. (1998) Children's use of computers in their homes, unpublished D.Phil. thesis, Australia: University of Western Sydney Macarthur.

Durant, A. (1990) A new day for music? Digital technologies in contemporary music-making, in P. Hayward (ed.), *Culture, Technology and Creativity in the Late Twentieth Century*, London: John Libbey.

Durbin, C. (2003) Creativity – criticism and challenge in geography, *Teaching Geography*, 28(2): 64–9.

Facer, K., Furlong, J., Furlong, R. and Sutherland, R. (2003) *Screenplay: Children and Computing in the Home*, London, New York: RoutledgeFalmer.

Fairclough, N. (2004) *Analysing Discourse*, London: Routledge.

Folkestad, G., Hargreaves, D.J. and Lindström, B. (1998) Compositional strategies in computer-based music-making, *British Journal of Music Education*, 15(1): 83–97.

Freedman, D. (2006) Internet transformations: 'old' media resilience in the 'new media' revolution, in J. Curran and D. Morley (eds), *Media and Cultural Theory*, London: Routledge.

Gall, M. and Breeze, N. (2005) Music composition lessons: the multimodal affordances of technology, *Educational Review*, 57(4): 415–33.

—— and —— (2007) The subject culture of music and ICT in the classroom, ICT, *Pedagogy & Education*, 16(1): 41–56.

Gee, J. (2003) *What Video Games Have to Teach Us About Learning and Literacy*, New York: Palgrave Macmillan.

Gibbs, M. (2007) Classroom, mathematical learning with computers; the mediational effects of the computer, the teacher and the task, unpublished doctoral thesis, Bristol: University of Bristol.

Godwin, S. and Sutherland, R. (2004) Whole class technology for learning mathematics: the case of functions and graphs, *Education, Communication & Information (ECi)*, 4(1) (March): 131–52.

Goldhaber, M. (1997) The attention economy and the net, *First Monday*, available online: www.firstmonday.dk/issues/issue2_4/goldhaber, accessed 3 July, 2007.

Goldstein, S. (1997) *Ofsted Report on IT Use in Secondary Schools, 1995–7*, London, HMSO.

Goodson, I. (1991) Studying curriculum: towards a social constructionist perspective, in I. Goodson and M. Mangan (eds), *Qualitative Educational Research Studies: Methodologies in Transition* (Research Unit on Classroom Learning and Computer Use in Schools, RUCCUS), London, ON: Faculty of Education, University of Western Ontario, pp. 49–90.

Green, B. (1988) Subject-specific literacy and school learning: a focus on writing, *Australian Journal of Education*, 32(2): 156–79.

—— (2004) Curriculum, English and Cultural Studies: or changing the scene of English teaching?, *Changing English*, 11(2), October.

—— and Bigum, C. (1994) Aliens in the classroom, *Australian Journal of Education*, 37(2): 119–41.

Gregory, D. (1981) Towards a human geography, in R. Walford (ed.), *Signposts for Geography Teaching*, London: Longman.

Habermas, J. (1987) *The Theory of Communicative Action*, Boston, MA: Beacon Press.

Haddon, L. (1992) Explaining ICT consumption: the case of the home computer, in R. Silverstone and E. Hirsch (eds), *Consuming Technologies: Media and Information in Domestic Spaces*, London: Routledge.

Halliday, M. (1989) *Spoken and Written Language* (2nd edition), Oxford: Oxford University Press.

Hassell, D. (2002) Issues in ICT and geography, in M. Smith (ed.), *Teaching Geography in Secondary Schools*, London: RoutledgeFalmer.

Heath, S.B. (1983) Ways with words: language, life and work in communities and classrooms, New York: Cambridge University Press.

Heath, S. (1986) What no bedtime story means: narrative skills at home and school, across cultures, in B.B. Schieffelin and E. Ochs (eds), *Language Socialization Across Cultures*, Cambridge: Cambridge University Press.

Hoggart, R. (1957) *The Uses of Literacy: Aspects of Working Class Life*, London: Chatto.

Holloway, S.L. and Valentine, G. (2003) *Cyberkids: Children in the Information Age*, London: RoutledgeFalmer.

Huckle, J. (1985) School geography, in R.J. Johnston (ed.), *The Future of School Geography*, London: Methuen.

Hughes, T. (1957) 'The Thought Fox' in *Hawk in the Rain*, London: Faber & Faber.

Hutton, W. (2006) At last a chance for every child, *Observer*, 5 March 2006.

Inglis, F. (ed.) (2004) *Education and the Good Society*, Basingstoke: Palgrave Macmillan.

Jewitt, C. (2006) *Technology, Literacy and Learning: A Multimodal Approach*, London, New York: Routledge.

Johnston, R.J. (1986) *On Human Geography*, Oxford: Blackwell.

Jupp, V. (1996) Documents and critical research, in Roger Sapsford and Victor Jupp (eds), *Data Collection and Analysis*, Thousand Oaks, CA: Sage Publications.

Kaplan, N. and Moulthrop, S. (1990) Computers and controversy: other ways of seeing, *Computers and Composition*, 7: 89–102.

Keller, S. (2003) *Community Pursuing the Dream, Living the Reality*, Princeton, NJ: Princeton University Press.

Kitchen, S., Finch, S. and Sinclair, R. (2007) *Harnessing Technology Schools Survey 2007*, Coventry: Becta, available online at http://partners.becta.org.uk/index.php?section=rh&catcode=re_rp_02&rid=14110.

Kress, G. (1996) *Reading Images: The Grammar of Visual Design*, Routledge Press, NJ.

—— (2003) *Literacy in the New Media Age*, Abingdon, New York: Routledge.

—— and Van Leeuwen, T. (1996) *Reading Images – The Grammar of Visual Design*, London: Routledge.

Landow, G. (1994) *Hyper/Text/Theory*, Baltimore, MD: Johns Hopkins University Press.

Lankshear, C. and Knobel, M. (2003) *New Literacies: Changing Knowledge and Classroom Learning*, Buckingham: Open University Press, p. 109.

—— and —— (2003) *New Literacies*, Buckingham: Open University Press.

—— and —— (2005) Digital literacies: policy, pedagogy and research considerations for education, Opening Plenary Address to ITU Conference, Oslo, Norway.

Latham, R. (1994) The economics of attention, Proceedings from the 124th Annual Meeting of Association of Research Libraries, available online at sunsite.berkeley.edu/ARL/Proceedings/124/ps2econ.html, accessed 3 July, 2007.

Latham, R. and Sassen, S. (2005) *Digital Formations: IT and New Architectures in the Global Realm*, Princeton, NJ: Princeton University Press.

Lave, J. and Wenger, E. (1991) *Situated Learning: Legitimate Peripheral Participation*, Cambridge: Cambridge University Press.

Macaro, E. (2001) *Learning Strategies in Foreign and Second Language Classrooms*, London: Continuum.

McFarlane, A.E., Sparrowhawk, A. and Heald, Y. (2002) *Report on the Educational Use of Games*, TEEM/DfES, available online at www.teem.org.uk/publications/teem_gamesind_full.pdf/.

McGavin, H. (1997) Blunkett fears two tier cyberspace, *Times Educational Supplement*, no. 4202, pp. 2–4.

McNeill, M. (1991) The old and new worlds of information technology in Britain, in J. Corner and S. Harvey (eds), *Enterprise and Heritage: Crosscurrents of National Culture*, London: Routledge, pp. 116–36.

Mariotti, M.A. (2002) Influence of technologies advances on students' maths learning, in L. English, M. Bartolini Bussi, G. Jones, R. Lesh and D. Tirosh (eds), *Handbook of International Research in Mathematics Education*, Mahwah, NJ: Lawrence Erlbaum Associates, pp. 695–721.

Marsh, J. (ed.) (2005) *Popular Culture, New Media and Digital Literacy in Early Childhood*, London: RoutledgeFalmer.

Matthewman, S. and Triggs, P. (2004) Obsessive compulsive font disorder: the challenge of supporting students writing with the computer, *Computers & Education*, 43(1–2): 125–35.

Matthewman, S., with Blight, A. and Davies, C. (2004) What does multi-modality mean for English? Creative tensions in teaching new texts and new literacies, *Education, Communication & Information (ECi)*, 4(1): 153–76.

Mills, J. and Murray, A. (2000) Music technology inspected: good teaching in Key Stage 3, *British Journal of Music Education*, 17(2): 157–81.

Mills, S. (2004) Who's a Smartie?, *Micromath* (Autumn): 20(3): 17–23.

Moore, A. (2006) *Schooling, Society and Curriculum*, London: RoutledgeFalmer.

Morgan, J. and Tidmarsh, C. (2004) Re-conceptualising ICT in geography teaching, *Education, Communication & Information (ECi)*, 4(1) (March): 177–92.

Morgan, J. and Lambert, D. (2005) *Teaching School Subjects: Geography 11–19*, London: Routledge.

National Advisory Committee on Creative and Cultural Education (NACCCE) (1999) *All Our Futures: Creativity, Culture and Education*, Sudbury: DfEE.

New London Group (1996) A pedagogy of multiliteracies: designing social futures, *Harvard Educational Review*, 66(1) (Spring): 60–92.

Nonaka, I. and Takeuchi, H. (1995) *The Knowledge-Creating Company*, New York: Oxford University Press.

Norman, D. (2000) *The Design of Everyday Things* (originally published as *The Psychology of Everyday Things*), London/New York: MIT Press.

—— (1993) *Things that Make Us Smart*, Cambridge, MA: Perseus Books.

Ofsted (2003) *Modern Foreign Languages in Secondary Schools* (Ofsted Subject Report Series 2001/2), London: Ofsted.

Olivero, F. (2006) Students' constructions of dynamic geometry, in C. Hoyles, J.B. Lagrange, L.H. Son and N. Sinclair (eds), *Proceedings of the 7th ICMI Study Conference 'Technology Revisited'*, Hanoi: Hanoi University of Technology, pp. 433–42.

——, Sutherland, R. and John, P. (2004) Seeing is believing: using videopapers to transform teachers' professional knowledge and practice, *Cambridge Journal of Education*, 34(2) 179–91.

Ong, W. (1982) *Orality and Literacy*, London: Methuen.

Pawson, R. (2002) Evidence-based policy: the promise of realist synthesis, *Evaluation*, 8(3): 340–58.

Pea, D. (1993) Practices of distributed intelligence and designs for education, in Salomon, G. (ed.), *Distributed Cognition*, Cambridge: Cambridge University Press.

Perkins, D. N. (1993) Person-plus: a distributed view of thinking and learning, in G. Salomon (ed.), *Distributed Cognitions: Psychological and Educational Considerations*, Cambridge: Cambridge University Press, pp. 88–110.

—— (1985) The fingertip effect: how information-processing technology changes thinking, *Educational Researcher*, 14(7), 11–17.

Prensky, M. (2001) *Digital Game-based Learning*, New York: McGraw-Hill.

Prior, G. and Hall, L. (2004) *ICT in Schools Survey*, ICT in Schools Research and Evaluation Series No. 22, Coventry, London: Becta/DfES, also available online at www.becta.org.uk/page_documents/research/ict_in_schools_survey_2004.pdf.

Reid, W. (1993) Literacy, orality, and the functions of curriculum, in B. Green (ed.), *The Insistence of the Letter: Literacy Studies and Curriculum Theorising*, London: The Falmer Press.

Ricoeur, P. (1992) *Oneself as Another*, K. Blamey (trans.), Chicago, IL: University of Chicago Press.

Robertson, S., Shortis, T., Todman, N., John, P. and Dale, R. (2004) ICT in the classroom: the pedagogical challenge of respatialisation and re-regulation, in Mark Olssen (ed.), *Culture and Learning*, Greenwich, CT: IAP.

Saljo, R. (1999) Learning as the use of tools: a sociocultural perspective on the human-technology link, in K. Littleton and P. Light (eds), *Learning with Computers, Analysing Productive Interaction*, London: Routledge.

Salomon, S. (1993) *Distributed Cognitions, Psychological and Educational Considerations*, Cambridge: Cambridge University Press.

Sandford, R. and Williamson, B. (2005) *Games Handbook*, Bristol: Futurelab.

Sandford, R., Ulicsak, M., Facer, K. and Rudd, T. (2006) *Teaching with Games: Using Commercial Off-the-Shelf Computer Games in Formal Education*, Bristol: Futurelab.

Sasken, S. (2006) *Territory, Authority, Rights: From Medieval to Global Assemblages*, Princeton, NJ: Princeton University Press, pp. 7–8.

Saussure, F. (1974) *Course in General Linguistics* (Introduction by Jonathan Culler, edited by Charles Bally and Albert Sechehaye, translated from the French by Wade Baskin) (revised edition), Glasgow: Fontana/Collins.

Saville-Troike, M. (2003) *The Ethnography of Communication*, Malden, MA: Blackwell Publishing.

Sawyer, R.K. (2003) Emergence in creativity and development, in R.K. Sawyer, V. John-Steiner, S. Moran, R. Sternberg, D.H. Feldman, M. Csikszentmihalyi and J. Nakamura, *Creativity and Development*, New York: Oxford Press, pp. 12–61.

Schon, D. (1983) *The Reflective Practitioner: How Professionals Think in Action*, New York: Basic Books.

Schostak, J. (1988) *Breaking into the Curriculum*, London: Methuen.

Selwyn, N. (1999) 'Gilding the grid': the marketing of the National Grid for Learning, *British Journal of Sociology of Education*, 20(1), pp. 55–68.

Selwyn, N. and Facer, K. (2007) *Beyond the Digital Divide*, Bristol: Futurelab.

Simon, H. (1971) Designing organisations for an information rich world, in M. Greenberger (ed.), *Computers, Communication and the Public Interest*, Baltimore, MD: Johns Hopkins University Press.

Slater, F. (1973) *Learning Through Geography. Pathways in Geography 7*, Indiana: National Council for Geographic Education.

Smith, P. (1988) *Discerning the Subject*, Minneapolis, MI: University of Minnesota Press.

Smith, M. (2002) *Teaching Geography in Secondary Schools*, London: Routledge Falmer.

Snyder, I. (1994) Re-inventing writing with computers, *The Australian Journal of Language and Literacy*, 17(3): 183–97.

Stables, A. (2003) *Conditional Literacies in Education for Diversity: Making Differences*, Aldershot: Ashgate Publishing.

Stravinsky, I. (1947) *The Poetics of Music: In the Form of Six Lessons* (trans. A. Knodell and I. Dahl), New York: Vintage Books.

Sutch, D. (2004) From 'knowledge giver' to 'advanced learner': changing pedagogy within an ICT integrated classroom, unpublished M.Sc. thesis, University of Bristol.

Sutherland, R., Olivero, F. and Weeden, M. (2004) Orchestrating mathematical proof through the use of digital tools, *Proceedings of the 28th Conference of the International Group for the Psychology of Mathematics Education, (PME) 2004*, Vol. 4, Bergen: Bergen University College, pp. 265–72.

Sutherland, R. (2007) *Teaching for Learning Mathematics*, Milton Keynes: Open University Press.

Taylor, A., Lazarus, E. and Cole, R. (2005) Putting languages on the (drop down) menu: innovative writing frames in modern foreign language teaching, *Educational Review*, 57(4): 435–55.

Trouche, L. (2003) From artifact to instrument: mathematics teaching mediated by symbolic calculators, *Interacting with Computers*, 15(6): 783–800.

Tuman, M. (1992) *Wordperfect: Literacy in the Computer Age*, London, Washington, DC: Falmer Press.

Turkle, S. and Papert, S. (1990) Epistemological pluralism: styles and voices within the computer culture, *Signs*, 16(1): 345–77.

Tyack, D. and Tobin, H. (1994) The 'grammar of schooling': why has it been so hard to change?, *American Educational Research Journal*, 31(3): 453–79.

Verillion, P. and Rabardel, P. (1995) Cognition and artifacts: a contribution to the study of thought in relation to instrumented activity, *European Journal of Psychology of Education*, 10: 77–101.

Vygotsky, L.S. (1978) *Mind in Society: The Development of Higher Psychological Processes*, edited by M. Cole, V. John-Steiner, S. Scriber and E. Souberman, Cambridge, MA: Harvard University Press.

Wajcman, J. (2002) Addressing technological change: the challenge of social theory, *Current Sociology*, 50: 353.

Weber, M. (1978) *Economy and Society: An Outline of Interpretive Sociology*, Vol. 1, edited by Guenther Roth and Claus Wittich, Berkeley, CA: University of California Press.

Weeden, M. (2002) Proof, proof and more proof, *Micromath* (18)3: 29–32.

Wenger, E. (1998) *Communities of Practice: Learning, Meaning and Identity*, Cambridge: Cambridge University Press.

Wertsch, J. (1985), *Culture, Communication and Cognition: Vygotskian Perspectives*, Cambridge: Cambridge University Press.

—— (1991) *Voices of the Mind: A Sociocultural Approach to Mediated Action*, London, Sydney, Singapore: Harvester Wheatsheaf.

—— (1998) *Mind as Action*, New York: Oxford University Press.

Williams, R. (1961) *The Long Revolution*, Harmondsworth: Penguin.

Williamson, B. and Sandford, R. (2005) *Games Handbook*, Bristol: Futurelab.

Woolgar, S. (ed.) (2002) *Virtual Society? Technology, Cyberbole, Reality*, Oxford: Oxford University Press, p. 13.

Index